A HISTORICAL
Edgar Allan Poe

The Historical Guides to American Authors is an interdisciplinary, historically sensitive series that combines close attention to the United States' most widely read and studied authors with a strong sense of time, place, and history. Placing each writer in the context of the vibrant relationship between literature and society, volumes in this series contain historical essays written on subjects of contemporary social, political, and cultural relevance. Each volume also includes a capsule biography and illustrated chronology detailing important cultural events as they coincided with the author's life and works, while photographs and illustrations dating from the period capture the flavor of the author's time and social milieu. Equally accessible to students of literature and of life, the volumes offer a complete and rounded picture of each author in his or her America.

A Historical Guide to Ernest Hemingway
Edited by Linda Wagner-Martin

A Historical Guide to Walt Whitman
Edited by David S. Reynolds

A Historical Guide to Ralph Waldo Emerson
Edited by Joel Myerson

A Historical Guide to Henry David Thoreau
Edited by William E. Cain

A Historical Guide to Edgar Allan Poe
Edited by J. Gerald Kennedy

A Historical Guide to Nathaniel Hawthorne
Edited by Larry Reynolds

A
Historical Guide
to Edgar Allan Poe

EDITED BY

J. GERALD KENNEDY

OXFORD
UNIVERSITY PRESS

2001

OXFORD
UNIVERSITY PRESS

Oxford   New York
Athens   Auckland   Bangkok   Bogotá   Buenos Aires   Calcutta
Cape Town   Chennai   Dar es Salaam   Delhi   Florence   Hong Kong   Istanbul
Karachi   Kuala Lumpur   Madrid   Melbourne   Mexico City   Mumbai
Nairobi   Paris   São Paulo   Shanghai   Singapore   Taipei   Tokyo   Toronto   Warsaw

and associated companies in
Berlin   Ibadan

Copyright © 2001 by J. Gerald Kennedy

Published by Oxford University Press, Inc.
198 Madison Avenue, New York, New York 10016

Oxford is a registered trademark of Oxford University Press.

Library of Congress Cataloging-in-Publication Data
A historical guide to Edgar Allan Poe / edited by J. Gerald Kennedy.
p.   cm. — (Historical guides to American authors)
Includes bibliographical references and index.
ISBN 0-19-512149-X; ISBN 0-19-512150-3 (pbk.)
1. Poe, Edgar Allan, 1809-1849—Criticism and interpretation.
2. Literature and society—United States—History—19th century.
I. Kennedy, J. Gerald   II. Series.
PS2638 .H54   2001
818'.309—dc21   00-020192

1 3 5 7 9 8 6 4 2
Printed in the United States of America
on acid-free paper

Contents

Abbreviations   vii

Introduction:
Poe in Our Time   3
J. Gerald Kennedy

Edgar Allan Poe, 1809–1849:
A Brief Biography   19
J. Gerald Kennedy

POE IN HIS TIME

Poe and the American
Publishing Industry   63
Terence Whalen

Spanking the Master:
Mind-Body Crossings in
Poe's Sensationalism   95
David Leverenz

Poe and Nineteenth-Century
Gender Constructions   129
Leland S. Person

Poe and the Issue of
American Privacy   167
Louis A. Renza

Illustrated Chronology   189

Bibliographical Essay:
Major Editions and Landmarks of
Poe Scholarship   209
Scott Peeples

Contributors   233

Index   235

Abbreviations

ER   Poe, Edgar Allan. *Essays and Reviews*. Ed. G. R. Thompson.
      New York: Library of America, 1984.
 L   Poe, Edgar Allan. *The Letters of Edgar Allan Poe*. Ed. John Ward
      Ostrom. 2 vols. 1948. Reprint, New York: Gordian Press,
      1966.
 P   Poe, Edgar Allan. *Poems*. Ed. Thomas Ollive Mabbott. Vol. 1 of
      The Collected Works of Edgar Allan Poe. Cambridge, Mass.:
      Harvard University Press, 1969.
PL   Thomas, Dwight, and David K. Jackson. *The Poe Log: A
      Documentary Life of Edgar Allan Poe, 1809–1849*. Boston:
      G. K. Hall, 1987.
PT   Poe, Edgar Allan. *Poetry and Tales*. Ed. Patrick F. Quinn. New
      York: Library of America, 1984.

A HISTORICAL GUIDE TO
Edgar Allan Poe

Introduction

Poe in Our Time

J. Gerald Kennedy

Despite persisting disagreement about Edgar Allan Poe's literary achievement, no American writer of the antebellum period enjoys greater current popularity and recognizability. One hundred fifty years after the author's death, cartoon characters Garfield and Bart Simpson entertain young television viewers by reciting "The Raven," and the new National Football League team in Baltimore owes its team nickname and logo to that famous poem. The compact disc "Tales of Mystery and Imagination" by the Alan Parsons Project has dazzled rock fans with its pulsating interpretations of Poe texts; such Roger Corman films as *The Fall of the House of Usher* and *The Masque of the Red Death* (both featuring Vincent Price) have become cult classics; and Generation-X readers, especially those attracted to the "Goth" counterculture, revel in Poe's dark fantasies. Apart from Frederick Douglass, he is the only American writer of his era yet featured on the popular Arts and Entertainment "Biography" series. Why does his work from the 1830s and 1840s seem so fresh and compelling to readers in the new millennium? Why has his influence on popular culture remained pervasive and enduring? Why does Poe haunt us still?

Like the enigma of "The Purloined Letter," the answers to these questions are both obvious and subtle. In the most immedi-

3

ate sense, Poe appeals to the popular imagination because he scares us to death. The yen for sensation feeds our fascination with terror; just as moviegoers rush to the latest horror film to be frightened out of their minds, so too they read Poe's hair-raising tales of shipwreck or premature burial to experience the frisson of near-encounters with annihilation. Long ago Aristotle speculated that tragedy produced catharsis through an audience's sympathetic identification with the doomed hero: the spectacle of agony and death on some level frightens us, yet we feel cleansed by the sacrificial scene we have witnessed. Symbolically someone else has suffered in our place. Perhaps for the same reason a sensational tale like "The Masque of the Red Death" produces exhilaration when we emerge from its absorbing horror unscathed by the deadly pestilence. "Sensations are the great things after all," Poe's Mr. Blackwood advises Psyche Zenobia, the aspiring magazinist in "How to Write a Blackwood Article" (*PT*, 281). Psychiatrist Herbert Hendin called the 1970s the "age of sensation," and his analysis of American life still seems accurate enough at century's end. Hendin contends that in a materialistic, success-oriented culture, the desire to be impervious to unsettling feelings, to control one's personal life by avoiding emotional commitments, produces a craving for escapist sensation: "Through different ways and in many forms people seek out fragmented sensory experience as a way of . . . escaping completely the involvement with feeling" (325). If Hendin's theory does not pertain to all readers of Poe, it nevertheless characterizes our own epoch in a way that explains the contemporaneity of the author's sensationalism.

But the reasons for Poe's continuing appeal are in fact more deeply rooted in American history and culture. Writing in the wake of Charles Brockden Brown, Catherine Maria Sedgwick, and James Fenimore Cooper, all of whom depicted episodes of bloody cruelty, Poe was yet the first important American writer to foreground violence and to probe its psychological origins. Especially in stories like "The Tell-Tale Heart" and "The Black Cat," he portrayed brutality from the subject position of the perpetrator, fetishizing the desire for power or "ascendancy" over an adversary. If, as Richard Slotkin has argued, the violence of

American culture was initially imported in the name of God, wealth, and Anglo-Saxon civilization, then exercised in wresting the land itself from Native peoples, and finally domesticated in cruelties enacted upon African slaves to make that land profitable, then Poe's emphasis on murder, revenge, mutilation, and torture patently mirrors a deep-seated national disposition. We need to remind ourselves that he produced his violent fiction in the 1830s and 1840s, when the U.S. government was either confining Indians to reservations, "removing" them west of the Mississippi, or (in the case of the Seminoles) remorselessly decimating them; this was the same era when the perpetuation and extension of slavery were being defended by Southern apologists and challenged by abolitionists determined to expose the barbarities of the "peculiar institution." As we see unmistakably in *The Narrative of Arthur Gordon Pym* (1838) and the unfinished "Journal of Julius Rodman," Poe was keenly conscious of both controversies and the hostilities they aroused.

As a crucial component of American identity, the "internal flaw of violence" has been traced by historian Richard Maxwell Brown to the frontier ethos of standing one's ground and meting out personal justice. Connecting the "glorified gunfighters" of the Wild West with U.S. military interventions in Korea, Viet nam, Grenada, and the Persian Gulf, Brown shows how the American repudiation of English common law, and specifically its obligation "to retreat 'to the wall' at one's back" before killing in self-defense, became in the nineteenth century, at fabled places like the O.K. Corral, a fierce cultural imperative to confront the enemy and slay him—not only to defend one's life but also to protect private property and capitalist values (4, 39, 156). If Poe prefers European settings and avoids explicitly nationalistic subjects, his tales nevertheless render in graphic detail the quick American impulse to violence. When the narrator of "The Black Cat" buries an ax in his wife's brain or when Hop-Frog (in the tale by that name) incinerates the king and his seven ministers dressed as apes, Poe anatomizes the psychology of revenge, flaunts atrocity, and depicts the recrudescence of our national "internal flaw."

In a culture of hate crimes, automatic weapons, high school

slaughter, and gang wars, violence seems ubiquitous and conta-
gious, the handiest form of instant self-empowerment. Violence
has now perhaps become so commonplace in American life that
many cannot perceive its strangeness or singularity as a cultural
trait. (Such is the ongoing frustration of those who would ban
handguns and restrict the availability of all firearms.) The glorifi-
cation of Rambo, the Terminator, or John McClane (the *Die Hard*
hero)—all cool exponents of redemptive violence—temporarily
fosters the illusion of blood justice and assuages our anxiety
about the gratuitous, random violence abroad in the real world
around us. Meanwhile, movies like *Pulp Fiction* or *Natural Born
Killers* glamorize cold-blooded murder as the ultimate entertainment, while *Fargo* turns the shredding of a body into a visual gag.
We need only return to Poe tales like "The Man That Was Used
Up," which playfully reveals a military hero to be no more than a
mutilated lump, or "A Predicament," which makes a joke out of
the narrator's decapitation, to appreciate the author's stunningly
modern treatment of violence.

The curious modernity (or postmodernity) of Poe's writing
derives, however, from more than his reliance upon sensation
and violence. For example, his fascination with madness and perverseness resonates with our heightened Western, post-Freudian
awareness of the unconscious and the irrational. From the Holo-
caust to Jonestown and Kosovo, much of the century's history
seems inspired by mass insanity. Foucault argues that after Sade
and Goya, we can trace the emergence of a madness in modern
art that constitutes a judgment on the unreason of modernity itself: "The world that thought to measure and justify madness
through psychology must justify itself before madness, since in
its struggles and agonies it measures itself by the excess of works
like those of Nietzsche, of Van Gogh, or Artaud" (289). In *Madness and Modernism*, psychologist Louis A. Sass describes a
provocative parallel between schizophrenia and modern culture,
suggesting that the twentieth century, characterized by "the
pursuit of extremes, by exaggerated objectivist or subjectivist
tendencies, or by unrestrained cerebralism or irrationalism," has
assumed on a vast social scale many of the features of schizo-
phrenic experience (38). As one of the first writers to treat mad-

ness as a recurrent subject, Poe explores the varieties of insanity and illustrates symptomatic phobias, obsessions, and hallucinations in such narratives as "Berenice," "Ligeia," and "William Wilson." His most famous tale, "The Fall of the House of Usher," presents a multilayered allegory of the disordered mind in which the house itself may be understood as the domain of unreason, its physical collapse analogizing the psychological disintegration of Roderick Usher, who in turn metaphorizes his loss of reason in the poem "The Haunted Palace." The analogy extends to the burial of Usher's sister Madeline and her return from the underground vault, for the utter madness that she represents cannot be indefinitely repressed in the unconscious. Poe thus portrays in "Usher" a distinctly modern world that seems (to borrow Sass's terms) altogether solipsistic, dehumanized, and "derealized" (32)—a realm of the bizarre.

While he probed the individual experience of irrationality, Poe was also attentive to the social and cultural meanings of madness. A comic piece, "The System of Doctor Tarr and Professor Fether," satirizes nineteenth-century treatments for insanity and indeed inverts the power relations of the asylum by depicting a curious French *maison de santé* in which inmates circulate freely, acting out their delusions, while the guards have been tarred, feathered, and locked up. At one point the supposed superintendent, Monsieur Maillard (subsequently revealed to be insane himself), comments on the cunning of a lunatic: "When a madman appears *thoroughly* sane, indeed, it is high time to put him in a strait jacket" (*PT*, 1018). Relentlessly problematizing the distinction between madness and sanity, Poe anticipates the unreality of the twentieth century, in which megalomaniacs such as Adolf Hitler, Joseph Stalin, Pol Pot, Saddam Hussein, and Slobodan Milosovic have reconstructed entire societies as paranoid formations, and in which deranged killers like Charles Manson or Jeffrey Dahmer have briefly become media celebrities in part because they personify the psychopathology of our own century of atrocity. When the narrator of "The Black Cat" describes the "spirit of perverseness" ("this unfathomable longing of the soul *to vex itself*—to offer violence to its own nature—to do wrong for the wrong's sake only" [*PT*, 852]), he may be said to describe a defining force in modern culture.

Poe's appeal to late-twentieth-century readers, however, derives not only from his projections of violence or insanity but also from his articulations of estrangement and doubt. It has been nearly fifty years since David Riesman's *Lonely Crowd* described the alienation of modern urban life, and more recent studies—like Robert N. Bellah's much-discussed *Habits of the Heart*—have documented the fragile, often superficial nature of postmodern community, as well as the recurrent American tendency toward solitude about which Crèvecoeur worried two centuries ago. Estrangement figures importantly, of course, in Poe's narrative scheme, and his isolated, reclusive protagonists rarely participate in the activities of a larger society. While this tendency may be ascribed to his Gothic models, it also reflects contemporary cultural and socioeconomic changes. The foster son of a dry-goods merchant, Poe witnessed the "market revolution" (as Charles Sellers terms it) that saw a family-based subsistence economy give way to an aggressive capitalist system bringing entrepreneurial opportunity but also cutthroat competition and profit-driven exploitation. These same pressures gripped the literary world: without international copyright laws, publishers "pirated" works by celebrated British novelists and compelled American authors to write for the periodical market. As he continued the futile quest for support of his own monthly journal, Poe proclaimed: "The whole tendency of the age is Magazineward" (*ER*, 1414). In satires like "The Business Man" and "Diddling," however, he exposed the crass, rapacious nature of nascent capitalism, and he recognized the intractably adversarial nature of economic rivalries—including conflicts between periodical owner-publishers and authors like himself, obliged to labor in what he bitterly called "the magazine prison house" (*ER*, 1036–38). In "The Literary Life of Thingum Bob, Esq.," he travestied his vocation as a magazinist, exposing the base strategies to which writers were reduced in a capitalist economy sustained by mechanical reproduction. As if suspecting that he has become a mere writing machine producing literary commodities, Thingum reports: "Through joy and sorrow, I—*wrote.* Through hunger and through thirst, I—*wrote.* Through good report and through ill report, I—*wrote.* Through sunshine and through moonshine, I—*wrote*" (*PT*, 786). A decade before Melville's "Bartleby, the Scrivener," Poe sarcastically portrayed the alienating consequences of the market revolution.

As a denizen of Philadelphia and New York, the author was also fascinated by the material aggregation of capital—the construction of the modern industrial city—and wrote about such phenomena as the omnibus, street paving, and cabs, although he surmised at once the social consequences of urban growth and the anomie that it would foster. His tale "The Man of the Crowd" conveys a prescient awareness of metropolitan alienation, in which a voyeuristic narrator regards passersby simply as social types, describes the city as a desolate, dehumanized place, and fixes his attention upon a singular character who seems paradoxically to personify both absolute loneliness and fear of solitude. This stranger who speaks to no one is said to be "the type and the genius of deep crime" because he "refuses to be alone" (*PT*, 396). As we see in the Dupin detective stories, all set in Paris, Poe associated the modern city with the proliferation of crime and the detective forces required to contend with the volume, variety, and impersonality of urban felonies. The mutilation of Madame L'Espanaye and her daughter in "The Murders in the Rue Morgue" and the discovery of a young woman's waterlogged corpse in "The Mystery of Marie Rogêt" associate horrific violence with a specifically urban context. In this sense Poe anticipates the grim vision of contemporary television cop shows like *N.Y.P.D. Blue* or *Homicide*, in which the city figures as a lonely, dangerous place inhabited by ruthless, inhuman types ready to kill anyone who gets in their way.

Although C. Auguste Dupin advises the prefect of police and gathers information from the Parisian newspapers, there is little sense here or elsewhere in Poe of productive social relations. Indeed, the vast majority of his tales represent alienated figures ensconced in remote, indefinite settings, absorbed in private fantasies or obsessions—the nineteenth-century equivalent of cyberspace. Jean Baudrillard has declared that the dominance of electronic mass media and the profusion of mass culture in postmodernity mark the end of the social and the disruption of the political through the proliferation of "simulacra," digitized images that problematize the real as they construct a virtual reality. As Shawn Rosenheim and Terence Whalen have both suggested in recent books, Poe brilliantly foresaw the information age, the computer, and the use of code or encryption to achieve new forms of privileged communication. Rosenheim has emphasized the connections between Poe's obsession with cryptography and the development of modern surveillance and intelligence gathering. Whalen underscores the author's complicated desire to protect his privacy while appealing to a mass public, and his discussion of Poe and Charles Babbage (who devised an early calculating machine) suggests that the magazinist anticipated the rise of an economy based on the use-value of information. Now that the Internet has made this unimaginable flow of data a reality, more people communicate with each other than ever before, but they do so privately and electronically, gazing at a cathode-ray tube that simulates presence and social interaction while leaving the user in perfect solitude.

There is yet another aspect of the estrangement prefigured by Poe and actualized in our time: the modernist dislocation from history. While contemporaries like Hawthorne and Cooper evoked the conflicts of seventeenth-century colonial New England or the border wars of eighteenth-century New York, respectively, Poe largely ignored the materials of the American past. Two exceptions come to mind: the aforementioned "Journal of Julius Rodman" borrows from the 1814 chronicle of the Lewis and Clark expedition to construct a fictive travelogue, and "Mellonta Tauta" includes a joking reference to Lord Cornwallis's surrender to George Washington. But otherwise, Poe had little use for American history and, indeed, recalled episodes from the past (as in the opening paragraph of "The Premature Burial") mainly as legendary atrocities, injustices, or natural disasters from the Old World. Although this circumstance might seem to argue for the author's indifference to the American cultural context, in fact Poe's antihistoricism is perfectly consistent with the Emersonian temper of his time. Lewis Perry has argued that, despite gestures of historical remembrance (such as the nineteenth-century "creation" of Plymouth Rock), the antebellum era felt itself increasingly divorced from the colonial and Revolutionary past and in the throes of momentous changes. Tracing the origins of a modern, "supersessive" sense of history back to the Renaissance and Reformation, Anthony Kemp similarly describes an accelerating estrangement from the past between the 1830s and the end of the century, launched by Emerson and culminating in Henry Adams. Like many Americans of his day and our own, Poe was more interested in the present than the past, and more fascinated still by a future that would include South Sea exploration, aeronautical adventure, and mesmeric revelation. He populated his tales not with avatars of American history but with eccentric, protomodern characters of obscure European origin, more responsive to novelty than to recognizable tradition.

While registering profound sociohistorical changes through images of isolation and alienation, Poe also represented the deepening spiritual uncertainty of the nineteenth century. He wrote at a time when modern science and social science began to establish empirical methods that challenged religious beliefs, as (for example) when geologists of the 1830s first questioned the accuracy of scriptural accounts of the creation of the world. Exponents of German "higher criticism" subjected the Bible to skeptical interpretation, and despite nineteenth-century revival movements, the secularism fostered by Enlightenment rationalism continued to supplant religious piety. Although the early poem "Sonnet—To Science" expresses alarm at the intrusion of scientific research into the realm of fancy, Poe subsequently became interested in astronomy and natural science—as well as the pseudosciences of phrenology and mesmerism—and he confronted the stark implications of a naturalistic world stripped of belief in a spiritual afterlife. When the speaker in "The Raven"— already anticipating the bird's fateful negation—asks whether there is "balm in Gilead" (spiritual salvation) or whether "within the distant Aidenn" (or heavenly afterlife) he will embrace his lost beloved, he poses the chief anxiety questions of the epoch (*PT*, 85). Poe's late love, Sarah Helen Whitman, wrote that he "sounded the very depths of the abyss" of nineteenth-century unbelief, and in tales like *The Narrative of Arthur Gordon Pym* and "The Facts in the Case of M. Valdemar," he portrayed death as a disgusting spectacle devoid of metaphysics: putrefaction without transcendence. As I have argued elsewhere, Poe's many fantasies of death—including such narratives of reincarnation or revivification as "Morella" or "Ligeia"—reflect his susceptibility to the dread evoked by contemporary religious doubt.

In this sense Poe prefigured the skepticism and uncertainty that spread from the nineteenth century into our own era. Nietzsche's scandalous proclamation of the death of God in *The Gay Science* (1882) only made explicit a pervasive earlier suspicion. In the works of Kafka, Hemingway, Sartre, and Pynchon, we have grown accustomed to the black void that seems to define the condition of modern being. From *The Waste Land* to *Waiting for Godot*, much of twentieth- century literature has been steeped in the radical doubt articulated by Satan at the end of Twain's *Mysterious Stranger*: "There is no God, no universe, no human race, no earthly life, no heaven, no hell. It is all a dream—a grotesque and foolish dream. Nothing exists but you. And you are but a *thought*—a vagrant thought, a useless thought, a homeless thought, wandering forlorn among the empty eternities!" (151). Twain's cynical vision seems a direct response to Poe's poetic question, "Is *all* that we see or seem / But a dream within a dream?" (*PT*, 97). Such uncertainty tormented Poe and magnified the threat of death, which in "The City in the Sea" he personified as a figure that "looks gigantically down" upon "gaping graves" (*PT*, 67). In "The Conqueror Worm," the famous poem inserted into "Ligeia," a writhing, "blood-red" emblem of decomposition dominates the human "tragedy," which is starkly reduced to three elements: "Madness," "Sin," and "Horror" (*PT*, 77–79). As these poems suggest, Poe sometimes projected death as a totemic presence, a savage god brooding over a kingdom we now recognize as the darkened landscape of modernity.

Those conversant with contemporary music will recognize the similarities between Poe's phantasms and the gruesome themes explored by hard rock and "heavy," "black," or "death metal" groups such as Autopsy, Carcass, My Dying Bride, Black Sabbath, and Judas Priest. Without hyperbole, we may speak of a postmodern cult of death that revels in fantasies of sadism, masochism, and annihilation; in place of a loving God, it reveres a hypostatized figure of universal destruction, similar to the one evoked in the closing sentence of "The Masque of the Red Death." To be sure, the beshrouded mummer of that tale is no Satan. Although Poe toyed (in "Usher" and "Ligeia") with the theme of vampirism, he never channeled his recurrent dread into diabolism, and, as we see in *Eureka*, he struggled mightily to sustain a rational belief—if not a buoyant faith—in "the Divine Being" (*PT*, 1358). But in giving memorable shape to his intractable fears, he also created images that still stir our own deepest anxieties about mortality and immortality.

Poe's peculiar appeal to the late twentieth century does not rely entirely, however, upon his preoccupation with the dark side of the imaginary. When he was not gazing into the abyss, he created compensatory fantasies of escape from or triumph over "the one Sepulchral idea" (*PT*, 674). The aforementioned detective story, in which the consummate rational intelligence of C. Auguste Dupin prevails over chaos and fear, provided one kind of apotheosis. Science fiction offered another alternative, and Poe's earliest contribution to the form, "The Unparalleled Adventure of one Hans Pfaall," depicted a fanciful balloon flight to the moon; but the framing tale undercut the travelogue's verisimilitude by exposing the narrator as a drunken trickster. In *The Narrative of Arthur Gordon Pym*, Poe subsequently recounted a perilous journey to the remote South Seas, where his narrator flees hostile black natives on a mysterious island and then sails into a milky polar sea, only to vanish, as it were, on the verge of a cataract, possibly an opening into the center of the earth. The derivative "Journal of Julius Rodman" purported to offer in serial form an account of the first crossing of the Rocky Mountains by a "civilized" man, but Poe dropped the project after six installments, leaving Rodman far from his Yukon destination. The most plausible of Poe's imaginary voyages, "The Balloon Hoax," initially appeared as a newspaper report, and its seemingly meticulous observations persuaded readers in 1844 that the first successful transatlantic balloon crossing had just taken place. As H. Bruce Franklin and others have shown, the modern genre of science fiction grew out of Poe's narrative inventions: his practice of extrapolating imaginary details from scientific facts and his anticipation of previously unimaginable geographic and astronomical discoveries inspired Jules Verne, H. G. Wells, and a legion of subsequent writers. That is, Poe shared with our own century a futuristic imagination that has envisioned brave new worlds of scientific conquest.

In addition to fantastic explorations of the physical world or outer space, Poe also pondered the twilight zone of metaphysics, the boundary between life and death. In dialogues such as "The Conversation of Eiros and Charmion" and "The Colloquy of Monos and Una," he imagined exchanges between disembodied spirits reflecting upon the nature of the universe or the terms of mortal existence. His "Mesmeric Revelation" offers an instructive contrast to "Valdemar" in its depiction of a mesmerized, dying patient who delivers psychic insights on matter, spirit, life, and death before slipping happily into "the region of the shadows" (*PT*, 727). Poe's passion for metaphysics and cosmological speculation culminated, of course, in *Eureka*, the long "prose poem" of 1848 that elaborated his most sanguine vision of futurity. In that treatise he contemplated the universe as an expression of the will of God and described impulses of diffusion and unity—the outward radiation of matter and its eventual return to oneness—as the systole and diastole of the "Heart Divine" (*PT*, 1356). He well understood how profoundly terrifying a universe without hope might be—which is perhaps why he tried to "prove" God's existence in his last major work. Poe's mystical, visionary side, which inspired intermittent efforts to imagine the unimaginable, the realm beyond death, appeals to the same yearning within contemporary culture that has produced such recent films as *What Dreams May Come* and *City of Angels*, as well as a legion of popular books devoted to near-death experiences and celestial visions.

The very tension between Poe's lurid Gothic imagination and his transcendental idealism, which was for many years a crux of critical debate, may ultimately explain the writer's singular appeal to denizens of the millennial era. Writing at the advent of the so-called post-Christian epoch, at the historical moment when public education and a secular, capitalistic mass culture had begun to supplant organized religion as the principal influences on private thought and belief, Poe gave memorable literary form to the conflicted imaginary of the modern consciousness. As instanced by his powerful hold on twentieth-century illustrators and artists, musical composers, and film makers, as well as such celebrated authors as John Barth, Joyce Carol Oates, and Paul Auster, Poe remains an inescapable presence in contemporary culture. And although academic disagreements about his achievement persist, his place in the pantheon of enduring American authors is secure.

Such was not always the case. When Poe died in 1849, his reputation was far from distinguished, and Rufus W. Griswold's scandalous obituary in the *New York Tribune* precipitated a ferocious debate in American periodicals. In fact, Griswold (whom Poe unwisely appointed his literary executor) brought out an early multivolume edition reprinting his scurrilous portrait. Friends such as N. P. Willis, George Graham, and Henry B. Hurst rushed to defend Poe in print from charges of madness, immorality, and dissolution. Abroad, the symbolist poet Charles Baudelaire published two tributes in the *Revue de Paris* in 1852 and subsequently produced a brilliant French translation of Poe's works that launched the persisting veneration of the American writer in France. Mrs. Whitman added her memorial in 1859 in a little book called *Edgar Poe and His Critics*, and in 1875 Walt Whitman (no relation) delivered an appreciative address at the dedication of Poe's tomb. But Poe remained disreputable enough in the later nineteenth century that he was excluded from manufactured sets of "Authors" cards. By the mid-1870s, the first full-length biography of Poe was published, and in 1903 the first complete scholarly edition of his writings appeared. Although author-critics such as T. S. Eliot, Aldous Huxley, and Yvor Winters disparaged Poe's work—especially the poetry—in the early twentieth century, an impressive body of modern scholarship, produced by Killis Campbell, T. O. Mabbott, and others, heralded the outpouring of important critical work from 1950 onward that has confirmed the significance of Poe's achievement.

Throughout the subsequent biographical essay, I have situated Poe's life and career in relation to the signal developments in American culture during four decades of extraordinary change. In his concluding bibliographic review, Scott Peeples sketches the historical growth of Poe studies and identifies the essential primary and secondary publications. The four intervening historical essays present focused studies of important aspects of Poe's literary life. Terence Whalen examines the complex, inescapable problem of Poe's relationship to the American publishing industry, notably the magazine world in which he remained an embattled figure for more than a dozen years. Whalen shows how economic forces in America profoundly affected the unfolding of Poe's career—and none more so than the implicit imperative to appeal to an emerging mass audience. The chapter by David Leverenz extends this line of inquiry, delving into the specific cultural and economic implications of the "tale of sensation." Leverenz indeed argues that antebellum avidity for sensationalism prodded Poe into writing great short fiction, turning him from insipid homosocial burlesques (like "Lionizing") to heterosexual horror tales such as "The Fall of the House of Usher." Likewise investigating Poe's responses to nineteenth-century constructions of gender, Leland S. Person pursues connections between the fiction and poetry, on the one hand, and Poe's contemporary relationships with men and women, on the other. In the biographical facts Person locates implacably gendered patterns of response, symptomatic of contemporary notions of masculinity and femininity that recur in surprising ways in the tales and poems. Louis A. Renza's chapter finally engages the issue of privacy in American culture as Poe responded to the emergence of public and private spheres in the 1830s and 1840s. Renza suggests that Poe's ambiguous relationship to the mass audience—he sought both fame and secrecy—produced (as we see in "William Wilson" and "The Man of the Crowd") a narrative method that compulsively exposes private action to a public gaze. Taken together, these four chapters reflect crucial intersections in Poe between the literary and the historical, collectively redefining the imprint of American culture upon tales and poems often assumed to represent a realm "out of space—out of time."

WORKS CITED

Baudrillard, Jean. *Simulations.* New York: Semiotext, 1983.
Bellah, N. Robert. *Habits of the Heart: Individualism and Commitment in American Life.*Berkeley: University of California Press, 1985.

Brown, Richard Maxwell. *No Duty to Retreat: Violence and Values in American History and Society.* New York: Oxford University Press, 1991.

Foucault, Michel. *Madness and Civilization: A History of Insanity in the Age of Reason.* Trans. Richard Howard. New York: Vintage, 1973.

Franklin, H. Bruce. *Future Perfect: American Science Fiction of the Nineteenth Century.* New York: Oxford University Press, 1966.

Hendin, Herbert. *The Age of Sensation.* New York: McGraw-Hill, 1977.

Kemp, Anthony. *The Estrangement of the Past: A Study in the Origins of Modern Historical Consciousness.* New York: Oxford University Press, 1991.

Kennedy, J. Gerald. *Poe, Death, and the Life of Writing.* New Haven, Conn.: Yale University Press, 1987.

Perry, Lewis. *Boats against the Current: American Culture between Revolution and Modernity, 1820–1860.* New York: Oxford University Press, 1993.

Riesman, David. *The Lonely Crowd: A Study in the Changing American Character.* New Haven, Conn.: Yale University Press, 1950.

Rosenheim, Shawn. *The Cryptographic Imagination: Secret Writing from Edgar Poe to the Internet.* Baltimore: Johns Hopkins University Press, 1997.

Sass, Louis A. *Madness and Modernism: Insanity in the Light of Modern Art, Literature, and Thought.* New York: Basic Books, 1992.

Sellers, Charles. *The Market Revolution: Jacksonian America, 1815–1846.* New York: Oxford University Press, 1991.

Slotkin, Richard. *Regeneration through Violence: The Mythology of the American Frontier, 1600–1860.* Middletown, Conn.: Wesleyan University Press, 1973.

Twain, Mark. *The Mysterious Stranger: A Romance.* New York: Harper and Brothers, 1916.

Whalen, Terence. *Edgar Allan Poe and the Masses: The Political Economy of Literature in Antebellum America.* Princeton, N.J.: Princeton University Press, 1999.

Whitman, Sarah Helen. *Edgar Poe and His Critics.* New York: Rudd and Carleton, 1859.

Edgar Allan Poe
1809–1849

A Brief Biography

J. Gerald Kennedy

While the nation's capital awaited the inauguration of James Madison as fourth president of the United States, Edgar Allan Poe was born in Boston, on January 19, 1809, the second son of actor David Poe Jr. and actress Elizabeth Arnold Hopkins Poe. David Poe Sr., Edgar's paternal grandfather, was of Irish-American stock and had been a major in the American Revolution, serving as assistant deputy-quartermaster general for Baltimore. Of English origin, Eliza came to America in 1796 with her mother, also an actress. Nine months after Edgar's birth, hard-drinking David Poe made his last theatrical performance, and he apparently abandoned his family soon after the birth of daughter Rosalie in December 1810. Presumably he died of consumption (tuberculosis) a year later. Entrusting her elder son, Henry (b. 1807), to the care of relatives in Baltimore, Eliza Poe—a favorite with audiences—struggled valiantly to sustain her theatrical career in Charleston, Norfolk, and Richmond with two small children in tow. In failing health she made her final stage appearance in Richmond on October 11, 1811; she died there of consumption on December 8. Orphaned by two itinerant stage performers, Poe in later life sometimes tried to obscure his humble origins, although he faithfully preserved a locket containing a miniature painting of his mother.

Poe was born at a time when transatlantic relations between the United States and Great Britain were quickly eroding, after twenty-five years of peace. Indignant at the continuing impressment of American sailors, the fledgling nation declared war in 1812. While battles erupted in Canada, along the Great Lakes, and at sea, the British blockaded the Chesapeake Bay and kept the Atlantic seacoast, including tidewater Virginia, in a state of alarm. In Richmond, where everyday life largely followed familiar routines, the Mackenzie family had adopted baby Rosalie Poe, while Edgar found a home with the Allans. John Allan was a tobacco and dry-goods merchant from Scotland, and Frances Valentine Allan had herself been an orphan. A childless couple, the Allans reared the boy as a son but never adopted him. Edgar nevertheless attached himself emotionally to Frances, who, like his natural mother, was slender, delicate, and prone to chronic illness. In his early years, at least, the lad was coddled and spoiled; he visited nearby plantations, where he played games with slave children, and he traveled to fashionable mountain spas with the Allans. One source (Weiss) plausibly mentions a black "Mammy" who took care of him. He received an early schooling and reportedly could read a newspaper by the age of five, though he was too young to worry that, one hundred miles to the north, British forces in 1814 had captured Washington and burned the Capitol. In Baltimore, three weeks later, his grandfather, the aged Revolutionary veteran, helped to organize the defense that repelled the British attack and inspired the "Star-Spangled Banner."

Following the war's conclusion, John Allan and his partner, Charles Ellis, decided to open a London office to capitalize on the renewal of trade, and in 1815, at the beginning of the so-called Era of Good Feelings, Allan took his family to England. Edgar asked to be reported, in one of Allan's letters, as "not afraid coming across the Sea" (PL, 26). The boy visited his foster father's relatives in Ayrshire, Scotland, and then—as "Edgar Allan"—settled into his new home in the Bloomsbury section of London and began to see the legendary sights of the great city. During the five years of Allan's English sojourn, Poe attended two different boarding schools, the first in Chelsea, run by the Misses Dubourg, and the second in the outlying village of Stoke

Newington, operated by the Reverend Bransby. Twenty years later Poe would base his famous tale "William Wilson" on haunting childhood memories of the latter school. During his years abroad from ages six to eleven, the young prodigy earned high marks as a student of Latin and became acquainted with Shakespeare and other British authors, doubtless including Sir Walter Scott; he probably also thumbed through such popular monthly magazines as *Blackwood's*, reading as a schoolboy the hair-raising fiction he later spoofed in "How to Write a Blackwood Article." The recurrent images of ancient European mansions and abbeys in tales such as "Ligeia" and "The Fall of the House of Usher" likely also owe something to his travels with the Allan family during the years in England. Although the British branch of Allan and Ellis initially prospered through tobacco sales, the collapse of the London tobacco market—which coincided with the American panic of 1819—doomed the venture, and in 1820 Allan and family returned to Richmond, there to salvage the home office, if possible.

That same year Congress negotiated the Missouri Compromise, debating for the first time the morality of slavery and addressing the diverging interests of free and slave states. Richmond continued to thrive as a center of tobacco production, and the industry's growing reliance on hired-out slaves was not yet a source of apprehension. Edgar Poe—for he resumed use of that name in the city where so many remembered his mother— enrolled in Joseph H. Clarke's academy on Broad Street and there excelled in Latin and Greek. His gift for satire and verse revealed itself to Clarke, who when quizzed by Allan about the wisdom of publishing a volume of Poe's juvenilia, counseled that such attention might turn the boy's head. When Clarke left Richmond in 1822, young Poe resumed his academic training under a new instructor, William Burke, and again distinguished himself in classical literature and French. But after years of enjoying Allan's favor as a "verry fine boy," the teenaged Poe grew mischievous and about this time incurred Allan's wrath for shooting "a lot of domestic fowls" on a nearby plantation (*PL*, 42, 49). One evening he dressed as a ghost and tried to frighten members of the Gentleman's Whist Club, which then included the military hero General Winfield Scott. As a youth, Poe indited poems to several Richmond girls, but his strongest feelings were directed toward an older woman, Jane Stith Stanard, the sympathetic mother of a Richmond friend. She presumably inspired his great lyric "To Helen," and her derangement and sudden death in 1824 so grieved him that in ensuing months he often visited her grave at the Shockoe Hill Cemetery. Yet he was not quite the gloomy outcast of legend: to flaunt his athletic skills, Poe challenged his schoolmates to footraces, boxing matches, and jumping contests; possibly on a bet, he undertook a dangerous swim, six miles down the James River against the tide on a sweltering summer day. When a Revolutionary War hero, the Marquis de Lafayette, visited Richmond in 1824, young Poe and fellow members of the Morgan Junior Riflemen formed part of the honor guard. In the throes of adolescence, though, Poe clashed increasingly with John Allan, who complained that his foster son felt "not a Spark of affection for us nor a particle of gratitude" (PL, 61).

Allan's irritability partly stemmed from financial problems, and unpayable debts compelled him to end his partnership with Ellis in 1824. But in March 1825 the death of his wealthy bachelor uncle, William Galt, suddenly left him the owner of three grand plantations, as well as "the slaves, stocks, and property belonging thereto" (PL, 64). Galt's bequest moreover provided stock in the Bank of Virginia and restored Allan's partnership in the mercantile business. This stunning windfall, equivalent to several million dollars today, enabled Allan to buy a Richmond mansion called "Moldavia," which probably aroused in Poe fantasies of one day owning a great house himself and becoming a member of the Southern gentry.

Although by nature imperious and aloof, Poe enjoyed friendships with several Richmond boys, and his closest companion was perhaps Ebenezer Burling, an adventurous lad with an early fondness for drink. Burling occasionally invited Poe to sleep overnight and then tempted him into midnight rambles. A temporary summer visitor arrived in 1825: Poe's older brother, Henry, a sailor who had grown up in Baltimore. Henry met Sarah Elmira Royster, the fifteen-year-old girl with whom Edgar had lately fallen in love. She later remembered Poe as a "beautiful boy," melancholy and somewhat laconic (Quinn, 91). Poe wrote poems for her, delivered them to her door, sketched her portrait, and apparently proposed to marry her when he returned from college.

By the mid-1820s, Poe looked forward, like many an American of that era, to a glowing future. Freed from the threat of foreign war, the United States was enjoying a new prosperity facilitated by an "American system" of "internal improvements"—the creation of roads, canals, and railroads constructed to open up the American frontier to settlement and cultivation while providing an outlet for marketable goods. A postwar cotton boom entrenched the plantation system and chattel slavery across the Old Southwest, committing the region irrevocably to an institution that was opposed by many subsistence farmers in the South. Improvements in transportation, printing technology, and paper production led to the emergence, mostly along the Atlantic seaboard, of a periodical trade that expanded rapidly and produced new opportunities for aspiring writers, editors, and publishers. Newspapers, magazines, and reviews, together with publishing houses, bookstores, and itinerant booksellers, created the framework for an emerging American mass culture. Guidebooks and gazetteers provided information for prospective emigrants to "The Great West," as land ownership and economic opportunity offered powerful incentives. Without regard for the ethics of displacing Native American populations, pundits and prophets hailed the spread of "Anglo-Saxon civilization," while educators from Maine to Georgia, encouraged by the *Dartmouth College v. Woodward* ruling of 1819 (which established the independence of private colleges from state control), hastened to organize colleges and universities for young white men eager to join the educated elite.

When Poe entered the University of Virginia on Valentine's Day, 1826, he arrived bearing John Allan's high expectations but precious little of his ample fortune. During his first semester the young scholar pursued language studies exclusively—in Greek, Latin, French, Spanish, and Italian. The university established by President Jefferson was still under construction, and the student body then consisted of a rowdy, ill-mannered contingent.

Drinking and gambling offered diversion, scuffles and fistfights abounded, and in one melee Poe sustained several nasty bites on his arm. Many students kept pistols at the ready to defend their honor, and in the later tale "Mystification," Poe portrayed this atmosphere of hot-blooded collegiate confrontation. A stillness settled over the campus, however, when on the fiftieth anniversary of the Declaration of Independence, the great founder passed away—an event that denied Poe the opportunity to dine that autumn (as he had been scheduled to do) with the architect of American freedom. During the fall semester Poe again excelled in classical languages and French, and he entertained fellow students by reading an early story (now lost) called "Gaffy." He also won several long-jumping contests, amused himself by covering his walls with charcoal illustrations, hiked about the surrounding countryside (depicted in "A Tale of the Ragged Mountains"), and wagered heavily at cards. The gambling finally undid him: John Allan refused to cover his many debts, estimated to exceed two thousand dollars—two years' salary in that era— and when Poe returned home for the Christmas holiday, Allan announced that he would no longer subsidize the education of a dissolute wastrel.

Poe was also stunned to learn that while he was away, Sarah Elmira Royster had become engaged. Having never received Poe's love letters from Charlottesville (because her father intercepted them), Sarah had bowed to family pressure and accepted the proposal of a budding local entrepreneur. With his education halted and his romantic hopes dashed, Poe was brimming with indignation yet forced to work, probably without pay, at Allan's business office. On March 18, 1827, the conflict between Poe and Allan apparently erupted; obliged to vacate the Allan residence, Poe vowed to leave Richmond: "My determination is at length taken—to leave your house and indeavor [*sic*] to find some place in this wide world, where I will be treated—not as *you* have treated me" (L, 7). His furious parting messages rebuked Allan for his lack of affection, although Poe also sought a "loan" to defray his passage to Boston. In reply Allan offered no cash and instead scored Poe's lack of "perseverance and industry," chiding him for reading such nonsense as *Gil Blas* and *Don Quixote* (PL,

78). Shortly thereafter, with a trunk of belongings that included his early poems, Poe slipped out of Richmond aboard a sailing ship, accompanied by Ebenezer Burling down the James River as far as the port of Norfolk. During a hasty visit to Baltimore, he saw his brother, Henry, and recounted for magazinist Lambert Wilmer the details of his ill-starred romance with Elmira Royster; he then made his way to Boston, the city of his birth. There is no evidence whatsoever to support the myth, circulated by Poe to forestall his university creditors, that after leaving home he had gone to Europe and—like his hero Lord Byron—fought for liberty in Greece.

We know precious little about Poe's activities in Boston. On one occasion he encountered by mischance a certain Peter Pindar Pease with whom he had gambled in Charlottesville and begged Pease not to expose his identity. Poe likely found employment as a store clerk and may have picked up some journalistic work as well; he spent part of his time completing and arranging his first volume of poetry, *Tamerlane and Other Poems*, which was published in Boston that summer. (This book remains one of the rarest and most valuable of early U.S. imprints.) By mid-1827 Poe had also enlisted in the U.S. Army under the pseudonym Edgar A. Perry (again to evade creditors) and was billeted for several months at Fort Independence. But when Battery H, First Artillery, was ordered to report to Charleston, South Carolina, Poe and the rest of his unit narrowly escaped shipwreck off the shoals of Cape Cod in a raging November storm. Such harrowing experiences at sea would later provide material for "MS Found in a Bottle" and *The Narrative of Arthur Gordon Pym*. After eleven days on the Atlantic, the brig *Waltham* safely reached Charleston, and during the next year the nineteen-year-old poet carried out military duties at Fort Moultrie.

Poe seems to have flourished during his sojourn in South Carolina. He later wrote to Allan: "At no period of my life, have I regarded myself with deeper satisfaction—or did my heart swell with more honorable pride" (*L*, 10). He continued to write poetry and pursued his desultory reading of Shakespeare and the English poets, and he probably made the acquaintance William Gilmore Simms and Hugh Swinton Legaré, both editors of

Southern literary journals. On leave he undoubtedly made a nostalgic visit to the Charleston Theater, where his parents had performed. The geography of the flat, coastal landscape so etched itself in Poe's mind that sixteen years later he would make Sullivan's Island the setting of his most popular tale, "The Gold-Bug." Despite commendations for his military performance, the young soldier nevertheless began to grow restless, and in December, when his unit was reassigned to Fortress Monroe, Virginia, Poe sought Allan's consent for an early discharge so that he could fulfill his literary destiny. "I must either conquer or die—succeed or be disgraced," he declared *(L,* 10). He alternately begged forgiveness for past errors and crowed that Allan's neglect fueled his personal ambition. A few weeks later, however, a promotion to the rank of sergeant major may have altered Poe's plans: although he continued to seek release from active duty, he also broached the idea to Allan of obtaining an appointment to the U.S. Military Academy, there to become an officer. Allan was too distracted, though, by the last illness of his wife to consider the proposal, and on February 28, the long-suffering Mrs. Allan expired. Poe arrived in Richmond too late for the funeral but achieved a brief, partial reconciliation with Allan, who was apparently mollified by his recent apology for "infamous conduct" at the university *(L,* 14).

Poe's homecoming coincided closely with the rowdy inaugural reception in Washington that marked the beginning of Andrew Jackson's presidency and the advent of a new era in American life. The contest of 1828 had transformed presidential elections forever by introducing national political tactics, fierce partisanship, and the appeal to a popular electorate through campaign spending. The politics of personality and party loyalty had arrived, and Jackson quickly adopted a "spoils system" in the federal government to reward allies and punish enemies. Although he vetoed the Maysville Road project in Kentucky (to spite his nemesis, Henry Clay), Jackson encouraged settlement of the West and in 1830 promoted the Removal Bill that authorized the "transfer" of eastern Indian tribes to lands west of the Mississippi. Most tribes signed treaties of evacuation for cash settlements and offers of uncontested land. In the South, however, the

Cherokees resisted for several years until U.S. troops forced them west along a "Trail of Tears," and, despite the capture of Chief Osceola, the Seminoles of Florida actually withstood federal efforts to remove them from the Everglades. During the Jackson administration, enforcement of Indian policy—which led to such episodes as the Black Hawk War— was one of the army's primary tasks.

In Virginia, Sergeant Major Poe, a two-year veteran with a quick wit and a flare for eloquence, seemed on the brink of a promising career: before he returned to Fortress Monroe, Allan outfitted him with a new suit and wrote letters on his behalf to request an appointment to West Point. On April 15, 1829, the young poet received his discharge from the army after hiring a replacement, Sergeant Samuel "Bully" Graves. Poe returned to Richmond to visit Allan again and then went on to Baltimore, where he called on Allan's old friend, William Wirt, a U.S. attorney general from Richmond who was later to become the 1832 presidential candidate of the Anti-Masonic Party. A man of letters—though not a poet—Wirt read the work Poe had recently composed, "Al Aaraaf," and offered candid advice about the importance of appealing to "modern readers" (PL, 92). Poe then showed the poem to Robert Walsh, a Philadelphia editor who worked for publishers Carey, Lea, and Carey, and while Isaac Lea considered the manuscript, Poe pleaded with Allan to underwrite any loss the volume might incur. In reply Allan chastised Poe and refused aid, but shortly thereafter he did write to Secretary of War John Henry Eaton, urging him to approve Poe's application to the Military Academy. Unbeknownst to Poe, Allan also pointedly denied any paternal responsibility for the poet, callously remarking to Eaton, "Frankly Sir, do I declare that He is no relation to me whatever" (PL, 92).

While in Baltimore awaiting an appointment, Poe sought out his paternal grandmother, Elizabeth Cairnes Poe, but her meager domestic circumstances obliged him to lodge in cheap hotels and boardinghouses. He was at this time reunited with his brother, Henry, a worldly young man so "entirely given up to drink" (L, 29) as to be more a worry than a comfort for Edgar. Poe spent the remainder of 1829 in the port city, where he cadged meals from relatives, composed poetry, sent manuscripts off to journals, and negotiated terms for his second volume of verse. Just before year's end, the firm of Hatch and Dunning published *Al Aaraaf, Tamerlane, and Minor Poems*. By now declaring himself "irrecoverably a poet" (*L*, 19), Poe brought his work to the attention of the cranky but influential New England critic John Neal, who opined in the *Yankee* that the author of *Al Aaraaf* could become "*foremost* in the rank of *real* poets" (*PL*, 103).

But Poe deferred a literary career because the long-awaited appointment to West Point arrived in March. After visiting Richmond, where his relations with John Allan remained chilly, Poe took his place among the new cadets in June, passed an entrance examination, and attended summer encampment. In September he enrolled in courses in mathematics and French, earning high marks in both. Scribbling witty verses that circulated among the cadets, Poe quickly acquired a reputation as class satirist. High-spirited, alternately diligent and dissolute, mirthful and morose, Poe conspired with classmate Thomas W. Gibson to hoax cadets into believing that Gibson, wielding a bloody knife, had just murdered a man (Silverman, 62). Poe may have been displacing his own anger: Because Allan had again sent him to school with inadequate funds, Poe found himself in financial difficulties. And while he was withstanding with the rigors of West Point training, back in Richmond his old "Pa," at the age of fifty-one, was transferring his affections from Mrs. Elizabeth Wills (with whom he had recently fathered illegitimate twin sons) to Louisa Patterson, a thirty-year-old woman from New Jersey. Allan's marriage to Miss Patterson in New York on October 5, 1830, had immediate, dire implications for Poe, who—given Allan's eagerness for legitimate heirs—saw his prospects for future inheritance vanishing.

Just after Christmas, his foster father delivered the final blow: after reviling Poe for his insinuations about Allan's drinking (imprudently conveyed to "Bully" Graves), he refused any further support and suspended communications with his erstwhile ward. Poe nevertheless replied, blaming his foster father's "mistaken parsimony" for his misfortunes at the University of Virginia and blasting Allan for sending him to West Point "like a beggar"

(L, 40). He also requested (but never received) a letter granting Allan's permission to resign. With independent wealth then the sine qua non of a military commander's career, Poe thus shortly began to neglect his responsibilities, ignoring roll call and absenting himself from mandatory drills. Abandoning all hope of reconciliation or patrimony, Poe sought a speedy, inglorious release from his appointment. On January 28, 1831, he appeared— physically ill and sick at heart—before a court-martial that expelled him for "gross neglect of duty" and "disobedience of orders" (PL, 113). Sustained by intellectual self-respect, however, Poe performed well during final examinations in mathematics and French, and as a parting gift the cadets collected $170 to underwrite publication of his next book of poetry. Making a break with the army, Poe departed on February 19, sailed down the Hudson to New York, and there soon located a publisher, Elam Bliss, who agreed to print *Poems by Edgar A. Poe*, a book dedicated to the "U.S. Corps of Cadets." Unfortunately for those at West Point expecting a jest book filled with satirical verses, strange lyrics like "The Valley of Nis" and "The Doomed City" constituted the poetic fare of the new volume.

Stricken with a "violent cold" and an infection so acute that his ear "discharge[d] blood and matter continuall[y]," Poe spent several weeks in New York; desperate for money, he appealed to both Allan and West Point's commandant, Sylvanus Thayer, rehearsing for the latter a half-baked (and never-realized) plan to obtain in France a military appointment through the Marquis de Lafayette to fight in the Polish Revolution (L, 43–45). By early May, however, Poe had migrated to Baltimore, where he found shelter with his grandmother, Mrs. David Poe, and his aunt, Maria Poe Clemm. Once again reunited with Henry, a sailor-poet given to alcohol and now wracked by consumption, Poe witnessed the shocking decline of his sibling. Separated in infancy, the brothers apparently both experienced (like Roderick and Madeline Usher) a preternatural sense of shared identity and perhaps even composed a few poems together (Silverman, 84-85). But they had little opportunity for collaboration: during the long hot summer Henry's condition became grave, and on August 1 he died. That year Poe looked without success for temporary work about the city, and in the midst of a cholera epidemic that swept the East, he responded to an announcement in the Philadelphia *Saturday Courier* offering one hundred dollars for the best original tale. Drawing on his eclectic reading, Poe produced a series of short, quirky narratives, mostly send-ups of the styles and forms popular in the monthly magazines. His desperate letters to Allan during the last three months of 1831 dramatize his abject need; repenting his "flagrant ingratitude" and—perhaps aware that the new Mrs. Allan had indeed given birth to a legitimate son and heir—Poe acknowledged that he had "deservedly lost" any claim to his foster father's affections (*L*, 46). Allan, who aged rapidly after his remarriage, may have sent funds in November, but they were insufficient to relieve Poe's "wretchedness" (*L*, 49).

Although the *Saturday Courier* sagaciously awarded first prize to Delia S. Bacon, the newspaper published Poe's Gothic fantasy "Metzengerstein" on January 14, 1832, five days prior to his twenty-third birthday. He received little or no compensation for the tale, nor is it certain when he learned that he had become a published writer of fiction. Before the end of the year, however, the newspaper had published four other tales by Poe, all parodies of such magazine types as the religious tale ("A Tale of Jerusalem") and the sensational tale ("A Decided Loss"). His spoof "The Duc de l'Omelette" was actually reprinted in the Baltimore *Minerva* in March, producing local evidence of his breakthrough as a magazinist. But Poe realized at most a pittance for his stories, perhaps nothing at all, and although he continued to live on Wilks Street with his grandmother, his aunt, and her young daughter, Virginia, his source of income for day-to-day expenses remains altogether uncertain. He apparently sought temporary work as a teacher and later as an editorial assistant. In August he perhaps received the painful news from Richmond that his childhood friend Ebenezer Burling had succumbed to cholera. That same month Poe presented a sheaf of stories (some already published) to Lambert Wilmer, editor of the Baltimore *Saturday Visiter*. But Wilmer, embroiled in legal troubles, soon abandoned the journal and could not help his young friend.

Baltimore was at this time a thriving port and a center of shipbuilding. Various industries were also flourishing, and Poe may have found employment for a time as a kiln worker in a brick-yard. He was then (in 1832) living in the Fell's Point area, near the docks, on what was called "Mechanic's Row." It is worth noting that a few streets away, closer to the harbor, Hugh and Sophia Auld resided with their son Thomas and a plucky domestic slave named Fred Bailey, who six years later escaped north in the guise of a sailor and achieved fame as the antislavery editor and orator, Frederick Douglass. In that era Baltimore marked a volatile con-tact zone on the margin of Southern culture, a city regarded by many Maryland slaveholders as "unsound" on the question of slavery (Fields, 49). Proximity to the North complicated the re-gime of slavery by providing short escape routes and an abun-dance of nearby sympathizers willing to assist fugitives. More-over, it brought to Baltimore a stream of Northern transients importing new ideas of abolition and emancipation. Slavery was also complicated there by the presence of a significant popula-tion of free blacks and, as Stephen Whitman has shown, by the growing practice in local industry of hiring slaves who then used their wage-earning power to bargain for freedom. Unrest also simmered as a result of the Virginia slave insurrection of 1831 led by Nat Turner—an episode that sent vicarious panic throughout the South. Poe's contact with slavery seems at this period to have been mostly incidental, although he had acted (in 1829) as Maria Clemm's agent in the hiring out of a slave named Edwin (*PL*, 100). Given the family's destitution, it seems highly unlikely that Mrs. Poe or Mrs. Clemm still retained domestic slaves in the 1830s.

Without employment or income, Poe must nevertheless have drawn occasional, ironic comparisons between his circumstances and those of the slave. His utter impoverishment continued for nearly three more years. He saw a few poems appear in the *Satur-day Visiter* in 1833 and that spring removed with Mrs. Poe, Mrs. Clemm, and Virginia to a tiny brick rowhouse on Amity Street. Having found a usable formula, Poe continued to compose short, grotesque satires and had accumulated eleven such squibs by the middle of the year. Little can be verified about his per-sonal life during this epoch; Poe apparently tutored Virginia, wrote flirtatious verses to his cousin Elizabeth Herring and several other young ladies, and for a few months romanced a girl named Mary Starr. In April he sent a final entreaty to Allan, portraying himself as "without friends, . . . absolutely perishing for want of aid," and begging to be saved "from destruction," but Allan apparently never replied (*L*, 49–50). When in June the *Saturday Visiter* announced premiums for the best tale and best poem—the prizes to be awarded by a committee that included Baltimore novelist John Pendleton Kennedy—Poe submitted a poem and six stories from a collection that he had lately begun calling "The Tales of the Folio Club." He framed the narratives with a brief, comic introduction depicting a fictitious club of oddball raconteurs like "Mr. Horribile Dictû" and "Mr. Convolvulus Gondola." Impressed by the "wild, vigorous" imagination of these pieces, the committee selected "MS Found in a Bottle" for the premium in fiction, while Poe's "The Coliseum" took second prize in the poetry competition (*PL*, 133). The story appeared on October 19, and the newspaper later announced an entire volume of "Folio Club" tales to be published by subscription. Before the work went to press, however, Poe managed to insult the editor (who had won the poetry contest using a pseudonym) and thus derailed the project, prompting Kennedy as literary patron to recommend the book to the well-known Philadelphia publishers Carey and Lea.

Still living with relatives and shackled by poverty, Poe submitted another "Folio Club" story, "The Visionary" (later called "The Assignation"), to Louis Godey's *Lady's Book*, a popular Philadelphia monthly, and the tale's publication in January 1834 marked Poe's debut on the national literary scene. After learning—perhaps from his sister, Rosalie—that John Allan's health was quickly failing, Poe made an unannounced call at his old Richmond home in mid-February in a last bid to regain Allan's favor (and perhaps a small inheritance). Ignoring the protest of the second Mrs. Allan (who had just delivered a third child), he bounded upstairs to Allan's room, only to confront the invalid, who brandished a cane and threatened to strike Poe if he did not withdraw. A scant six weeks later Allan died, leaving behind a will that scandalized Richmond by providing not only for his three sons by Louisa but also for the one surviving son by Mrs. Wills *and* for her daughter, apparently fathered by Allan before the death of Frances. The document did not, however, mention the young man Allan had raised as a son from 1811. Thus formally disinherited, Poe persisted in his magazine writing, awaiting word from Carey and Lea and looking for opportunities to display his intelligence and learning. In November he traveled to Philadelphia to visit Henry C. Carey, who seemed willing to publish the stories (possibly as a favor to Kennedy) but doubtful about the market appeal of an esoteric volume by an unknown author. He advised Poe to publish the tales piecemeal in the periodicals and gift books and even tried to place one of them himself but shortly lost interest in the larger project. To the end of Poe's ill-starred career, the "Tales of the Folio Club" never appeared in print as such.

But Poe's luck was, for a brief interval at least, about to change. In the early 1830s the country was undergoing dynamic change, making the transition from a largely agricultural, subsistence economy to a capitalist, market economy fueled, in part, by an emerging factory system. Once a champion of hard currency, Andrew Jackson easily won a second term in 1832 by promising entrepreneurs greater availability of paper bills. He accomplished this by vetoing the recharter of Nicholas Biddle's Second National Bank (its federal charter would expire four years later) and by shifting government deposits from the Second Bank to state banks, thereby triggering a rapid proliferation of regional banks that began issuing paper notes. His liberal money policy prompted what Edward Pessen has called a "frenzied race for riches" through investment and speculation (103), and Jackson's laissez-faire approach also encouraged new forms of production and transportation. The growth of American cities during the 1830s was little short of phenomenal: the population of New York more than doubled (from 123,000 to around 310,000) between 1820 and 1840, as the annual arrival of new immigrants from Europe spiked upward in the 1830s sixfold from averages typical of the mid-1820s. With Philadelphia, Boston, New Orleans, and Cincinnati also boasting populations in excess of 100,000, the rise of metropolitan culture was palpable, and the spread of both money and public education (a great theme during the decade) produced a new reading public. The expanding periodical trade of the 1830s—which saw the founding of such high-quality journals as *Godey's*, the *New England Magazine*, the *Democratic Review*, and the *Knickerbocker*, among others—aimed to capitalize on this audience while shaping its political, economic, and literary inclinations. Religious life was likewise affected: Charles Sellers has noted that the market revolution "pushed insecure clerics of all denominations toward a loving Christianity of middle-class respectability and capitalist effort" (375). The mythology of middle-class striving was promoted on all fronts.

In Baltimore, the wealthy Kennedy gave Poe a link to this milieu of rising prosperity. He offered encouragement, found him odd jobs, outfitted him with new clothes, invited him to dinner, and even loaned him a horse for the sake of outdoor recreation. It seems likely that Kennedy also wrote on Poe's behalf to Thomas W. White, an ambitious Richmond printer who decided in late 1834 to profit from the boom by establishing a new periodical, the *Southern Literary Messenger*. Poe sent an original manuscript, and the March 1835 issue featured the gruesome "Berenice," a story of such questionable taste that Poe, in proposing further tales each month, felt compelled to assure White that he would "not sin quite so egregiously again" (*L*, 58). In the months to follow he supplied the *Messenger* with book reviews and previously published tales from the "Folio Club" series, works such as "Lionizing" and "Bon Bon." To ingratiate himself with White, Poe also composed for the Baltimore *Republican and Commercial Advertiser* unsigned laudatory notices of the new journal, which included appreciative comments about his own contributions. Seizing on local interest in balloon ascensions, he concocted for the June *Messenger* a madcap science fiction tale, "The Unparalleled Adventure of One Hans Pfaall," depicting an imaginary trip to the moon. In a letter that same month he hinted broadly that he would be pleased to work for White. "At present a very small portion of my time is employed," he reported (*L*, 63). The following month Poe purchased ink for White in Baltimore, and in early August he journeyed south to lend personal assistance, for White was then ill and shorthanded after dismissing his editor. The visit—Poe's first to Richmond since the death of John Allan—marked the beginning of his seventeen-month employment with the *Messenger*, a stint that would make him famous, or at least infamous, in the American publishing world.

Poe's return to Richmond proved unexpectedly traumatic. Shortly before departing Baltimore he had helped to bury his grandmother, Elizabeth Cairnes Poe, and leaving behind his aunt Maria and cousin Virginia, he gave up the only domestic affection he had known in years. In Richmond he apparently sought solace in drink and also found comfort in the presence of lovely Eliza White, the proprietor's daughter. A romance quickly developed, despite the qualms of the publisher, who suspected that his new assistant was "rather dissipated" (*PL*, 167). Perhaps cognizant of Poe's sudden infatuation, Mrs. Clemm in late August sent him a heartrending letter, explaining that in her destitution, she felt obliged to entrust care of Virginia to cousin Neilson Poe, owner of the *Baltimore Chronicle*. After sheltering Edgar for four years, Maria clearly expected her nephew to reciprocate once he had established himself professionally, and her manipulative letter had the desired effect. Devoted to Virginia (then thirteen), whom he called his "darling," "Sissy," and "little wifey," Poe feared that he would "never behold her again" if she came under the charge of the detested Neilson and his wife, Josephine Clemm, who happened to be Virginia's half sister and Neilson's own first cousin (*L*, 69–71). Poe implored Mrs. Clemm and Virginia to move immediately to Richmond, and fighting off deep depression he hurried to Baltimore in September, procured a marriage license, and perhaps impulsively wedded his young cousin in a private ceremony. Stunned by his assistant's hasty departure, White believed that Poe had "[flown] the track already" and guessed correctly that he was "a victim of melancholy" (*PL*, 170–71). Begging reinstatement two weeks later, Poe received a stern temperance lecture from his employer before resuming his position as editorial subaltern. With Mrs. Clemm and Virginia now under his protection, he took up residence in a Richmond boardinghouse.

On the evidence of editorial responses to the *Messenger* from other journals, one can trace Poe's meteoric rise in the literary world. Identified simply as White's assistant, he received accolades for improving the journal's literary tone; papers from Maine to Georgia hailed his originality as a writer of tales and noted the sometimes acerbic tone of his critical notices. In December he ignited a controversy with his savage review of Theodore Fay's *Norman Leslie*, a novel "bepuffed" by the *New-York Mirror*, which employed Fay as associate editor. In that same issue Poe published his unfinished drama, *Politian*, based on the notorious Beauchamp murder in Kentucky. Although his workload apparently impeded the composition of new tales (he reprinted only old ones through the end of 1836), Poe proved a clever magazinist: posing as a handwriting expert, he interpreted the signatures of fellow authors in "Autography," and in "Maelzel's Chess Player" he disclosed the secret of a mysterious automaton. Upon learning that novelist James Kirke Paulding had praised him to White as "the best of all our going writers," Poe unabashedly forwarded his "Folio Club" manuscripts, begging Paulding to find a publisher (*PL*, 184). About this time he also began to represent himself in letters as editor of the *Messenger*, and critical notices reprinted in the journal so identified him as well, but—and the point is crucial—White never confirmed the appointment by changing the masthead to reflect Poe's control over editorial matters.

A thorny problem for Poe and the journal itself emerged from the slavery crisis of the 1830s. Since William Lloyd Garrison had launched the abolitionist movement in 1831 with his fiery newspaper, the *Liberator*, Southerners who had been divided themselves about the "peculiar institution" felt under increasing scrutiny in their public discourse. If the Virginia legislative debates of 1831–32 had exposed sharp regional differences, the proliferation of pamphlets by the American Anti-Slavery Society in 1835—tracts aimed at Southern readers—produced defensive reactions, as well as a new, pro-slavery ideology. In Virginia, as John Ashworth notes, "laws were passed forbidding blacks from preaching or from circulating incendiary pamphlets" (140). In South Carolina, a mob led by a former governor stormed a post office and destroyed several bags of antislavery propaganda. The increasingly anti-Southern abolitionist rhetoric complicated the editorial handling of commentary on slavery in a nationally circulated journal like the *Messenger*. Ordinarily White and Poe tried to avoid the subject, but certain valuable contributors felt compelled to register their sentiments. In an April 1836 review frequently misattributed to Poe, Nathaniel Beverley Tucker waxed eloquent on the "moral influences flowing from the relation between master and slave" and defended slavery as a "much abused" institution from which the South derived "much more of good than of evil." Two months earlier, however, Poe had aligned himself with "all men of sense" (*L*, 87) in lauding Lucian Minor's "Liberian Literature," which recalled the "horrors of the Middle Passage" and celebrated advances in Liberia by way of endorsing colonization, the strategy favored by "gradualists" opposed to both "immediatist" abolition and the indefinite perpetuation of slavery. As Poe discovered in Richmond, there was mounting pressure to present a united Southern front on slavery, as well as increasing surveillance of newspapers and journals; but Poe (and White) also wanted to retain the support of Northern subscribers and so endeavored to articulate what Terence Whalen has called an "average racism," a lukewarm view of slavery that offended as few (white) readers as possible (111–46).

While negotiating the tightrope of editorial politics, Poe tried to silence local gossip in May 1836 by betrothing Virginia in front of witnesses, including White and his daughter Eliza. Not quite fourteen years old, "Sissy" looked even younger, and doubtless for some years the couple maintained a chaste relationship. (Not until his 1841 tale "Eleonora" did the author portray an intimacy transformed by Eros.) Poe perhaps thought the nuptials would demonstrate his own steadiness and respectability, for White had serious doubts about his young assistant. Now producing a large share of the editorial fillers and critical notices, Poe apparently lapsed into occasional intemperance. In reality his homecoming had proved more complicated than expected; stories about his earlier prodigality at Charlottesville resurfaced, and the sight of John Allan's mansion (and young sons) must have fueled chronic resentment. Moreover, he received disappointing news from Harper and Brothers: they were rejecting his "learned and mystical" Folio Club tales and advised him to produce "a single and connected story" of one or two volumes—as if a writer of his temperament could grind out a plodding tale (*PL*, 212). By September, disturbed by Poe's alcoholic "illnesses" and by objections to his "cutting and slashing" reviews, White thought seriously about firing him (*PL*, 222, 236).

A chastened Poe remained in place, however, and offered his "mystical" tales to the British firm of Saunders and Otley, which had opened a New York office. But dubious about his prospects and intrigued by Jeremiah Reynolds's report to Congress on a proposed South Seas expedition, Poe began working on a long story ostensibly narrated by the survivor of fantastic adventures at sea. The first two issues of the 1837 *Messenger* carried the opening episodes of "The Narrative of Arthur Gordon Pym," depicting Pym's escape from "Edgarton" in terms resembling Poe's own 1827 departure from Richmond. That his young hero gains his freedom by hiding in a ship's hold may have historical resonance, for as Marie Tyler-McGraw and Gregg D. Kimball have observed, "the most common form of [slave] escape from Richmond involved hiding out in the storage spaces of a ship" (69). Pym's eagerness to leave home probably recalls Poe's feud with John Allan, but it also anticipates his quarrel with White, who discharged his editorial "Tomahawk Man" at the beginning of 1837, just before Poe's twenty-eighth birthday. In less than a year and a half, the author-editor-critic had nevertheless transformed the *Messenger* into a much-noticed periodical, and even if he exaggerated his impact on circulation (Whalen, 58–75), he had indeed achieved a certain celebrity.

However much Poe's alcoholic absences or acerbic opinions figured in his dismissal, White also fired his editorial genius in response to financial distress. The publisher was deeply in debt, his wife was ill, and a strike by his press crew had disrupted production of the *Messenger*. In late November he begged a friend in New York to send currency from one of the city banks: "Send it on as soon as you can get it—for we are all without money in Richmond" (*PL*, 234). White's dilemma was symptomatic of a national money problem, and at its crux was the circulation of in-

creasingly worthless bank notes, the bitter fruit of Jackson's plan
to destroy the Second Bank of the United States. Indeed, the
bank's national charter had expired in 1836, and by then so many
unregulated, state-chartered banks were issuing bills that Jackson
was forced in July to issue his Specie Circular requiring payment
of gold or silver for public lands. The boom was suddenly over:
the very edict designed to protect the federal government against
fraud and to discourage the circulation of unsound bank notes
actually produced a run on specie, led to the hoarding of sound
bills, and undermined public confidence in state banks. As Jackson's handpicked successor, Martin Van Buren fought off a challenge from the newly formed Whig Party in the 1836 presidential
election, but he was faced with the grim consequences of Jackson's fiscal policies. Interest rates began to rise, businesses failed,
and Britain (facing a specie shortage of its own) stopped buying
cotton from the South. Sellers tersely observes of this epoch:
"Bad cotton debts brought down 93 New York firms with over
$60 million in capital" (354). Hard times were at hand.

Soon after his dismissal, Poe received an invitation from Rev.
F. L. Hawks to join the staff of the *New York Review,* and (after
"pestering" White for back pay) he departed Richmond in early
February to take up residence with Virginia and Mrs. Clemm in an
apartment on Sixth Avenue in Manhattan. Few details about Poe's
year in the city can be confirmed, but we know that in the midst of
pervasive economic uncertainty the position with Hawks never
materialized. Unemployed men were then demonstrating in the
streets of New York, and about the time of Poe's arrival, a mob
broke into a warehouse to seize city-owned flour. In a tight market, the author published very little in the magazines that year except an esoteric review of a travel book and two slight tales, "Von
Jung the Mystific" (later "Mystification") and "Siope. A Fable"
(later "Silence—a Fable"). He attended a booksellers' dinner on
March 30 that allowed him to rub elbows briefly with Paulding,
Washington Irving, and William Cullen Bryant; no doubt hoping
to attract a job offer, he toasted "the *Monthlies* of Gotham" (*PL,*
243). He filled his time, apparently, by searching for work and by
expanding to novel length *The Narrative of Arthur Gordon Pym,* a
book listed by Harper and Brothers as virtually set for publication

in May 1837. But that same month disaster struck: New York banks suspended specie payments, paper notes became nonnegotiable, and the Panic of 1837 was under way. Harper and Brothers postponed publication of Poe's novel, leaving the writer jobless and penniless, except for the trivial sums he obtained for his two magazine contributions. Probably to economize, Poe and his family moved to 113½ Carmine Street, where they weathered the opening months of a depression that would last six full years.

Early in 1838, amid short-lived hopes of renewed business activity, Poe moved to Philadelphia and with Virginia and Mrs. Clemm took up residence in a boardinghouse on Arch Street (now Mulberry). Nationally, anti-British sentiment raged as state governments and private companies defaulted on loans from British creditors, and along the St. Lawrence, New York frontiersmen conspired to foment insurrection in Canada. Sustained by foundries and factories, and especially by the manufacture of steam engines and locomotives, Philadelphia suffered less than New York from the banking crisis, partly because in 1837 Nicholas Biddle had obtained a charter from Pennsylvania to keep his well-run bank in operation there. In 1838 the country's first public high school opened in Philadelphia, and the new Museum Building provided an elegant setting for the display of natural specimens and cultural artifacts. Poe arrived in the City of Brotherly Love, however, at a time of violent local agitation about the slavery crisis: in May a mob opposed to abolition burned to the ground Pennsylvania Hall, where black and white women attending the Anti-Slavery Convention of American Women had scandalously marched arm in arm. That same year, simmering resentment of blacks in Philadelphia had led the Pennsylvania legislature to revoke the voting rights of free black men. As Poe was uncomfortably aware, similar public fury was sometimes directed against recent Irish immigrants, which perhaps inspired his effort at that time to claim German ancestry (*L*, 113).

How the writer planned to sustain his family is uncertain: he had some slight acquaintance with such publishers as Henry Carey, and Philadelphia (like New York) supported an impressive array of newspapers and periodicals, including the newly founded *Gentleman's Magazine*. But reduced to writing occasional filler, Poe had little hope of recapturing prominence as a magazinist, and in July 1838 he appealed to Paulding, the recently appointed secretary of the navy, requesting even "the most unimportant Clerkship," to free him from "the miserable life of literary drudgery" (*L*, 681) pursued with so little recent success. Delayed by the banking panic, *The Narrative of Arthur Gordon Pym* finally appeared at the end of July, and a pirated English edition followed soon thereafter. Depicting the massacre of white explorers by black natives on a remote island, the novel unmistakably exploited the racial anxieties of the 1830s. It also capitalized on current discussion about Antarctica, and in what may have been a marketing ploy, the book's American publication coincided closely with the departure of the Wilkes Expedition. But although Poe evoked a polar region of "novelty and wonder" (*PT*, 1176), the book did not sell well. Harper and Brothers nevertheless must have compensated Poe, for by early September he claimed to have "nearly" extricated himself from his recent financial "embarrassments" (*L*, 112) and moved with Virginia and Mrs. Clemm to a small house on Sixteenth Street. He also brought in a few dollars through his arrangement with Professor Thomas Wyatt to "edit" a textbook on seashells, which was published (as something of a legal dodge by Wyatt) under his assistant's name in 1839. Poe made a more important connection that year with Nathan C. Brooks, then launching a new journal in Baltimore, the *American Museum*, whose September issue included Poe's strange tale "Ligeia." It was one of his greatest stories and the first original tale of consequence to appear in almost three years. Two months later the magazine carried his two-part burlesque, "The Psyche Zenobia" ("How to Write a Blackwood Article") and "The Scythe of Time" ("A Predicament"). Audacious, inventive, and replete with self-mockery, "Blackwood" satirized his own sensationalism as the author again displayed the verve that typified his rise to national prominence.

Once more, however, Poe found himself in arrears, and by early 1839 he was seeking loans from acquaintances. His literary effusions early that year were limited to a column of "Literary Small Talk" and a new poem, "The Haunted Palace," both in the

Museum, as well as a piece in the Philadelphia *Saturday Chronicle*, "The Devil in the Belfry," which parodied the Knickerbocker persona of Washington Irving. Since he encountered the great man at the booksellers' dinner in 1837, Irving had become something of an emblem for Poe of the "overrated" author of "surreptitious" reputation (*L*, 112). He obviously envied Irving's wealth as well as his huge popularity. In May, Poe met William Burton, an actor and theater manager who had in 1837 founded the *Gentleman's Magazine*. Burton in fact blasted *Pym* in September 1838 as a "mass of ignorance and effrontery" (*PL*, 254), but he recognized Poe's skill as a magazinist and hired him, initially, to perform odd jobs. By June 1839, however, the magazine listed him as an assistant editor, and thereafter Poe's name appeared beside Burton's as coeditor. Drawing a meager salary of fifty dollars per month, Poe handled the "critiques" and quickly resumed the savage reviewing style that was becoming his hallmark, taking on such revered figures as Henry Wadsworth Longfellow. In August he asked Joseph Evans Snodgrass, the physician, editor, and abolitionist, to reprint a flattering review of Poe in a Baltimore newspaper and brazenly flaunted his scorn for literary "enemies": "I intend to put up with nothing that I can *put down*" (*L*, 114). The following month he assured Philip Pendleton Cooke: "As soon as Fate allows I will have a Magazine of my own—and will endeavor to kick up a dust" (*L*, 119). His growing sense of prowess (heralded by "Ligeia") led to the September publication in *Burton's* of "The Fall of the House of Usher," a tale of dramatic intensity, psychological subtlety, and symbolic complexity. He followed it one month later with a dazzling tale of conscience, "William Wilson," which had already been sold to an annual, *The Gift*. Still eager to see his stories in a single volume, Poe negotiated an agreement with Lea and Blanchard to publish *Tales of the Grotesque and Arabesque*. Issued in early December, the book featured twenty-five tales (including the original "Folio Club" stories), and Poe's preface addressed an imputation of "Germanism" by declaring that "terror is not of Germany, but of the soul" (*PT*, 129). At the age of thirty, Poe regarded his tales as the result of "matured purpose and very careful elaboration" (*PT*, 130). In less than a year he returned from literary oblivion to command new influence in American letters.

As approving notices of the *Tales* began to appear, the author looked to display his inventiveness in other ways. To showcase his analytical acumen, he boasted to readers of *Alexander's Weekly Messenger* that he could solve any cryptogram submitted to him, and for five months he deciphered coded messages to back his claim. Simultaneously *Burton's* trumpeted the publication of a sensational discovery—a manuscript composed by the "first white man" to cross the Rockies (*PL*, 277). In January 1840, the magazine featured the first of six installments of "The Journal of Julius Rodman," a chronicle purportedly documenting the earliest exploration of the Far West in the 1790s. Poe sustained the hoax by cribbing passages from Alexander Mackenzie's *Voyages* (1801), the history of the Lewis and Clark expedition (1814), Irving's *Astoria* (1836), and other sources. Although a February 1840 Senate document cited its potential historical importance (*PL*, 288), the serialized narrative did not fool most readers for very long. Perversely, while he was ransacking historical sources for "Rodman," Poe intensified his attack on Longfellow by accusing him of plagiarism—thus touching off a controversy that raged several years. Overworked and underpaid, Poe dashed off reviews for *Burton's* with increasing carelessness; he resented the owner's wealth, his lordly manner, and his refusal to pay premiums for a competition announced earlier. When he learned that Burton was building a new theater and preparing to sell the journal, Poe decided to seize the day and found a monthly of his own. Privately he drew up a prospectus for the *Penn Magazine* and began soliciting subscriptions. Perhaps worried about the consequent salability of his own journal, Burton reacted to the prospectus as a betrayal and on May 30 dismissed his assistant. Poe fired back an indignant letter that warned: "If by accident you have taken it into your head that I am to be insulted with impunity I can only assume that you are an ass" (*L*, 130). Rejecting the claim that he owed Burton one hundred dollars, he calculated the number of magazine pages he had supplied in twelve months to show how underpaid he had been.

During the ensuing year, Poe labored mightily to amass the financial capital and literary commitments needed to establish the *Penn*, which he conceived as "somewhat on the plan" of the *Southern Literary Messenger* (*L*, 153). Animated by the sincere desire to "produce some lasting effect upon the growing literature of the country," he felt he must "do or die . . . in a literary sense" (*L*, 141, 152). Poe solicited contributions from John Pendleton Kennedy, Thomas Holley Chivers, Robert T. Conrad, and Dr. Joseph Snodgrass, and—hoping to secure a wealthy patron—called upon the recently retired Nicholas Biddle, who paid for a four-year subscription but (with an old banker's caution) withheld further support (*PL*, 311). Poe's timing was, as usual, wretched: the depression that began in 1837 was still wreaking havoc on the money supply, and bank failures multiplied. The national election of 1840 reflected discontent with the fiscal policies of Van Buren: the Whig Party, generally representing business and commercial interests—as well as antipathy toward Jacksonian leveling—swept into power by promising a new national bank and principled leadership under "Tippecanoe and Tyler, too." But General William Henry Harrison, the old Indian fighter, died of pneumonia one month after taking office and was succeeded by John Tyler, a states' rights man so dubious about a central bank that even with Whig majorities in Congress, no meaningful economic reform could be effected. By the end of the following year, Tyler (an erstwhile Democrat) had been abandoned by his new party. The Whig victory nevertheless raised new hopes for Poe—who claimed to be a Harrison supporter—of escaping what he later called "the magazine prison house" (*ER*, 1036).

Likewise disenchanted with the periodical business, Burton sold his *Gentleman's Magazine* in October 1840 to George Graham, owner of the *Casket*, who merged the two periodicals in December to create *Graham's Magazine*. To the first issue Poe contributed a tale of surveillance and analysis, "The Man of the Crowd," which evoked both the London of Dickens and the city of his childhood memories. Just as he was arranging the inaugural issue of the *Penn*, however, he became seriously ill and was bedridden for several weeks, forcing a postponement. The delay was fatal: the national monetary crisis that began on February 4, 1841, dashed any hope of soon issuing the projected journal. All banks in Philadelphia suspended specie payments on bills larger than five dollars, and the Bank of the United States closed its doors permanently. With the country sliding into a deeper depression, Poe pragmatically accepted a temporary position with George Graham, an association that brought steady income and a renewed reputation as an inventive magazinist. Unveiling the first of his so-called tales of ratiocination, an April feature titled "'The Murders in the Rue Morgue," Poe added a new genre to the realm of prose fiction: the detective story. To the May issue he contributed the horrific story "A Descent into the Maelstrom" and later provided a much-discussed piece, "Secret Writing," as well as a sequel to his earlier study of "autography." In a review of Dickens's *Barnaby Rudge*, then in serialization, he correctly predicted that the idiot Barnaby would be revealed as the murderer's own son. Impressed by Poe's talent, Graham offered his partnership in producing a high-quality literary monthly, and during the summer of 1841, Poe wrote to such respected authors as Irving, Cooper, Kennedy, and even Longfellow, describing the proposed journal and soliciting contributions. But while he touted the new venture, Poe also grumbled privately about Graham's fondness for "namby-pamby" features and fashion plates (*L*, 197) and so—encouraged by his friend Frederick W. Thomas—initiated inquiries about a government appointment from President Tyler.

During this season of anticipation Poe also composed "Eleonora," a prophetic and surprisingly hopeful tale about a young man's quest for new love after the demise of his cousin-wife. The story would soon come to haunt the author: while performing a song after dinner, possibly on the evening of Poe's thirty-third birthday in 1842, Virginia suffered a pulmonary hemorrhage and almost died. It was the first undeniable evidence of the consumption that would send her to an early grave. Agonized by her subsequent relapses, Poe fell ill himself, sought forgetfulness in drink, and largely neglected his magazine work. Still pursuing a larger goal, though, he wrote to Thomas in February, proposing to make the *Penn* a political instrument of the embattled Tyler (whose cabinet, aside from Daniel Webster, had recently resigned en masse) if the president's son could be recruited as a benefactor (*L*, 192). In the troubled aftermath of Virginia's collapse, he also composed "Life in Death" ("The Oval Portrait"), a guilt-driven tale about a painter whose obsession with his own art causes the death of his wife. In early April, when he returned to *Graham's*, Poe discovered at his desk an interim editorial assistant, took umbrage at being "replaced," and promptly resigned. Graham shortly offered the position to Rufus W. Griswold, the anthologist who became Poe's literary executor and nemesis. The May issue (prepared in April) nevertheless included the famous review of Hawthorne's *Twice-Told Tales*, introducing Poe's idea that every word of a tale should contribute to the "outbringing" of a "single *effect*" (*ER*, 572). Obsessed by his wife's subjection to a fatal disease, he also produced his shocking allegory of contagion, "The Masque of the Red Death."

In May, Thomas wrote to suggest a new scheme to sustain Poe's literary career—an appointment to the Philadelphia Custom House. Poe broached the idea to another Washington friend, James Herron, who called on President Tyler's son to promote the notion. Virginia was again "dangerously ill with hemorrhage from the lungs" when Poe journeyed to New York in June 1842 in quest of editorial employment (*L*, 199). Succumbing to despair, he drank mint juleps with a Kentucky poet named William Wallace and then embarrassed himself in the presence of several literary men, including editor William Snowden and the Langley brothers, publishers of the *Democratic Review*. When Poe returned to Philadelphia, though, he found a letter from Herron conveying Rob Tyler's assurance of an appointment. A sinecure seemed his only hope; musing on his predicament, Poe told Thomas: "Literature is at a sad discount. . . . Without an international copyright law, American authors may as well cut their throats " (*L*, 210). In the absence of such protection, pirated British literature still flooded the American market, reducing opportunities for native writers. To this circumstance Poe attributed his recent failure to find a publisher in New York for a second volume of tales called *Phantasy-Pieces*. He managed, however, to sell a new story, "The Pit and the Pendulum," to *The Gift*, and he sold his second detective story, "The Mystery of Marie Rogêt" to Snowden's *Ladies Companion*. Using details gleaned from New York newspapers, Poe attempted in the latter piece to unriddle the mysterious death of a salesgirl named Mary Rogers through the cogitations of his fictional detective, C. Auguste Dupin. (While the story was in serialization, however, new information suggested that the young woman had died from an unsuccessful abortion.) In his next composition Poe apparently tapped his residual contempt for John Allan to create the chilling murder story "The Tell-Tale Heart," which appeared in James Russell Lowell's *Pioneer*. With his two dependents—one now chronically ill—he moved at the end of the summer to a house on Coates Street in the Fairmount section.

Dismayed by his failure in November to receive the custom house job—and even more so by a glimpse of the Whig "ruffians and boobies" who received political appointments ahead of him (*L*, 219)—Poe entered a partnership in January 1843 with Thomas C. Clarke, editor of the weekly *Saturday Museum*, who agreed to publish a monthly magazine now called the *Stylus*. In a revised prospectus Poe declared the "leading object" of the journal to be "absolutely independent criticism," uncompromised by the practice of indiscriminate puffing (Quinn, 376). Hoping to enlist new subscribers—and to wangle a government post if possible—Poe took the train to Washington in March, got drunk repeatedly, and embarrassed his friends. He expected a meeting with President Tyler himself but never received one. In an apologetic letter to Thomas and Jesse E. Dow, he alluded to a sorry episode in which his cloak was "turned inside out" (*L*, 229). Among other "peccadilloes" he offended Thomas Dunn English, a Philadelphia writer visiting on business, and English took revenge by satirizing Poe as a drunken literary man in his temperance novel *The Doom of the Drinker* (1843). Having sought in alcohol an escape from private grief, Poe soon found himself—in an era of zealous reform—reduced to public caricature. In disgrace he returned from Washington, hoping to salvage his dream of publishing the *Stylus*. He made inquiry about purchasing the *Southern Literary Messenger* (Thomas White had recently died) and spoke boldly of collaborating with a Philadelphia "capitalist" (*L*, 243), but soon thereafter Clarke—who had commissioned English's novel for serialization—withdrew his support.

Sometime during these troubled months, Poe moved his family to a house on North Seventh Street in an area called Spring Garden. Defying the ongoing national depression, which reached its depths around February 1843, Philadelphia was experiencing rapid growth and urbanization. The Whigs controlled local politics, and hundreds of Philadelphians had amassed enough wealth in real estate speculation and manufacturing to be the equivalent of today's millionaires. In 1842, Democrat George Lippard began publishing his muckraking newspaper, *Spirit of the Times*, while Graham and partner Charles Peterson established *Peterson's Lady's National Magazine*. Eliza Leslie and T. S. Arthur likewise founded *Miss Leslie's Magazine* in January 1843, the year that two foreign opera companies enjoyed long-running engagements at the Chestnut Street Theatre. Yet despite these cultural adornments, the city was wracked by ongoing racial and ethnic conflict. As a major stop on the Underground Railroad, Philadelphia experienced a constant influx of refugees from slavery and a widening gap between the rich and the poor. In August 1842 a white mob attacked the Negro Young Men's Vigilant Association, then marching to commemorate the abolition of slavery in the West Indies; many blacks (including women and children) were beaten, and two buildings associated with abolitionist meetings were burned. Noting that Philadelphia was both a "Garrison stronghold" and the "most southern of northern cities," Elizabeth M. Geffen remarks that the conflicting "twin traditions of brotherly love and white racism" had by the 1840s become a problem whose "moral dimensions" had reached "major proportions" (355). Moreover, oppression of blacks accompanied an anti-Irish, anti-Catholic crusade organized in late 1842 by a group of Protestant clergymen. A related phalanx calling itself the Native American Party began to coordinate national anti-Catholic demonstrations and to establish newspapers like the *Daily Sun* to promote Nativist political candidates and an agenda of ethnic hatred that eventually incited rioting in Philadelphia.

In this climate of violence Poe finally received welcome news in June 1843: his treasure-hunting tale "The Gold-Bug" won a prize of one hundred dollars offered by the *Dollar Newspaper* and brought belated fame. Given contemporary racial tensions in Philadelphia, his portrayal of the relationship between cryptographer William Legrand and his manumitted slave, Jupiter, possesses more than passing interest. By August, a dramatic adaptation of the story was performed at the Walnut Street Theatre, and that same month the *Saturday Evening Post* published "The Black Cat," a veritable temperance tale with an indelicate emphasis—given Virginia's invalidism—on domestic brutality. Poe perhaps also derived some proceeds from a pamphlet called *The Prose Romances of Edgar A. Poe,* which featured the incongruous pairing of "The Murders in the Rue Morgue" and an 1839 satire, "The Man That Was Used Up." Despite the prize and the pamphlet, Poe was soon pressed for cash, and in November, just before Clarke's newspaper began serializing *The Doom of the Drinker,* he presented (for the William Wirt Institute) a lecture on "American Poetry" before a huge crowd at a local church. It was, we should recall, the great age of the lyceum movement, which during the 1830s spread from New England (where Emerson attained fame as a lecturer) across the nation, bringing learning, inspiration, and sometimes reformist ideas to middle-class audiences. Containing a mix of clever ideas, complimentary nods, and scathing denunciations, Poe's speech created excitement; he repeated it several times over the next two months in nearby cities that included Wilmington and Baltimore. Perhaps to capitalize on his new celebrity as a lecturer, Poe resumed more regular reviewing in *Graham's,* although the owner pocketed his "savage" critique of Longfellow's verse drama "The Spanish Student" and privately assured Longfellow that he planned to "part company" with Poe after publishing some less "venomous" reviews in hand (*PL,* 452). Though Poe could still find local outlets for his tales and received extravagant praise from Democrats John S. Du Solle in the *Spirit of the Times* and George Lippard in the *Citizen Soldier,* he had concluded that his aim of owning a high-quality magazine could never be realized in Philadelphia. On March 30 he wrote to James Russell Lowell: "How dreadful is the present condition of our literature! To what are things tending? We want two things, certainly:—an International Copyright Law, and a well-founded Monthly Journal, of sufficient ability, circulation, and character, to control and so give tone to, our Letters" (*L*, 247).

Poe's growing preoccupation with the copyright question may also help to account for his return, in April 1844, to New York. An American Copyright Club had been formed there in 1843 by writers associated with Everett Duyckinck and Cornelius Mathews, and Poe himself was asked to join (Widmer, 99). There, perhaps, he could form that secret "coalition" among the literary elite—a scheme just outlined to Lowell—to establish a great national journal. On the morning of April 6, Poe and Virginia took the train to Perth Amboy, New Jersey, and from there a steamer that shuttled them to the New York harbor. Joined by Mrs. Clemm a few days later, Poe quickly caused a commotion by publishing as a news article in the *New York Sun* the piece now known as "The Balloon-Hoax." The story's appearance drew a crowd clamoring for more details about a reported transatlantic balloon flight. Soon after arriving he also agreed to provide for the *Columbia* (Pennsylvania) *Spy* a series of gossipy letters called "Doings of Gotham." The series gave Poe a forum (albeit obscure) for opinions on diverse matters; he sauntered about the burgeoning city, commenting on the crumbling old mansions of Manhattan, the commodity value of street garbage, the "great raree-show" of an early department store, and the sheer din of street noise (Poe, 48). Alluding to the presidential election of 1844, he noted that "'Polk Houses,' 'Polk Oyster Cellars,' and 'Polk hats, gloves, and walking-canes,' are already contending with their rivals of Clay" (48). Perhaps in deference to Virginia's health, Poe soon found lodging for his family in a farmhouse just north of the city. A July letter to Lowell suggests that the semi-rural setting proved agreeable; Poe himself had apparently experienced a recent, creative surge, "a sort of mania for composition," and was eager to sketch out his philosophy about life, death, and God (*L*, 256–57). The *Dollar Newspaper* featured his hoaxing "bugaboo tale," "The Premature Burial," in July; the *Columbian Magazine* for August included his visionary "Mesmeric Revelation"; and soon thereafter *The Gift* published the dazzling, final Dupin story, "The Purloined Letter." In early October, Nathaniel Parker Willis hired Poe as an assistant at the *Evening Mirror*.

By then the fever of the 1844 election was rampant. Without party hacking, Tyler abandoned hope of reelection, and the Whigs seemed poised for victory with Henry Clay as their standard-bearer and with consensus on banking reform and a return to internal improvements. Territorial issues, however, dominated the campaign: the annexation of Texas aroused strong feelings, although it was the dispute between Britain and the United States over the Oregon Territory north of the Columbia River that provoked the famous slogan "Fifty-four forty or fight." Misgivings about Texas annexation (which threatened to further extend slavery) cost Van Buren the support of Andrew Jackson and hence the Democratic nomination, which went to James K. Polk, a Tennesseean prepared to embrace the party's expansionist platform. Resisting the Whig taunt, "Who is James K. Polk?" the Democrats won a close election in December, thanks to the abolitionist Liberty Party, which drew votes away from Clay, especially in the Empire State. As he made his way in the New York literary world, Poe (who usually disdained party politics) aligned himself the Democrats. During the fall he composed a campaign song for a Democratic political club (*PL*, 472), and in November he began to contribute his "Marginalia" to John Louis O'Sullivan's influential *Democratic Review*.

Poe also used his position at the *Mirror* to attack Longfellow again and to demand an international copyright law. After the January 1845 publication of "The Raven," a poem widely reprinted and parodied, he became nationally famous. The February issue of *Graham's* featured an engraved portrait of the author with a flattering sketch by Lowell—based ultimately on misinformation from Poe—sponsoring the untruths that he had "graduated with the highest honors" from the University of Virginia and that he went abroad to aid the "insurgent Greeks" but (lacking a passport) was sent home from St. Petersburg. As indicated by his 1844 satire, "The Literary Life of Thingum Bob," Poe understood the strategies of self-promotion. In February he resigned from the *Mirror* and moved back into the city (154 Greenwich Street) to join Charles F. Briggs and John Bisco in publishing the *Broadway Journal*. There he supplied literary reviews and—most controversially—renewed his prosecution of Longfellow for plagiarism, eventually alienating Briggs and even Lowell. On February 28, he lectured at the Society Library on the "Poets and Poetry of America," delivering trenchant judgments on native versifiers. In the ensuing months he developed friendships with many literary women, attended their salons (where he sometimes recited "The Raven"), and carried on a public flirtation with Mrs. Frances S. Osgood in the pages of the *Broadway Journal*.

Meanwhile the annexation of Texas riveted public attention. Partly to halt British designs on Texas, Congress had passed a joint resolution in February admitting Texas to immediate statehood, stipulating that up to four additional states might be formed from its territories. The admission of Texas solved one problem but created several others by raising the issue of slavery's extension, by provoking Mexican hostility, and by exposing sectional conflicts within both major parties—the fault lines that led to the Civil War. Annexation also brought to the fore the contentious issue of imperialism, for Polk's ultimate goal was the accession of New Mexico and California. In 1845, O'Sullivan (hardly a defender of slavery) introduced the concept of Manifest Destiny in the *Democratic Review* and in "increasingly aggressive editorials" sponsored the belief that Americans were destined to occupy and settle the entire continent (Widmer, 51). Despite the opposition of Northern Whigs and Democrats, such imperialist ideology became infectious and subsequently propelled the United States into a war with Mexico.

Although Poe published "The Power of Words" amid the jingoism of the June *Democratic Review*, his own view of Manifest Destiny remains a matter of conjecture. Virtually since his arrival in Gotham, he had been linked to Evert Duyckinck's Young America group by his vehemence about the copyright issue and his contempt for Lewis G. Clark and the Whiggish *Knickerbocker* magazine. Although he still criticized the "indiscriminate laudation of American books" (*L*, 281), Poe's passion to found a national journal and to protect the rights of American authors persuaded him to make common cause with Young America, a group of mostly "Loco-Foco" (radical) Democrats. Duyckinck thus included a volume of twelve tales by Poe in his patently nationalistic "Library of American Books," issued by Wiley and Putnam. The book appeared in late June, and two weeks later (after Briggs resigned) Poe assumed full editorial control of the *Broadway Journal*. Then boarding at a house on Broadway, Poe was in fact "dreadfully unwell" (L, 290) and distracted by Virginia's precarious condition. Ending eighteen months of sobriety, he reverted to drink and started behaving erratically. He apparently made a fugitive journey to Providence to see Mrs. Osgood and (on the same trip) caught a glimpse of Sarah Helen Whitman, with whom a later romance developed. Soon after moving to Amity Street, he embarrassed himself before the Boston Lyceum in October by reciting (to the perplexity of many) his early, arcane poem, "Al Aaraaf," instead of a promised new composition. But somehow Poe persevered in his magazine work and through a series of loans acquired Bisco's share of the *Broadway Journal*, becoming on October 24 its sole proprietor; through the end of the year he kept it afloat, blaming "enemies" who plotted its destruction (L, 304). Wiley and Putnam brought out *The Raven and Other Poems* in November, and Poe created another sensational hoax by publishing in George Colton's (Whig) *American Review* "The Facts in the Case of M. Valdemar." Such publicity did not, however, enable him to salvage the *Journal*, which ceased publication in January 1846—ironically, just as the American economy was rebounding from a long depression.

While saber rattling intensified along the Rio Grande, Poe found himself embattled in literary wars, as Lewis Gaylord Clark of the *Knickerbocker* continued his editorial sniping. Mrs. Elizabeth F. Ellet circulated the rumor that Mrs. Osgood had written indiscreet letters to Poe, and when Poe (at the request of Margaret Fuller and Anne C. Lynch) tried to end the controversy by returning the fawning letters of Ellet and Osgood, he got into a bigger tangle. After Mrs. Ellet's brother threatened mayhem, Poe sought a pistol from Thomas Dunn English, who scuffled with him and then launched a series of journalistic attacks in the *Evening Mirror,* prompting a lawsuit by Poe. Seeking rural tranquillity, the author that spring moved his family to the country, renting a house on the East River and then a cottage in Fordham. Across the Atlantic, his work was at last receiving attention in English and French periodicals. Poe still planned to launch a monthly magazine (*L*, 312), but by April, stories circulated in the newspapers that he had become "deranged" (*PL*, 634–35). In May, while Congress was declaring war on Mexico, his series "The Literati of New York City" captured national attention in *Godey's Lady's Book*; running through October, the portraits were sometimes flattering, sometimes wickedly satirical. He praised the "high genius" of Margaret Fuller and declared Caroline M. Kirkland "one of our best writers," lauding her "freshness of style" (*ER*, 1173, 1182–83). English, Clark, Briggs (his former partner), and Hiram Fuller (editor of the *Evening Mirror*) all felt Poe's sting, though. English began serializing a roman à clef called *1844*, which lampooned Poe as the pugnacious drunk Marmaduke Hammerhead. Perhaps covertly inspired by his conflict with English, Poe's brilliant revenge tale, "The Cask of Amontillado," appeared in *Godey's* in November. By that time, though, both Poe and Virginia were "dangerously ill" with consumption (*PL*, 672).

While the U.S. Army attacked Mexico, and Congress debated the Wilmot Proviso, Mrs. Clemm and Marie Louise Shew (a doctor's daughter) tried to relieve the final suffering of Virginia, who expired on January 30, 1847, of "pulmonary consumption." Ailing and grief-stricken, Poe attended her funeral on February 2 at the Dutch Reformed Church and the burial in the Valentine family vault. In a letter to a new follower, George Evelith, he enclosed an obituary notice rather than rehearse the "painful" details (*L*, 343). Poe perhaps took some comfort that month in winning his lawsuit against the *Mirror* and with the $225 settlement apparently bought new furnishings for the Fordham cottage. With Mrs. Shew's attentions he gradually recovered his health and dedicated to her a poem called "The Beloved Physician." Now the object of sympathy and generosity, Poe received an offer of lifetime support from poet Thomas Holley Chivers if he would "come to the South to live" (*PL*, 691–92). By July he shook off illness and melancholy sufficiently to travel to Philadelphia and Washington. But he did little writing during this period of mourning; perhaps the only notable composition of 1847 was his stunning poem "Ulalume," likely inspired by nocturnal visits to Virginia's tomb.

While Poe struggled to recapture the sense of literary purpose he had expressed in December 1846 to Evelith and Nathaniel P. Willis (*L*, 333, 339), General Winfield Scott was leading an American assault west from Vera Cruz toward the capital of Mexico, routing Santa Anna at Cerro Gordo. Younger officers such as Lee, Grant, Jackson, and Sherman were sharpening the command skills they would display in a later, deadlier war. The defeat in 1847 of the Wilmot Proviso (which would have outlawed involuntary servitude in territories gained from Mexico) forced the problem of slavery again to the forefront of public discussion. Another troublesome conflict concerned fugitive slaves: the *Prigg v. Pennsylvania* decision (1842) freed Northern states from any obligation to assist Southern slaveholders in recovering their "property," and subsequent "personal liberty" laws further impeded the work of slave catchers. The rapid formation of a provisional American government in California after the defeat of Mexican forces there compelled lawmakers to face an impending crisis. Since the Missouri Compromise, the issue of slavery's extension had stirred little concern, as free and slave states had been added in equal numbers until the annexation of Texas. But with the status of Texas still unresolved and with California moving toward statehood, the future of slavery was now clearly on the line. Such was the climate as the election year approached.

At the beginning of 1848, Poe wrote to Evelith: "My health is better—best. I have never been so well" (*L*, 355). It was a year of great expectations, for gold had just been discovered that January in California. Determined to become his own publisher and to launch the *Stylus* at last, Poe simultaneously began writing a vast, cosmological "prose poem" titled *Eureka*. To subsidize a trip to promote his journal, he lectured in February on "The Universe" at the New York Society Library, outlining his grand theory of God and the cosmos. Although excluded from Anne C. Lynch's Valentine party, he nevertheless received through her a poem from his new admirer, Sarah Helen Whitman, and reciprocated by sending his 1831 poem "To Helen," followed by new verses for her. Another drinking spree began, however, about the time he completed *Eureka*. Disturbed by the seemingly heretical nature of Poe's new theories, Mrs. Shew declined further involvement in his affairs. Meanwhile, English renewed his Poe-baiting in the pages of the weekly newspaper, *John-Donkey*. Poe was thus eager for approbation and welcomed the invitation from Mrs. Jane Ermina Locke to lecture in Massachusetts. In July he spoke in Lowell on American poetry and there met Mrs. Nancy "Annie" Richmond, who quickly became his confidante and soul mate. His lecture coincided closely with the publication of *Eureka: A Prose Poem* and with the appearance in France of the first Poe translation ("Mesmeric Revelation") by a young poet named Charles Baudelaire. On returning from Lowell, Poe set out quickly for Richmond, seeking subscribers for the *Stylus*; among other visits, he called on his first love, Sarah Elmira Royster Shelton, by then a widow. Reportedly Poe drank heavily in Richmond, even declaiming passages from *Eureka* atop a saloon table (*PL*, 749). The arrival of ardent verses from Sarah Helen Whitman, however, hastened his return to New York. In his last letter to Mrs. Shew he had confessed his need to find a new wife: "Unless some true and tender and pure womanly love saves me, I shall hardly last a year longer, alone!" (*L*, 373). In September he thus traveled to Providence, and two days after meeting Mrs. Whitman in person, proposed to her in a cemetery. She declined, citing her age (forty-five) and ill health, but she also recognized Poe's erratic impulsiveness

Undeterred, Poe renewed his courtship of the widow in October and then visited Annie Richmond to unburden himself and extract a promise to attend him on his deathbed. He was emotionally dazed: he mourned Virginia; adored the mystical Mrs. Whitman; and desperately loved the securely married Mrs. Richmond. Depressed and "tormented" by a "demon," he ingested an overdose of laudanum, a common headache remedy, on November 5 in Providence and became wretchedly ill (*L*, 402). He nevertheless recovered, persisted in his romance with Mrs. Whitman, and finally won her consent, providing that he avoid strong drink. Curiously, he also wrote to Annie, the *"wife* of [his] soul," assuring her that he loved her "as no man ever loved woman" (*L*,

401). After his Providence lecture in December before a crowd of nearly two thousand, Mrs. Whitman and her suspicious mother seemed prepared to accept the nuptials. But reports of Poe's drinking caused her to cancel the wedding plans, and her crest-fallen suitor left immediately for New York, never to see her again.

The year of gold's discovery thus closed unhappily for Poe. But in the Southwest, the Mexican War was finally at an end; the Seneca Falls Convention in July marked the beginning of a long struggle to secure equal rights for women under the U.S. Constitution; and in France a new revolution ended the "bourgeois monarchy" of Louis Philippe. Because Polk declined to run for a second term, the presidential election of 1848 pitted conservative Democrat Lewis Cass against Mexican War hero Zachary Taylor, the Whig candidate, and Martin Van Buren, the favorite of the upstart Free-Soil Party, a group comprising antislavery Democrats, "Conscience" Whigs, and members of the abolitionist Liberty Party. Determined to halt the spread of slavery, the Free-Soil Party anticipated the formation of the Republican Party a few years later, and although Van Buren ran third, Free-Soil votes tilted the close election in favor of Taylor (whose political opinions were hard to discern) and exhibited the strength of Northern antislavery sentiment. Wrangling over House leadership in the next Congress revealed just how divided—and precarious—the Union had become.

As the new year began, Poe sent Annie Richmond intimate letters confessing his hopes and "dark forebodings" (L, 438). In March he published "Hop-Frog," a veiled narrative of slave revolt, in a Boston weekly, The Flag of Our Union, and the following month he sought to capitalize on gold fever with "Von Kempelen and His Experiment." He also composed his famous poem "For Annie," dedicated to Mrs. Richmond. New encouragement arrived from an unlikely source: a printer named Edward H. N. Patterson wrote from Oquawka, Illinois, to propose publishing the Stylus from that frontier outpost, an offer Poe took seriously. The author again departed for Richmond to raise funds, but in Philadelphia he became inebriated, went to jail, and suffered hallucinations that included a vision of "Mrs. Clemm being dismembered" (*PL*, 813). The new owner of the *Union Magazine*, John Sartain, took care of Poe until he could resume his travels, and in gratitude Poe offered Sartain his poem "Annabelle Lee." In Richmond, he was attentive to the wealthy Mrs. Shelton and in July proposed marriage. There he also delivered a lecture on "The Poetic Principle," and in late August, after many a debauch, joined the Sons of Temperance, possibly to gain the trust of Mrs. Shelton. Repeating his lecture in Norfolk, he spent a few days at Old Point Comfort, reciting "The Raven" and "Ulalume" for guests at the resort. By late September, Mrs. Shelton agreed to marriage, and Poe departed triumphantly for New York to bring Mrs. Clemm to the wedding. But just when he seemed ready to launch his magazine and wed his own first love, ill chance befell him. In Baltimore, Poe apparently fell into the hands of political thugs who plied him with drink, escorted him from precinct to precinct as a "repeat" voter, and then abandoned him in the street. He was taken to Washington College Hospital, where after four days of delirium, he died on October 7, 1849. His funeral was held the following day, and Poe was buried "without ostentation" in a Presbyterian cemetery (*PL*, 848). At the age of forty, he had at last conquered the fever called "living."

WORKS CITED

Ashworth, John. *Slavery, Capitalism, and Politics in the Antebellum Republic.* Vol. 1. Cambridge: Cambridge University Press, 1995.

Fields, Barbara Jean. *Slavery and Freedom on the Middle Ground: Maryland during the Nineteenth Century.* New Haven, Conn.: Yale University Press 1985.

Geffen, Elizabeth M. "Industrial Development and Social Crisis." In *Philadelphia: A 300-Year History,* ed. Russell F. Weigley. New York: Norton, 1982.

Pessen, Edward. *Jacksonian America: Society, Personality, and Politics.* Rev. ed. Urbana: University of Illinois Press, 1985.

Poe, Edgar Allan. *Doings of Gotham.* Ed. Thomas Ollive Mabbott. 1929. Reprint. Folcraft, Pa.: Folcraft Library Editions, 1974.

Quinn, Arthur Hobson. *Poe: A Critical Biography.* New York: D. Appleton-Century, 1941.

Sellers, Charles. *The Market Revolution: Jacksonian America, 1815–1846.* New York: Oxford University Press, 1991.

Silverman, Kenneth. *Edgar A. Poe: Mournful and Never-ending Remembrance.* New York: HarperCollins, 1991.

Tyler-McGraw, Marie, and Gregg D. Kimball. *In Bondage and Freedom: Antebellum Black Life in Richmond, Virginia.* Richmond: Valentine Museum, 1988.

Weiss, Susan Archer. *The Home Life of Poe.* New York: Broadway Publishing, 1907.

Whalen, Terence. *Edgar Allan Poe and the Masses: The Political Economy of Literature in Antebellum America.* Princeton, N.J.: Princeton University Press, 1999.

Whitman, T. Stephen. *The Price of Freedom: Slavery and Manumission in Baltimore and Early National Maryland.* Lexington: University Press of Kentucky, 1997.

Widmer, Edward L. *Young America: The Flowering of Democracy in New York City.* New York: Oxford University Press, 1999.

POE IN HIS
TIME

Poe and the American Publishing Industry

Terence Whalen

Poor Poe

When Poe died in 1849 at the age of forty, "Poor Poe!" was a common refrain in many obituaries and reminiscences of his life. George Lippard remembered him as "a man of genius, hunted by the world, trampled upon by the men he had loaded with favours, and disappointed on every turn of life." Magazine proprietor George Graham saw Poe's peculiar genius as the primary cause of his sufferings: "The passionate yearnings of his soul for the beautiful and the true, utterly unfitted him for the rude jostlings and fierce competitorship of trade." Given the events of his life and the tormented characters depicted in his tales, it is no surprise that eulogists seized upon the romantic outcast as a convenient symbol for Poe's career. An obituary in the *American Whig Review* summed up the general lament: "Poor Poe! It was a sad day for him when he was forced from dreams into the real world."[1]

Poe might have taken a perverse pleasure in this sad refrain, for in addition to the actual hardships of his life, he had at times sought to represent himself to the American public as a sort of dark visionary. Yet if we were to adopt the investigative method of "The Philosophy of Composition," we would discover that behind the veil of accursed genius, Poe had pursued a literary career of enormous vitality and breadth. By the year of his death, he had worked in Baltimore, Richmond, Philadelphia, and New York—the major publishing centers of the United States. He had acquired a substantial literary reputation not only as a poet and story writer but also as one of the preeminent literary critics in America. He had labored, moreover, in a variety of part-time and full-time positions in the publishing industry, which afforded him a practical familiarity with all aspects of newspaper and magazine production. In sum, by the time of his death, Poe had worked as proofreader, editor, reviewer, and—briefly—as the sole proprietor of his own journal; he had maintained a steady stream of business correspondence with subscribers, contributors, editors, and book publishers; and, in a never-ending effort to "fill up" the pages of periodicals, he had written articles on subjects ranging from road building to naval exploration to the "philosophy" of furniture. Finally, when neither fact nor fiction would do, Poe exploited the gray area in between by mastering the art—or perhaps the science—of the literary hoax.

It is this other Poe whom historicism can bring back to life. Unlike his tormented double, the practical Poe was poor primarily in an economic sense. This poverty, moreover, was not simply a negative force that crushed the spirit and sensibility of an aspiring artist. In the crucible of the antebellum publishing industry, it was also the force that transformed Poe into one of the most innovative writers of his day, chiefly by driving him into new fields of literary labor and by granting him startling insights into the artistic implications of capitalist development. By investigating the antebellum publishing environment, we shall be in a better position to understand Poe's significance as both cultural symbol and commercial writer.

The Economic Environment

By almost any measure, Poe's lifetime spanned one of the most tumultuous periods of expansion in American history. When Poe was born in 1809, the United States numbered seven million inhabitants; by the time of Poe's death in 1849, the population had more than tripled to twenty-two million. Much of this increase came from immigration. In 1820, for example, approximately eight thousand immigrants arrived in the United States; by 1849, the figure had swelled to nearly three hundred thousand. Aside from accelerating the growth of American cities, this rising population fueled westward development and the acquisition of new territory through purchase or conquest. The most notable territorial acquisitions during Poe's lifetime stemmed from the annexation of Texas (1845) and the Mexican War (1846–48), which added more than a million square miles to the United States and thereby fulfilled the imperial agenda of Manifest Destiny. Improved transportation facilitated both geographic expansion and intensified development in settled areas. During Poe's childhood, railroads were unknown in America, but by 1849 there were ten thousand miles of track serving to knit the country together—economically if not ideologically.

To convey the social meaning of such changes, historians have devised a variety of labels for the era in which Poe lived. Following the practice of naming historical periods by political rulers, some have identified the time of Poe's literary apprenticeship as the "Age of Jackson" or of "Jacksonian Democracy." Andrew Jackson, who began his presidency when Poe was nineteen and ended it when Poe was twenty-seven, rode the crest of a populist swell by repeatedly affirming the rights of the multitude and the wisdom of the common (white) man. Jackson's professed aim was to honor the infallible "will of the people" by restoring the virtues of the old Republic, such as honest work, simplicity, economy, and independence. In practice, this meant attacking the symbols of privilege and corrupt power, such as chartered corporations, paper money, expensive federal projects, and especially the Bank of the United States. Regardless of how one evaluates Jackson's achievement, his presidency would have offered Poe a formula for success (appeal to the masses) and an easy polemical target (the wealthy gentleman). The age of Jackson also provided the original context for Poe's occasional disparagement of mobs and mob rule. In other words, Poe's aristocratic pronouncements were to some extent protests against a pervasive and perhaps tiresome democratic rhetoric.

Other names for Poe's era place less emphasis on political discourse than on the momentous material changes in the antebellum economy. George Rogers Taylor, for example, has characterized the explosion in canals, turnpikes, and railroads as a "transportation revolution" that prepared the way for unparalleled capitalist development. Adopting a somewhat broader perspective, Charles Sellers has described a "market revolution" that was propelled by an unresolved tension between democracy and capitalism. Still others have used phrases such as "communications revolution" or "control revolution" to emphasize the way that information facilitated economic development by subsuming diverse peoples and practices into the world market.[2] This emphasis on information brings us closer to Poe and the rise of a publishing industry in the United States, for transportation networks enabled the dissemination of a wide variety of private correspondence and published texts. Many books and magazines were obviously intended as entertainment. But in order for the nation to develop and compete in the world market, the United States also required a swift, reliable system to disseminate information about prices, foreign markets, shipping schedules, labor disputes, trade regulations, patent laws, new manufacturing techniques, and innovations in the prevailing conditions for agricultural and industrial production.

Poe was a keen observer of the communications revolution. As the foster child of John Allan, a Scottish-born tobacco exporter and dry-goods merchant, Poe grew up speaking the language of commerce. Dinner conversations in the Allan household ranged from the perils of price fluctuations to the economic consequences of political instability in Europe. It is also significant that Allan's firm stocked books and periodicals alongside other merchandise (catering to the taste of his customers, Allan sold such popular publications as the *Edinburgh Review*, *Blackwood's*, and the *London Ladies' Magazine*). Young Edgar Poe would therefore have understood the economic value of information, just as he would have known that literature was a commodity produced for sale in the capitalist marketplace.

What effect did this formative environment have on Poe's writing? As I suggest later, there is no simple answer to this question, but here it is appropriate to sketch some rudimentary consequences. The inherent instabilities of capitalist development left Poe and other commercial writers in a perpetual state of uncertainty about the future of American literature and American mass culture. Sometimes, of course, commercial writers guessed wrong; Poe, for example, failed to capitalize on the rise of the novel and instead staked his hopes on the periodical press. But this should not detract from the fundamental issue, namely, the role that economic anticipations were exerting over literary decisions. For Poe, this sometimes meant tailoring literary themes to the tastes of a capitalist culture. In 1841, Poe noted that money is "a topic which comes home at least as immediately to the bosoms and business of mankind, as any which could be selected" (ER, 349). Later, in an anonymous review of himself, Poe attributed the popularity of his tale "The Gold-Bug" to the same materialistic predilections of the American mass audience: "The intent of the author was evidently to write a popular tale: money, and the finding of money being chosen as the most popular thesis" (ER, 869). A similar desire to exploit or control the mass audience underlies Poe's great innovations in literary form, such as the tale of "ratiocination" or, more specifically, the detective story (which Poe is credited with inventing). An attentiveness to the emerging mass market even informs Poe's aesthetic writings, for he is perpetually investigating the possibility of creating a single literary text capable of satisfying both "the popular and the critical taste."

Finally, Poe seems to have viewed the communication revolution as the cause of a transformation in human consciousness itself. In 1845, he explained how developments in the literary market were linked to more fundamental changes in the American economy and the American mind:

> The increase, within a few years, of the magazine literature, is
> . . . but a sign of the times, an indication of an era in which
> men are forced upon the curt, the condensed, the well-
> digested in place of the voluminous—in a word, upon jour-
> nalism in lieu of dissertation. . . . I will not be sure that
> men at present think more profoundly than half a century

ago, but beyond question they think with more rapidity, with
more skill, with more tact, with more of method and less of
excrescence in the thought. Besides all this, they have a vast increase in the thinking material; they have more facts, more to
think about. For this reason, they are disposed to put the
greatest amount of thought in the smallest compass and dis-
perse it with the utmost attainable rapidity. Hence the journalism of the age; hence, in especial, magazines. (*ER*, 1377)

Clearly, Poe believed that changes in the publishing environment
were accompanied by momentous and paradoxical changes in
the emergent mass culture. The issue, then, is not whether the
publishing industry exerted significant pressures over Poe's work,
but rather how this environment remains relevant to literary interpretation today.

Poe's Experiences in the Publishing Industry

When Poe landed his first full-time job in the publishing industry,
his professional life had been a series of mistakes and wrong
turns. Poe was twenty-six years old in 1835, and aside from his
service in the U.S. Army—which he viewed as an employer of
last resort—Poe had been decidedly unsuccessful in establishing
himself in a career. Nor was he particularly successful in educat-
ing himself for professional success, for by this point he had
dropped out of the University of Virginia and had provoked his
court-martial from West Point. Most important, he had grown
estranged, emotionally and financially, from his foster father, and
this threw him back upon the extremely meager resources of
relatives in Baltimore. So when Poe heard that an editorial position might open up at the *Southern Literary Messenger* in Richmond, he pursued the job with a characteristic combination of
bravado and desperation.

Poe's campaign to break into the editorial ranks is best illustrated by the incidents surrounding his tale "Berenice." The tale
was published in the March 1835 issue of the *Southern Literary
Messenger* while Poe still resided in Baltimore. Narrated by a

monomaniac who is obsessed with the teeth of his fiancée-cousin, the tale describes the death of Berenice and the narrator's midnight visit to her grave site in a trancelike fit of bereavement. The awful truth of his midnight vigil is revealed obliquely at the end of the tale: the narrator has exhumed the body and extracted the teeth of Berenice, who, in a final gruesome twist, turns out to have been alive when her grave and her mouth were violated. As might be expected, many readers were shocked by the tale, and some lodged complaints with Thomas W. White, proprietor of the *Messenger*. Recognizing that such complaints might jeopardize any job prospects, Poe defended himself by speaking a language that the proprietor could understand. Emphasizing the hard facts of literary business, Poe argued that a publisher—and by extension, a writer—must be less concerned with the "taste" of the reading public than with the circulation of the magazine:

> The history of all magazines shows plainly that those which have attained celebrity were indebted for it to articles *similar in nature to Berenice*—although, I grant you, far superior in style and execution. . . . But whether the articles of which I speak are, or are not in bad taste is little to the point. To be appreciated you must be *read*. . . . I propose to furnish you every month with a Tale of the nature which I have alluded to. The effect—if any—will be estimated better by the circulation of the Magazine than by any comments upon its contents.[3]

Coming from someone who was purportedly unfit for "the rude jostlings and fierce competitorship of trade," this is a startling insight. It is also startling that the author of "Berenice" would see fit to lecture a capitalist proprietor about the true nature of capitalism itself. Whether or not Poe was sincere, the passage reveals his willingness to adopt a calculating, aggressive stance toward literature and toward the mass audience whose "taste" would henceforth be measured by gross acts of purchase.

Poe sent this letter in April 1835, several months before he actually arrived in Richmond to commence editorial work at the *Messenger*. In all probability, then, he harbored few illusions about the magazine business. His new boss, moreover, had far more to teach Poe about the publishing industry than about literature per se. (As Thomas W. White freely admitted, he relied upon the literary taste and discernment of others because he possessed very little himself.) Poe's apprenticeship therefore encompassed the full range of tasks necessary to the survival of a new magazine: checking into available inks and papers; soliciting contributions from recognized authors; revising accepted manuscripts; correcting proofs; declining submissions from aspiring poets; striking deals with the editors of other publications regarding exchanges and favorable notices; drumming up new subscribers; and "filling up" the book review section of the magazine with a curious mixture of hackwork and brilliantly innovative criticism.

In addition to these varied tasks, Poe was occasionally called upon to alter controversial political articles to fit the ostensible "neutrality" of the *Messenger*. In February 1836, for example, a frequent contributor named Lucian Minor published an article purporting to review recent issues of the *Liberia Herald*. Minor's true purpose is to praise the work of the American Colonization Society and the success of American blacks in establishing an African colony. Colonization was praised and denounced by those on both sides of the slavery question, but in this review Minor embraces Liberia as a progressive enterprise. After discussing various signs of Liberian progress, Minor calls attention to the newspaper itself. According to Minor, "what heightens—indeed what *constitutes* the wonder" of the newspaper is the fact that the editors, printers and writers "are all *colored people*."[4] Minor realized that his review might upset *Messenger* readers, and he accordingly disavowed any radical intent: "What we especially had in view, however, when we began this article, was neither rhapsody nor dissertation upon the march of Liberia to prosperity and civilization—unparalleled as that march is, in the annals of civilization—but a notice (a *critical notice*, if the reader please) of the aforesaid newspaper" (158). Despite this disclaimer, White was worried about repercussions. Since Minor was a major supporter of the magazine, White could not simply reject the review. White did, however, order Poe to revise or delete the more controversial sections of the review (the disclaimer quoted above may in fact be Poe's work). White also gave Poe the job of informing Minor about these revisions, and Poe dutifully told Minor that "it was thought better upon consideration to omit all passages in 'Liberian Literature' at which offence could, by any possibility, be taken" (L, 1:83). Poe's revisions were not entirely successful. In a review of the February *Messenger*, the *Augusta Chronicle* denounced "Liberian Literature" as being "altogether unsuited to our Southern region, and as indicating a dangerous partiality for that most pestiferous and abominable parent of the Abolitionists, the *Colonization Society*."[5] The handling of Minor's article nevertheless reveals something of the ideological constraints that the *Messenger* imposed upon even its most valued contributors.

Two months later, Poe edited another article on the slavery question. The so-called Paulding-Drayton review appeared in the April 1836 issue of the *Southern Literary Messenger*. Although it purports to evaluate two recently published books, most of the unsigned review is devoted to justifying slavery not as a necessary evil (a position held by many Southern apologists) but instead as a positive good for master and slave alike. The review has long been the center of controversy, primarily because James A. Harrison and others have attributed it to Poe himself. Harrison printed the Paulding-Drayton review in the 1902 edition of *The Complete Works of Edgar Allan Poe,* and as a consequence many critics and literary historians relied upon it to document Poe's political views. It has now been conclusively demonstrated that the review was written by Beverley Tucker rather than Poe, but in two different ways, the original misattribution still undermines political interpretations of Poe's work.[6] First, some early literary histories created an image of Poe as a public advocate for an orthodox or even reactionary Southern politics, and even though doubt has been cast on the Paulding-Drayton review, many critics still accept the image that was derived almost entirely from this faulty evidence. Second, the controversy surrounding the authorship of the Paulding-Drayton review has obscured the distinction between a public advocate or political crusader, on the one hand, and a commercial writer or "magazinist," on the other. These roles can of course overlap, but Poe tended to shun involvement in the partisan political disputes of

his day. In addition, even if Poe had desired to become a political
activist, he would not have been encouraged to do so at the
Southern Literary Messenger. In fact, he was paid to do precisely
the opposite insofar as White required him to edit or "neutralize" controversial articles on colonization and slavery. Poe may
have perceived this as an awkward duty, but he understood the
economic constraints on free speech. His foster father, after all,
had been fond of advising young merchants to be "neuter" and
to "let Politics alone altogether" (PL, 33).

During this same period, Poe was also trying to interest book
publishers in a collection to be called "Tales of the Folio Club."
Characteristically making use of everything at his disposal, Poe
envisioned a volume combining his already published tales with
critical commentary by club members, thereby creating "a burlesque upon criticism generally" (L, 1:104). (Perhaps Poe was hoping that the kind of critical performance he had been practicing
at the *Messenger* would also succeed in the book market, or he
may have wanted to escape the control exercised by the proprietor of the *Messenger* by selling directly to a national audience.)
While negotiating with Harper and Brothers in 1836, however,
Poe learned that the commercial writer never made direct contact with the mass reader—or even with the refined reader. Instead, magazine and book publishers functioned as the first
reader for any prospective literary commodity, and their calculating "taste" determined which texts would attain physical existence in the literary market. Poe had asked James K. Paulding to
approach Harpers with his proposal; when the proposal was re-
jected, Paulding offered the following explanation:

> By the way, you are entirely mistaken in your idea of my influ-
> ence over these gentlemen in the transactions of their busi-
> ness. They have a Reader, by whose judgment they are guided
> in their publications, and like all other traders are governed by
> their anticipations of profit or loss, rather than any intrinsic
> merit of a work or its author.[7]

Poe is here a victim of the same economic logic he had used to justify "Berenice" just one year earlier. In Poe's relatively naive ver-

sion, however, there was no mediator between author and audience, whereas in Paulding's account, a profit-oriented "Reader" initiates and controls this relation. Going beyond a simple market model of buyers and sellers, Paulding's account exposes the capitalist foundations of the American publishing industry. In so doing, Paulding casually hints at a deep connection between gross economic forces and the creative activity of literary producers. Writers necessarily have some notion of audience that, above and beyond any actual feedback, guides them in the production of texts. Paulding's letter suggests that the first audience for a literary commodity is neither a genteel critic nor even an anonymous magazine subscriber but instead a capitalist publisher.

Poe lost his job at the *Messenger* near the beginning of 1837. Prior to this point, Poe and Thomas White had quarreled over a variety of issues. White had once complained about his editor's use of alcohol "before breakfast," but Poe's salary and tendentiousness probably had more to do with his dismissal. In any event, Poe left Richmond and traveled to New York with high hopes, but his only job prospect failed to pan out, and he was unable to find any other steady work. To compound his woes, a financial crisis commenced shortly after Poe arrived in the city. The Panic of 1837 marked the beginning of one of the more severe depressions in U.S. economic history. After several years of fast growth, excessive speculation, and high inflation, the overextended banking system began to collapse, and these bank suspensions sent shock waves throughout the entire economy. The collapse may have been triggered by the federal government's refusal to accept anything other than gold or silver specie in payment for western lands. The so-called Specie Circular was one of Andrew Jackson's last official acts, and in accord with his popularity and political good luck, the panic did not strike until the next president (Martin Van Buren) had assumed office.[8]

Regardless of the immediate cause, the panic had a major impact on the publishing industry, which had already been developing at an uneven and tumultuous rate. The negative effects of an economic crisis are fairly obvious, but in many ways the Panic of 1837 merely accelerated the rise of a mass publishing industry and a mass culture. On the one hand, then, the panic had a devastating impact on the high end of the book trade. During the 1820s books sold for an average of two dollars; during the depression of 1837–43, they sold for fifty cents. On the other hand, the decline in prices was partly matched by cheaper printing costs and increased sales. Religious texts and schoolbooks captured the main share of the market. Pirated British novels also sold well; due to the absence of an international copyright law, foreign texts could be reprinted without compensation to the original authors or publishers. For all these reasons, the output of the book industry increased in value from an estimated $2.5 million in 1820 to $5.5 million in 1840; by 1850 the output more than doubled again to $12.5 million.[9]

The growth of the newspaper industry was even more dramatic. The number of newspapers grew steadily throughout the antebellum period, from 375 in 1810, to 1,200, in 1835, and to 2,526 in 1850. This increase was partly due to the fixed postage rate for newspapers, which was so low that it amounted to a federal subsidy. There were, however, many other factors at work, including high literacy rates, improvements in transportation and technology, urbanization, and a growing cash (as opposed to subsistence) economy. Paradoxically, the Panic of 1837 may have increased the viability of newspapers because they could undersell other forms of information and entertainment. Not surprisingly, then, this was the heyday of the penny press. The first successful penny newspaper, the *New York Sun*, was founded in 1833; after the Panic of 1837, cheap dailies and weeklies assumed an unprecedented importance in American culture. In 1846, Poe retrospectively described how the *New York Sun* rose to prominence by supplying "the public with news of the day at so cheap a rate as to lie within the means of all." Poe believed that the consequences of this plan, on both the newspaper business and the nation itself, were "beyond all calculation" (*ER*, 1214). He had good reason to take notice, for during this period newspapers aspired to become a complete reading package by printing both news and what we today call literature. Especially noteworthy in this regard were the so-called mammoth weeklies, which frequently printed entire novels in the form of "extras." Due to the massive size of the newspaper page, whole books could be printed on two or three sheets, a capability that American weeklies like *Brother Jonathan* and the *New World* were quick to exploit, especially when they could obtain pirated editions of English works.

The burden of these developments fell heavily upon Poe and other commercial writers. Even though Poe had moved to New York, the heart of the American publishing industry, he could find no editorial employment. Nor was he thriving as a writer of books. *The Narrative of Arthur Gordon Pym* had been composed partly to satisfy Harper's demand for "a single connected narrative," but they would not publish *Pym* until the summer of 1838, and even then it brought Poe little recompense. Hence, during the early years of the panic, Poe and his family lived in dire poverty, "suffering from want of food" and forced to subsist "on bread and molasses for weeks together" (*PL*, 248). In an 1844 letter to Charles Anthon, Poe poignantly described the "sad poverty & the thousand consequent contumelies & other ills which the condition of the mere Magazinist entails upon him in America—where more than in any other region upon the face of the globe to be poor is to be despised."[10]

In the same letter, however, Poe claimed that he was "essentially a Magazinist," and that he was trying to cope with the chaos of the publishing industry by establishing a magazine of his own. This was a viable way to overcome the low pay for creative and editorial labor, but in order to achieve his dream—first called the *Penn Magazine* and later the *Stylus*—Poe needed capital. At one point he believed that magazine proprietor George Graham would back the project. Poe had become the book review editor of *Graham's Magazine* in 1841, and at the commencement of his employment, Graham had apparently agreed to support Poe's magazine at some later date. The support failed to materialize, causing Poe to speculate about the inherent conflicts between the "man of capital" and the commercial writer:

> As Mr. G. was a man of capital and I had no money, I thought it most prudent to fall in with his views. The result has proved his want of faith and my own folly. In fact, I was continually laboring against myself. Every exertion made by myself for the benefit of "Graham," by rendering that [magazine] a

greater source of profit, rendered its owner, at the same time, less willing to keep his word with me. At the time of our bargain (a verbal one) he had 6000 subscribers—when I left him he had more than 40,000. It is no wonder that he has been tempted to leave me in the lurch. (*L*, 1:205)

Given Poe's desperate poverty and his equally desperate desire to achieve creative freedom through magazine ownership, it is no surprise that he fantasized about a different kind of capitalist, namely, "a partner possessing ample capital, and, at the same time, so little self-esteem, as to allow me entire control of the editorial conduct" (*L*, 1:224).

Poe never found his fantasy partner, but despite the turmoil wrought by the Panic of 1837 and ensuing depression, he remained committed to his magazine project. From an economic perspective, this made sense, for Poe's expectations had been shaped by his work on one of the first successful Southern magazines (the *Southern Literary Messenger*) and on what has been identified as the first American magazine to attain a truly mass circulation (*Graham's*). Poe was quick to take credit for his past associations. In the prospectus for the *Stylus*, he suggested that a detailed description of his proposed magazine was obviated by "the editor's connexion, formerly, with the two most successful periodicals in the country" (*ER*, 1034). Poe's economic anticipations, however, were linked to deeper aspirations. First, a magazine would enable Poe to combine his diverse talents as critic, tale writer, and poet into a single package. As he realized, "unless the journalist collects his various articles he is liable to be grossly misconceived & misjudged" (*L*, 1:270). Second, Poe believed that a magazine would grant him the creative freedom that he had been denied by publishers and proprietors. Publicly, Poe claimed that in his work for previous magazines, his objects had been "at variance with those of their very worthy owners." Because he had lacked a "proprietary right" in these other magazines, Poe continued, he had been unable "to stamp, upon their internal character, that *individuality* which he believes essential to the full success of all similar publications" (*ER*, 1034). Privately, Poe was less charitable toward the "worthy" proprietors: "So far I have not only labored solely for the benefit of others (receiving for myself a miserable pittance) but have been forced to model my thoughts at the will of men whose imbecility was evident to all but themselves" (*L*, 1:154). From Poe's perspective, then, the magazine project promised to fulfill both economic and artistic desires. Whatever he may have thought about the psychological dimensions of "individuality," Poe had come to realize that in the new publishing environment, artistic individuality had become the prerogative of capital.

Cultural Consequences

The Working Poe

All of these changes in the publishing industry had profound cultural consequences, the most obvious being the emergence of Poe as a magazinist or commercial writer. In many literary studies, it is conventional to view economic forces as belated, external influences over writing. But as we have seen, Poe was intimately familiar with both the antebellum American economy and the specific conditions in the American publishing industry *before* he dedicated himself to a literary career. Partly in jest, he once observed that "the horrid laws of political economy cannot be evaded even by the inspired" (*ER*, 211). With greater seriousness, he claimed that many of his works had been written to "run" or to "supply a particular demand" (*L*, 1:287, 271). Such claims undermine the assumption the Poe was somehow "forced from dreams into the real world." Instead, all of the available evidence suggests that the Poe we know today was summoned into existence by the horrid laws of political economy.

The Mass Audience

By the 1830s, many of the preconditions for a mass literary market were already present, and many commercial writers expected that the United States would follow the example of Great Britain. In many ways, the Panic of 1837 fueled such expectations, for it accelerated the development of a mass culture and an ostensibly homogeneous mass audience. I say "ostensibly" because the homogeneity of this audience had far more to do with the exigencies of large-scale production than with any actual social or cultural similarities among readers. Thus it would be fair to say that in antebellum America, the mass reader was a kind of economic or ideological approximation who was conjured up to serve specific purposes. Poe sometimes invoked the mass reader to demonstrate his commercial acumen to prospective employers and investors, but he conjured up a somewhat different image of the mass reader in his critical essays and reviews. In these texts, Poe was not only attempting to sort through a daunting oversupply of literary texts; he was also striving to evaluate and anticipate new forms of writing for a new culture.

Poe understood that this was a perilous task. In fact, he often denounced the authors, texts, and readers who characterized the new culture. In many instances, Poe adopted a disdainful attitude toward the mass audience, characterizing it by such terms as the "mob," the "uncultivated taste," the "rabble," and the "demagogue-ridden public." This last phrase is important, for it shows how Poe was drawing from a long tradition of English and American political thought to distinguish between the errors and vicissitudes of mere public opinion and the less fallible wisdom of "the people."[11] Significantly, Poe characterized the publishing industry itself as a kind of demagogue. In the 1840 prospectus of the *Penn Magazine*, for example, he condemned the general corruption, claiming that with a magazine of his own, he could resist the pressures "to read through the medium of a publisher's will" (*ER*, 1024). Such pressures distorted and manipulated public opinion, and hence Poe denounced "those cliques which, hanging like nightmares upon American literature, manufacture, at the nod of our principal booksellers, a pseudo-public opinion by wholesale" (*ER*, 1025). Since public opinion could be the product of simple ignorance or deliberate manipulation, Poe sought to distinguish between popularity and literary value in many of his critical writings, especially in his writings about the more famous authors of his day. In an 1842 review of Charles James Lever, for example, Poe proclaimed that "the popularity of a book . . . is evidence of the book's *demerit*, inasmuch as it shows a 'stooping to conquer'—inasmuch as it shows that the author has dealt largely, if not altogether, in matters which are susceptible of appreciation by the mass of mankind—by uneducated thought, by uncultivated taste, by unrefined and unguided passion" (*ER*, 312).

Despite such protests, Poe could never escape the harsh logic outlined in his 1835 "Berenice" letter, where he concluded that "to be appreciated you must be *read*." In consequence, he admitted that "pecuniary policy" could compel a talented writer to conform to the exigencies of the mass market. Poe, however, tried to retain some role for artistic genius by developing a theory of the divided text. According to Poe, one part of a literary work could appeal to the popular taste (to achieve economic value), while another part could appeal to the critical taste (to achieve artistic value). In explaining this theory, he drew from both economic and political discourse: "The writer of fiction, who looks most sagaciously to his own *interest*, [will] combine all votes by intermingling with his loftier efforts such amount of less ethereal matter as will give general currency to his composition" (*ER*, 312).

This notion of the divided text was carried over into such key critical texts as "The Philosophy of Composition," where Poe describes the "necessity" of "composing *a* poem that should suit at once the popular and the critical taste." William Charvat, referring to Poe's designation of "*a*" poem, has asked if there is "significance in the italic."[12] When viewed from the perspective of literary creation, the significance is profound. The italics means that a single text must satisfy all segments of the audience, so Poe is effectively conceding that economic conditions determine which texts shall attain material existence during a given cultural moment. In other words, Poe understood that a work devoid of popular appeal would not just prove unprofitable; since it would also very likely fail to achieve publication, it would not even have a chance to reach the refined or fully sympathetic reader. The divided text, however, poses a significant artistic challenge insofar as it conflicts with Poe's theory of the single effect. In "The Philosophy of Composition" and elsewhere, Poe celebrates the "im-

mensely important effect derivable from unity of impression"
(*ER*, 15). It is likely that Poe was influenced by the so-called Aris-
totelian unities (the theory that dramatic plots should recount a
single event occurring in a single time and place). Since he emphasized the unity of effect *on a reader*, however, Poe created a serious practical problem, for the mass audience comprised many
different kinds of readers with different tastes and sensibilities. In
addition, he failed to explain how the popular poet could escape
the degradation attending the popular novelist who "stooped to
conquer." Perhaps the success of "The Raven" made Poe less
concerned about the conflict between economic and poetic
value, but prior to 1845 he had complained that "the higher order
of poetry is, and always will be, in this country, unsaleable."[13] In
a variety of ways, then, the rise of a mass audience had serious
implications for the commercial writer. Those whom Poe derided as the "gentlemen of elegant leisure" may have enjoyed the
luxury of creative freedom, but for commercial writers, there
was no escape from the rigors of a capitalist publishing industry.

Cultural Politics

The real and perceived limitation on creative freedom also ap-
plies to political expression. In this instance, however, the issue is
not so much what could be thought and said in antebellum
America, for the period witnessed a striking diversity of ideas. As
I shall demonstrate later, the real challenge is to explore how
Poe's writing links us—imaginatively or materially—to other
times and other worlds.

Significantly, Poe's "other worlds" have less to do with the partisan politics of his day than with the political economy of the
antebellum publishing environment. Both in public and in private, Poe tended to shun the issues that his own era regarded as
political. As a critic, he proclaimed that "political allusions" have
"no business in a poem" (*ER*, 302). He also objected to the use of
poetry as an instrument for moral instruction, a practice Poe denounced as "the heresy of *The Didactic* (*ER*, 75). As an editor, Poe
seems to have adopted the perspective of Charles F. Briggs, a
coeditor at the *Broadway Journal*. According to Briggs, magazine

owners judged "propriety by profit," and this compelled editors to eschew "horrifying because unprofitable doctrines."[14] Except when Poe was trying to win a patronage job or attack a literary competitor, he remained behind the convenient veil of poetical neutrality. This neutrality carried over into his private communications. In an 1844 letter to Thomas H. Chivers, for example, Poe suggested that his political views were represented by "no one of the present parties" (*L*, 1:215). Poe must have maintained his neutrality even in personal conversations, for in 1845 one of his closest friends found it necessary to ask, "What are your politics?"[15] In light of this political obscurantism, it is probably misguided to assign a straightforward ideological meaning to Poe's literary works, especially insofar as these works have long been celebrated for being ambivalent, subversive, and multivocal. Nor can much be gained by attempts to expose Poe's "real" intentions. Aside from the theoretical and evidentiary problems of reconstructing a stable authorial intent, there is with Poe the additional difficulty of reconstructing a stable author.

Despite such difficulties, there has recently been much stimulating discussion of Poe's cultural politics, that is, the way his literary writings relate to such broad issues as race, gender, slavery, and imperialism. As suggested earlier, these discussions are often undermined by a failure to acknowledge the disparity between the presumptive freedom of political expression and the manifest restrictions of political economy. To make any meaningful progress in this area, theories of Poe's cultural politics must confront three general challenges. The first is to avoid the interpretive temptation to take one of Poe's scandalous or shocking political pronouncements as coloring all of his writings. Such an approach is of dubious merit, especially when the shocking pronouncement was made by someone other than Poe (as in the case of Beverley Tucker's Paulding-Drayton review). The second challenge is to evaluate Poe's statements in relation to the espoused positions of his day. This is especially important for a writer like Poe, who was apt to repeat political statements offhandedly and to contradict himself when it served his purposes. The need for assessing the depth of Poe's convictions is borne out by his private correspondence, which is rather startling for its

lack of political introspection and comment. Third, those claiming a political significance in Poe's writings are obliged to document or at least specify the precise impact. If Poe's tales had an
effect on the political movements of his day, there should be
some evidence of it, as there is for the writings of Ralph Waldo
Emerson, George Fitzhugh, and Harriet Beecher Stowe. And if
Poe's political agenda is so hidden or elusive that it requires
painstaking decryption, it is fair to wonder precisely who is responsible for precisely what meanings.

In light of these challenges, an investigation into Poe's cultural politics should probably commence by considering his varied responses to the material conditions of the publishing industry. As indicated previously, Poe at times acted as an advocate for
the emergent publishing industry, either by disparaging out-
moded standards of literary evaluation or by justifying literary
texts that appealed to all segments of the mass audience. At
other times, he seemed like a literary hustler, hawking his own
productions and enticing magazine investors with false claims.[16]
Poe, however, was often incisively critical of the conditions
under which he labored. In "Some Secrets of the Magazine
Prison-House," for example, he derides book publishers for re-
fusing to pay, magazine owners for paying too late and too little,
and the "demagogue-ridden public" for being blithely complic-
itous in the whole affair. Later on in his career, Poe created revenge fantasies such as "Hop-Frog," in which a performing dwarf
destroys the small group of men (the king and his ministers) who
had abused and exploited him. Finally, Poe often dreamed about
new methods of communication that would enable artistic value
to triumph over economic value. This dream is embodied in tales
such as "The Power of Words" and, less grandly, in essays such as
"Anastatic Printing."

The 1845 article "Anastatic Printing" is particularly significant
insofar as it reveals Poe's sense of the deep connection between
literature and the material conditions of production. It describes
a fairly simple printing technology that allows plates to be made
directly from manuscript. According to Poe, this technology
will liberate authors by reducing their dependence on capital-

intensive methods of publication. This, in turn, will give readers access to a vast array of texts ordinarily suppressed by profit-oriented publishers, whose decisions are based on salability rather than literary merit. Under normal conditions, the high cost of publishing dooms "many excellent works" to oblivion because initial investments in stereotype plates can only be recouped for books that sell in larger quantities.[17] Capital—or the lack thereof—is for Poe an obvious impediment to the artistic independence of writers and the free choice of readers. As he explains later in the essay, the advantages of anastatic printing are more apparent if one realizes that "in several of the London publishing warehouses there is deposited in stereotype plates alone, property to the amount of a million sterling" (156). Because of the dramatic reduction of capital costs, Poe predicts that the alternative method of printing will "cheapen information," "diffuse knowledge and amusement," and "bring before the public the very class of works which are most valuable, but least in circulation on account of unsaleability" (156). In other words, Poe seeks to escape more than capital itself, more than "the expensive interference of the typesetter, and the often ruinous intervention of the publisher" (157); he also wants to liberate himself from what capital implies, namely, dependence on high-volume sales and on the tastes of the literate multitude. In Poe's ideal economy, the author would achieve independence from *both* capital and the mass reader, for these were merely two aspects of the same productive process.

In the remainder of the essay, Poe predicts that anastatic printing will change everything from handwriting (which will become more legible) to thought (which will become more precise) to the labor force (which will include more female workers). Poe saves his grandest claims for the end, where he asserts that a printing method that severs the link between capitalism and publication will ultimately inspire the emergence of a genuinely democratic culture:

The value of every book is a compound of its literary and its physical or mechanical value as the product of physical labor applied to the physical material. But at present the latter value immensely predominates, even in the works of the most esteemed authors. It will be seen, however, that the new condition of things will at once give the ascendancy to the literary value, and thus by their literary value will books come to be estimated among men. The wealthy gentleman of elegant leisure will lose the vantage-ground now afforded him, and will be forced to tilt on terms of equality with the poordevil author. At present the literary world is a species of anomalous Congress, in which the majority of the members are constrained to listen in silence while all the eloquence proceeds from a privileged few. In the new *régime*, the humblest will speak as often and as freely as the most exalted, and will be sure of receiving just that amount of attention which the intrinsic merit of their speeches may deserve.[18]

Economists ranging from Adam Smith to Karl Marx distinguish between two primary forms of value: the intrinsic worth, or use-value, of a commodity and the market worth, or exchange-value, it bears in relation to other commodities. In the preceding passage, Poe establishes a different opposition, not between use-value and exchange-value, but between literary value (produced by authors) and that portion of value contributed by raw material, machinery, and manual labor (all of which he saw as being controlled by capitalist publishers or "wealthy gentlemen of elegant leisure"). Poe accordingly transforms the technical distinction between literary and physical value into a political conflict between the mass of "poordevil" authors and the "privileged few." Since this inequality has a material basis, he hopes that it can be redressed through a material innovation. In other words, he hopes that anastatic printing will overthrow not only the form of value that dominates the literary commodity but also the class of people who dominate the literary world.[19] To be sure, the "new *régime*" is a democracy for authors only, for Poe nowhere suggests that suffrage should be extended to the common reader. "Anastatic Printing" may nevertheless be seen as an example of Poe's cultural politics insofar as it depicts a literary republic liberated from the dominion of capital.

Literary Form and Method

In a general sense, Poe's commitment to the magazine business helps to explain his preference for short literary works such as the tale, the scientific hoax, and even the critical polemic. These, after all, were the kinds of magazine articles that could attain the "celebrity" that Poe saw as a prerequisite to economic survival and artistic freedom. When it comes to his *specific* innovations in literary form and method, however, it is far more difficult to reconstruct a chain of historical causes and artistic effects. It is therefore worthwhile to consider the relation between art and environment in light of what Poe called "adaptation" or "the mutuality of adaptation." By this phrase, he meant that incidents (in fiction or life) may be so intimately arranged "that we cannot distinctly see, in respect to any one of them, whether that one depends from any one other, or upholds it" (ER, 1316). This is not to deny that literature is determined by economic conditions, especially when "determine" is understood as "setting limits and exerting pressures."[20] Unfortunately, however, this implies a fairly rigid sequence in which the artist is diverted from some prior and preferred artistic practice. Poe, in contrast, sometimes seemed as if he were summoned into being by the publishing industry, while at other times he seemed "determined" by social conditions that were emergent or imagined—that is, by social conditions that followed rather than preceded the act of artistic creation. At the rarefied level of literary form, moreover, the term *adaptation* offers some advantages, for the work of art produces its own version of the world, a world which then serves to create or enhance a variety of aesthetic effects. If we keep this in mind, it will be easier to see that Poe's formal and stylistic innovations are as worthy of historical interpretation as the themes and plots of more conventional works.

Poe's most obvious formal innovation is, of course, the detective tale. In 1841, Poe published "Murders in the Rue Morgue," in which an American narrator recounts the crime-solving genius of a fallen French aristocrat named C. Auguste Dupin. This tale, widely acknowledged as the first detective story, was followed by other tales of ratiocination and by two more Dupin stories ("The

Mystery of Marie Rogêt" and "The Purloined Letter"). Like
Poe's hoaxes, the detective tale imitates scientific discourse without delivering any "real" or (externally verifiable) information.
Unlike the hoaxes, however, the Dupin tales constitute a sort of
genre in miniature through which Poe explores the economic
predicament of intellectuals and the precarious status of truth in
the new publishing environment. The predicament of intellectuals is illustrated by the contrast between the first and last Dupin
tales. In "The Murders in the Rue Morgue," Dupin is not yet a
professional detective, and so he investigates the case to amuse
himself and (secondarily) to exonerate an innocent suspect. After
forming a hypothesis about the deaths of Madame L'Espanaye
and her daughter, Dupin commences a spirited quest for truth
rather than a calculated search for wealth. At the end of the
story, the owner of the orangutan offers him a financial reward,
but Dupin is after something else: "My reward shall be this. You
shall give me all the information in your power about these murders in the Rue Morgue" (*PT*, 427). Dupin therefore uses his analytical ability to uncover the whole truth (which is then conveyed
to baffled and appreciative readers). In "The Purloined Letter,"
on the other hand, Dupin pursues the letter for its cash value
rather than its truth content, and the story concludes without re-
vealing the epistolary secret to curious readers. By the end of the
series of Dupin tales, in other words, the detective has been
transformed from a free thinker into a hired intellectual, and like
a prototypical data processor, he functions as a conduit for information that can bring him no enlightenment.

"The Purloined Letter" also illustrates the precarious status of
truth in the new market economy. Since there was no international copyright law, and since domestic copyright legislation was
widely ignored by periodical publishers, the value of a new text
dropped precipitously as soon as it was published. For this reason, an author would have to guard the secrecy or privacy of a
text in order to retain any bargaining power. In addition, the publishing industry placed a great deal of emphasis on novelty (or
the appearance of novelty) in order to stimulate sales. These factors caused a relative devaluation in a common literary tradition
and in common knowledge, and Poe accordingly derided popu-

lar authors for reworking ideas that were already "the common property of the mob" (*ER*, 325). As we have seen, Poe was well aware of the dangers of conflating literary and market value, but in "The Purloined Letter" he develops the tendencies of the capitalist publishing industry to a logical and perverse extreme. Regardless of what it may have meant to the queen, the stolen letter retains its power only so long as its contents remain secret. If the letter were to be published, the minister could not continue his blackmail, the police could not curry favor with the queen, and Dupin could not exchange the letter for a financial reward. By the inner logic of both the tale and the emerging relations of production, information would lose all value the instant it became common knowledge. In the very extremity of its rationalism, the detective tale exposes the irrationality at the heart of the publishing industry.

It is far more difficult to ascertain how the publishing environment may have influenced Poe's literary style, but even here there is evidence of adaptation. Poe's style has been characterized as a version or precursor of symbolism, and generations of critics have noted the ambiguity at the literal level of his texts to justify psychological, mythic, or symbolic interpretations. More recently, poststructuralist and deconstructive critics have focused on some of the same features of Poe's literary method, often using Poe to illustrate the indeterminacy of literary language or the fundamental gulf between a literary text and the world of human thought and action (which is no longer seen as the controlling or limiting referent). It is not surprising that Poe's literary texts should support such approaches, but his own explanations for his style deserve greater attention, especially since he took the time to justify his literary method in his most rigorous critical writings. In the "Philosophy of Composition" for example, Poe argues that the richness of a poetic text depends on its possessing "some amount of suggestiveness—some under current, however indefinite, of meaning (*ER*, 24). And in "The Poetic Principle," he maintains that poetry (which he calls "*The Rhythmical Creation of Beauty*") should have "no concern whatever either with Duty or with Truth" (*ER*, 78). Significantly, Poe tended to see a connection between artistic autonomy and artistic productivity, especially in regard to prose fiction. For example, in the same review where he derides the popular novelist for rehashing tales that are "the common property of the bivouac," Poe commends the productivity of true genius:

> *Now the true invention never exhausts itself.* It is mere cant and ignorance to talk of the possibility of the really imaginative man's "writing himself out." . . . So long as the universe of thought shall furnish matter for novel combinations' so long will the spirit of true genius be original, be exhaustless—be itself.[21]

Not incidentally, this concept of endless productivity reappears in the "Power of Words," the last of Poe's angelic dialogues. As we learn from the mentoring angel, the primary purpose of the infinite material universe is to fulfill the angelic desire for infinite inquiry: "There are *no* dreams in Aidenn—but it is here whispered that, of this infinity of matter, the *sole* purpose is to afford infinite springs, at which the soul may allay the thirst *to know* which is for ever unquenchable within it—since to quench it would extinguish the soul's self" (*PT*, 822).

In a general sense, then, Poe would have favored any literary mode—including symbolism—whose productivity was adapted to the peculiar requirements of the emerging mass culture. But Poe's praise of indefiniteness or "under currents" of meaning can also be traced to his understanding of the (divided) mass audience. That is, although Poe believed that literature should achieve a single effect on the reader, he acknowledged that the commercial writer had to satisfy readers who differed markedly in ability, motive, and taste. As a magazinist, he could scarcely ignore such differences, and on occasion he attempted to categorize his "common" readers with sociological precision:

> To the uneducated, to those who read little, to the obtuse in intellect (and these three classes constitute the mass) these [popular] books are not only acceptable, but are the only ones which can be called so. We here make two divisions—that of the men who *can* think but who dislike thinking; and that of

the men who either have not been presented with the materials for thought, or who have no brains with which to "work up" the material. (*ER*, 177)

Such statements demonstrate the difficulty of Poe's professed aim to compose a single text to satisfy "the critical and the popular taste." In fact, it would seem that such a text would necessarily appear suggestive or indefinite to the more energetic readers. Poe's literary style may therefore be seen as an adaptation to one of the central contradictions of his publishing environment, namely, the contradiction between the material presence of the divided audience and the artistic imperative of the single effect.

There are, finally, several speculative links between Poe's literary method and the antebellum publishing industry. First, just as Poe sought to satisfy multiple tastes with a single poem, so too did he seek to combine multiple discourses into a single (literary) text. That is to say, he repeatedly distilled nonliterary discourses into the raw material for literary performances. (*The Narrative of Arthur Gordon Pym*, for example, draws from geology, biology, and exploration narratives, while *Eureka* makes use of astronomy, chemistry, natural philosophy, and other fields.) Second, in the present context, Poe's persistent dream of a material language would seem to be a response to the mediation of publishers and the capitalist publishing industry. This dream extends from the Tsalal chasms in *Pym* to the signifying universe "read" by angels in "The Power of Words." It also underlies the handwriting utopia of "Anastatic Printing" and Poe's invented epigraph for the *Stylus*: "Lo! this is writ / With the antique *iron pen*" (*ER*, 1033). The central issue involves control of the physical embodiments of the written word, and in each of these cases Poe imagines a material text that comes into being apart from the horrid laws of political economy. A final link between the publishing industry and Poe's literary method is signaled by his favor among postmodern critics.[22] Aside from questioning the nature of language and the stability of fundamental concepts of existence (life, death, the world), Poe challenges the adequacy of the traditional thinking subject in the new publishing environment. That is, Poe links an epistemological predicament (how to know the modern world) with a material condition (the overproduction of texts and discourses made possible by the capitalist publishing industry). The overabundance of publications was widely acknowledged in antebellum America, and Poe himself complained of the problem:

> The enormous multiplication of books in every branch of knowledge, is one of the greatest evils of this age; since it presents one of the most serious obstacles to the acquisition of correct information, by throwing in the reader's way piles of lumber, in which he must painfully grope for the scraps of useful matter peradventure interspersed.[23]

Unlike many intellectuals of his day, however, Poe did not support any implicit or explicit limits to the growth of the publishing industry. Instead, he became increasingly fascinated with alternative thinking subjects who could thrive in an information-rich environment. These new subjects of social knowledge range from human polymaths (Ligeia, Legrand, and especially Dupin) to collective entities (crowds, shadows, and police bureaucracies) to nonhuman or posthuman intellects (primitive computers, dead souls, and mathematically gifted angels). In *Eureka*, Poe even imagines that selves, like texts and discourses, will collapse into a single homogeneous mass. Near the end of *Eureka*, Poe foresees a "final ingathering" when the "myriads of individual Intelligences become blended" into a "general consciousness" (*PT*, 1350, 1358). In other words, Poe's attempt to adapt to the necessities of a new mass culture ultimately culminated, at the end of his career, in an apocalyptic embrace of the mass audience.

From what we have seen, it is clear that Poe was never sheltered from the "rude jostlings" of the expanding capitalist economy. Cut off from family support at a fairly young age, Poe energetically pursued a career as a commercial writer, adapting himself to the shifting conditions of the publishing industry at the same time that he sought artistic and economic solutions to his predicament. Living in impoverished conditions in Baltimore, he served a kind of literary apprenticeship by developing his skills as a story writer and by making connections with a variety of literary publications. This led to his position with the *Southern Literary Messenger*, which was for Poe a different sort of apprenticeship insofar as it afforded him a tantalizing glimpse of magazine ownership. He labored, unsuccessfully, on the magazine project for the rest of his life, but along the way he pursued a startling diversity of literary endeavors. He wrote a novel of exploration and first contact; he transformed literary criticism into a kind of scientific performance; he invented literary forms that could thrive in the new publishing environment; and in such tales as "The Power of Words" he propagated his strange dream of an omnipotent material language, a language that was in many ways the divine correlative of his magazine ventures.

I began this essay with the refrain of countless eulogies: "Poor Poe! It was a sad day for him when he was forced from dreams into the real world." From what we have seen, however, it is clear that Poe's very poverty led him into new fields of literary labor, which in turn inspired new dreams of artistic freedom and economic power. The instabilities of the publishing industry kept these dreams forever out of reach, but as Poe moved from city to city and job to job, he ceaselessly probed his environment for omens and opportunities. It is therefore crucial to understand this publishing environment, for in addition to illuminating Poe's life as a literary artist, it complicates the various terms I have used to describe his career as a working intellectual. "Author" seems too narrow a word in light of Poe's editorial and proprietary ambitions, ambitions epitomized when he claimed that he was "essentially a magazinist." The notion of Poe as a public intellectual or political advocate is equally problematic, especially insofar as his political ambitions were more or less confined to the political economy of literature. But in our attempts to label Poe, we are perhaps guilty of imposing overly rigid definitions of political, artistic, and even religious practice upon a writer who vacillated so wildly between the extremes of material necessity and imaginative freedom. To encompass these extremes, literary historicism must pay as much attention to capitalism as it pays to culture. This kind of historicism is often presumed to be grimly reductive, but it seems to me that such an approach can be outward tending, opening up the richness of Poe's achievement as if for the first time.

NOTES

1. Quotations from *Edgar Allan Poe: The Critical Heritage*, ed. I. M. Walker (London: Routledge, 1986), 318, 383, 347.

2. See George Rogers Taylor, *The Transportation Revolution* (New York: Holt, Rinehart and Winston, 1951); Charles Sellers, *The Market Revolution* (New York: Oxford University Press, 1991); Robert G. Albion, "The 'Communication Revolution,'" *American Historical Review* 37 (July 1932): 718–20; and James R. Beniger, *The Control Revolution: The Technological Origins of the Information Society* (Cambridge: Harvard University Press, 1986).

3. Poe to White, April 30, 1835 (*L*, 57–58).

4. Lucian Minor, "Liberian Literature," *Southern Literary Messenger* 2 (February 1836): 158.

5. March 6, 1836; cited in *PL*, 193. Poe called the *Chronicle* reviewer a "scoundrel," and in a personal correspondence he assured Minor that his article on Liberian writing had been "lauded by all men of sense" (*L*, 88).

6. For discussions of Tucker's authorship of the review, see J V. Ridgely, "The Authorship of the 'Paulding-Drayton Review,'" *Poe Studies Association Newsletter* 20, no. 2 (fall 1992): 2; and Terence Whalen, *Edgar Allan Poe and the Masses: The Political Economy of Literature in Antebellum America* (Princeton, N.J.: Princeton University Press, 1999), 116–21.

7. Paulding to Thomas W. White, March 3, 1836, in *The Letters of James Kirke Paulding*, ed. Ralph M. Aderman (Madison: University of Wisconsin Press, 1962), 173–174. On March 17, 1836, Paulding repeated these sentiments in a letter written directly to Poe: "Harpers . . . will be I presume, governed by the judgement of their *Reader*, who from long experience can tell almost to a certainty what will succeed. I am destitute of this valuable instinct, and my opinion counts for nothing with publishers" (*L*, 178). Eugene Exman identifies this reader as John Inman. See Exman, *The Brothers Harper* (New York: Harper and Row, 1965), 80.

8. Reginald Charles McGrane, *The Panic of 1837: Some Financial Problems of the Jacksonian Era* (1924; reprint, Chicago: University of Chicago Press, 1965), 1.

9. James J. Barnes, *Authors, Publishers and Politicians: The Quest for an Anglo-American Copyright Agreement, 1815–1854* (Columbus: Ohio State University Press, 1974), 1–29; Charles Sellers, *The Market Revolution* (New York: Oxford University Press, 1991), 371.

10. Poe to Charles Anthon, *ante* November 2, 1844 (*L,* 270).

11. For a discussion of how the British Romantics distinguished between the public and the people, see Raymond Williams, *Culture and Society* (New York: Anchor, 1960), 35–37.

12. William Charvat, *Literary Publishing in America* (1959; University of Massachusetts Press, 1993), 97.

13. September 27, 1842, letter to Thomas H Chivers (*L,* 216). For Poe's earlier aspirations to be a poet, see *L,* 19, 32.

14. Briggs to Lowell, March 19, 1845, and April 10, 1845; quoted in Bette S. Weidman, "The Broadway Journal (2): A Casualty of Abolition Politics," *Bulletin of the New York Public Library* 73 (February 1969): 108, 110.

15. Frederick W. Thomas to Poe, July 10, 1845, file 1053 of the Griswold Collection, Boston Public Library.

16. See Whalen, *Edgar Allan Poe and the Masses,* chapter 3.

17. "Anastatic Printing," *Broadway Journal* 1 (January 1845): 15; the article is reprinted in *The Complete Works of Edgar Allan Poe,* ed. James A. Harrison (1902–1903; reprint, New York: Ams Press, 1965), 14:153–59.

18. *Complete Works,* 14:158.

19. This corresponds to the coalition strategy outlined in Poe's 1844 letter to Lowell (*Letters,* 247), where the intent is to escape the domination of large publishers.

20. See Raymond Williams, *Problems in Materialism and Culture* (New York: Verso, 1980), 32.

21. Poe's review of *Charles O'Malley, The Irish Dragoon* by Harry Lorrequer (Charles James Lever), *Graham's Magazine,* March 1842, reprinted in *ER,* 319.

22. For a thorough and sometimes harsh survey of Poe and postmodern antihumanism, see David H. Hirsch, "Poe and Postmodernism," in *A Companion to Poe Studies,* ed. Eric W. Carlson (Westport, Conn.: Greenwood Press, 1996), 403–24.

23. Review of Theodorick Bland's *Reports of Cases Decided in the High Court of Chancery of Maryland,* in *Southern Literary Messenger* 2 (October 1836): 731.

Spanking the Master

Mind-Body Crossings in Poe's Sensationalism

David Leverenz

> I have argued that the longing for recog-
> nition lies beneath the sensationalism
> of power and powerlessness. . . .
> Jessica Benjamin, *The Bonds of Love*

Why do sensations make Poe's narrators feel supernaturally spanked?

In "The Imp of the Perverse" (1845), for instance, why does the narrator say we all want to jump from a precipice? It's not to kill ourselves; "It is merely the idea of what would be our sensations during the sweeping precipitancy of a fall from such a height." The idea of "rushing annihilation" crosses into our bodies: it "chills the very marrow of our bones" with the "fierceness of the delight of its horror" (*PT,* 829). At the end, when the narrator's presumptive "we" yields to his perverse leap from the precipice of gentlemanly reason, he satisfies his craving for a rush, along with his desire to be slam-dunked: "I turned—I gasped for breath. For a moment, I experienced all the pangs of suffocation; I became blind, and deaf, and giddy; and then, some invisible fiend, I thought, struck me with his broad palm upon the back."

Only then does the narrator birth his secret, which "burst forth from my soul" as "pregnant sentences" condemning him to "hell" (*PT,* 831). Mind-body crossings confuse male and female as well as life and death. If hitting bottom means getting born and slapped, that feels like being struck by a fiend who may be about to take his "prostrate" body to hell (*PT,* 832). If his soul has "burst forth" into words, his just-born "sentences" are still "pregnant" with uncontrollable meanings. As with so many other of Poe's narrators, such sensations bring not just "pleasurable pain" but punishment, from the Latin *poena,* the original meaning of pain.

In her 1995 essay "Humanitarianism and the Pornography of Pain," Karen Halttunen has explored the intimate links between the rise of sensational and sentimental fiction and the representation of flogging scenes. "Never Bet the Devil Your Head" (1841) is the only one of Poe's tales to mention flogging directly, and there he uses it for anti-Emersonian farce. Unfortunately, Toby Dammit's mother flogged him with her left hand, not her right, and so he grew up with a "black" and "evil propensity" (*PT,* 459) for transcendentally losing his head. But Poe's horror stories turn beatings from physical fact to internalized metaphor. For narrators who idealize intellection, sensations feel like whips, beating the mind into involuntary submission. Sensations induce the monstrous birth of subjectivity, then slap it down to hell.

To extend the terms of my epigraph from Jessica Benjamin, sensations in Poe signal not the stimuli for a continuous identity, in Lockean terms, but the collapse of precariously maintained hierarchical oppositions that sustain the narrators' illusion of power. The most obviously deregulated boundaries lie between mind and body, God and brute, life and death. These ontological crossings intimate other, more social ones: between male and female, honor and shame, white and black. As Joan Dayan, Dana Nelson, and Teresa Goddu have argued, Poe subverts various discourses shoring up white male mastery, even as his writings display recurrent racism.[1] Living on the margins of the Empire of Pure Reason, Poe's narrators become not only tainted with mortality, vulnerability, and passionate malice but also more shamefully amalgamated with a plebeian or feminized or blackened mass of chaotic and wayward impulses.

Poe's best horror stories represent sensory eruption as a mind-body crossing that leaves mastery enslaved. At the level of intellectual history, Poe's sensationalism dramatizes the last flailings of Enlightenment Reason, when Reason confronts its own lack of individuality as well as "the passions and the interests" becoming so ungovernable in the Jacksonian era.[2] At the level of gender and racial politics, sensations embody moments of crossing and doubling between masterful white males and abjected women or blacks. At the most personal psychological level, as Stanley Cavell has illuminated for King Lear as well as Poe, moments of crossing are moments of exposure, of knowing that your most basic self cannot possibly be loved, and deserves to be punished.[3]

The first part of this chapter explores how the soul-brute crossings in "Metzengerstein" and depersonalized body parts in "Loss of Breath" (both 1832) jostle with Poe's linguistic playfulness. Then, after sketching the rise of tabloid journalism from the late 1820s on, the second part argues that the emerging market for sensationalism hurt Poe into greatness. With "Berenice" and "Morella" (both 1835), Poe turns from his experiments with conventional modes of Gothic and satire, particularly his send-ups of the peculiarly Southern fascination with nose-pulling. Instead of presenting shameful gentry males as neoclassic figures of mockery, Poe links sensationalism with self-torture to make them romantic figures of sympathy. He discovers that male abjection sells.

The third part considers how mind-body crossings destabilize white male mastery. "The Premature Burial" serves as a lead-in to Roderick Usher's poem, "The Haunted Palace," which allegorizes Poe's sensationalism in slow motion. The final part suggests that as Poe's life started to fall apart in the mid-1840s, his play with sensationalism's subversive crossings becomes a more chaotic unsettling of the white-black binary underpinning ideals of manly honor. Here, before analyzing the complex crossings of god-like mind and brute body in "The Black Cat," I note various slave figures and tropes of blackness, from the two Pompeys in "How to Write a Blackwood Article" and "The Man That Was Used Up" to Jupiter in "The Gold-Bug" and Hop-Frog, along with some black-white crossovers in "The Facts in the Case of

M. Valdemar." As in "The Raven," the doubling of white mastermind and black brute body intimates a chiasmic inversion, at first
comic, then increasingly desperate.

My arguments differ from current critical approaches in at
least two respects. First, I question whether Poe's sensationalism
emerges from sentimental conventions, as Jonathan Elmer argues. Though sympathies of a scarcely intelligible nature do exist
between them, Poe's sensationalism buries the sentiments it
feeds on.[4] To take up Jessica Benjamin's epigraph again, Poe
loves to stage dramas of power and powerlessness. He shocks
readers with spectacles of dominance and abjection in which
highly cultivated men lose their mental controls. The result re-
masculinizes Poe's genius, which delights in creating a buzz by
playing with readers' cravings for sensations.[5]

Second, while Poe's sensationalism exploits anxiety about
crossings between life and death and between elite and popular
culture, as J. Gerald Kennedy and Terence Whalen have demonstrated, these crossings displace more socially dangerous threats
to manly control. Poe undermines from within the hierarchies
privileging the white male elite. Crossings between mind and
body, honor and shame, male and female, and mastery and abjection ultimately expose the tenuousness of his gentry heritage's
most pervasive and presumptive binary, the hierarchical subordi-
nation of black physical servitude to white leisured intellection.

I

Poe's most sensational moments depict bodies grotesquely transformed. A one-eyed, red-mouthed cat appears on top of a
woman's gashed skull. Hop-Frog's king and courtiers become a
fiery blackened mass. Psyche Zenobia parodically inventories her
own sensations as her severed head rolls into the street. In the
seventh month of M. Valdemar's coma, his tongue says, "I am
dead," just before his body dissolves into liquid putrefaction. Yet
throughout his stories, Poe's narrative uses of body parts and
transformations seem curiously depersonalized. Poe's bodies
that splatter don't quite matter. They evoke a strange, frag-

mented nobodyhood, like Berenice's thirty-two teeth or the body parts that Pompey reassembles into "The Man That Was Used Up."

Moreover, Poe's usually anonymous narrators have sensations without feelings. They crave sensations to make their disembodied minds feel real, not just words rattling around in the house of hyperliterary language. Noting the "disembodied voice" of Poe's first-person narrators, Jonathan Auerbach usefully suggests that Poe sacrifices selfhood to gain narrative control.[6] At least in Poe's horror stories, however, narrators crave sensations to make themselves feel real by losing control. Their minds then interpret the birth of their embodied selfhood as being spanked, assaulted, or invaded.

Poe's earliest tales rely on strategies of mockery and ironic control to keep those cravings and crossings at a distance. The comic unsettlings already display Poe's trickster delight in subversive crossings and highly depersonalized representations of body parts. From the beginning, he also shows considerable relish for destabilizing identity through language play. But two inherited traditions inhibited Poe's first ventures into Gothic sensationalism by encouraging him to exaggerate rather than undermine the mind-body split. Poe wanted to make a cosmopolitan splash in romantic lyric poetry, where he sought to elevate the mind above its passions and sensations. He also sought recognition through neoclassic burlesques, where he used body fragmentations to satirize the South's provincial code of manly honor. Much has been made of the violence to women's bodies in Poe's major tales, and too little of the violence to men's bodies in his earlier fictions.

In "Metzengerstein," Poe's first experiment in Gothic fiction, the climactic sensation comes from the revelation that a proud Hungarian aristocrat has been possessed by his rival's horse, whose fiery and demonic malignity terrorizes him into being burned to death in his own castle. The first paragraph signals Poe's interest in "Metempsychosis" (*PT*, 134), and the third paragraph's prophecy rather patly establishes the prospect of spiritual transformations: "'as the rider over his horse, the mortality of Metzengerstein shall triumph over the immortality of Berlifitzing'" (*PT*, 134). The reverse happens: Count Berlifitzing's immortality, embodied in his horse, triumphs over Baron Metzengerstein the mortal rider. In getting to that metempsychotic irony, the story dramatizes various doublings and crossings: from lord to brute, from immortality to mortality, from self-control to "perverse attachment" (*PT*, 140), from a commanding demeanor to an "ungovernable fire" (*PT*, 141) and "uncontrollable" shrieking (*PT*, 142), from haughty mind to "lacerated lips, bitten through and through in the intensity of terror" (*PT*, 142). Conversely, the horse crosses from near death to life, Berlifitzing to Metzengerstein, animal to human, subjected brute to godlike demon, and perhaps immortality to mortality.

These crossings animate Poe's sensationalism throughout his career. Yet the story does not shock or horrify, partly because the omniscient narrator never loses control, and partly because the climax features a smoke-and-mirrors contrivance: fiery smoke in the shape of a horse. Poe could do better. Also, the story's ironic reversals transpose rather than subvert gentry rituals of vengeance, by turning a physical duel into a supernatural haunting. After Count Berlifitzing has been killed in the stable fire probably ordered by the baron, the count's horse appears with fiery "human" eyes in the baron's tapestry, then materializes at the gate "'all smoking and foaming with rage,'" the count's initials branded on its forehead (*PT*, 137–38). The story's last sentence literalizes that fire and smoke.

At another level, Poe's play with linguistic crossings and implied puns mutes the shock effects. The story's first crossings of "soul," "seul," and "cheval" move from English to French. A not quite comprehensible French passage about the soul's variable embodiments and resemblance to animals crosses back to the prophecy in English about mortal rider triumphing over immortal horse. The ironic reversal at the climax also implies a bilingual pun. Baron Metzengerstein is a horseman, or chevalier, who becomes cheval-iest—horsier, then horsiest. Perhaps the story's last sentence is another implied pun, since the horse goes up in smoke. Or perhaps Poe was simply horsing around. In any case, the pat opening framing, the language play, and the comfortably controlling narrative voice rein in the spectral doublings and crossings, as well as the strenuous claims for terror.

If "Metzengerstein" is Poe's first venture into Gothic mind-body crossings, "Loss of Breath" (also 1832, expanded 1835) is his most flamboyant early experiment with mind-body separations to burlesque the emerging genre of sensationalism. As the subtitle indicates, this "Tale Neither in Nor out of 'Blackwood'" both reflects and parodies *Blackwood's Edinburgh Magazine*, the British magazine that first popularized the genre. In what is arguably Poe's most preposterous plot, his incessant depersonalizations feature fragmented body parts and life-death crossings, all grounded in male sexual anxieties.

On the morning after the narrator's wedding day, while the narrator is throttling his wife's neck and shouting in her ear, he would have "ejaculated" something more "to convince her of her insignificance" (*PT,* 153) when he discovers he has lost his breath. Looking for his voice in secret, he discovers only "a set of false teeth, two pair of hips, an eye, and a bundle of *billets-doux* from Mr. Windenough to my wife" (*PT,* 153). The partiality of "Mrs. Lackobreath" for Mr. Windenough is understandable, Mr. Lackobreath reflects, since his rival is so tall while he is so fat and short (*PT,* 153). To elude his wife's "penetration" (*PT,* 153), he trains his nonvoice to utter "deep guttural" sounds for the stage. With a double pun, Poe then puts Mr. Lackobreath on a "mail-stage," where the other passengers think he is dead. In throwing him out, the driver fractures the narrator's skull, and a surgeon starts to dissect the corpse.

At this point male sexual inadequacy converges with nose pulling. Two cats start to chew on his nose. The loss of Mr. Lackobreath's nose "proved the salvation of my body" (*PT,* 157); he bursts his bandages, only to be mistaken for a condemned prisoner and hanged. Placed in a public vault, he discovers a fellow corpse, Mr. Windenough. For several pages he soliloquizes while holding the nose of his rival, who awakes, displeased. After more nose-holding, Mr. Windenough admits that he has the narrator's lost breath, which he returns through an unmentionably "delicate, *so delicate*" process involving a third party (*PT,* 162). All's well that ends well, and Mr. Lackobreath concludes by advising "the *erection* of a shrine and temple" (*PT,* 163, emphasis added) to protect against other calamities.

To a much greater degree than "Metzengerstein," this story plays with sensationalism without being sensational. Poe mocks the contemporary relish for attending executions and other public spectacles, but with considerable self-censorship at moments of indecorum. At the moment of his hanging, for instance, Mr. Lackobreath refrains from recounting his sensations except to say, "My convulsions were said to be extraordinary. . . . The populace *encored*" (*PT*, 158). At the climactic moment, when male sexual rivalry yields to a homosocial breath exchange that fills Lackobreath with wind enough to talk about erections again, the narrator teasingly intimates a pact with the Devil, or perhaps a ménage à trois among male bodies living and dead, but refrains from mentioning particulars.

As in Poe's more well-known parody of sensationalism, "How to Write a Blackwood Article" (1838), the first-person narrator remains continuously and confidently self-identified while being detached from ears, or eyes, or limbs, or head. Though Psyche Zenobia, Poe's only female narrator, goes considerably further in representing herself as an arbitrary linguistic assemblage (*PT*, 278–79), Mr. Lackobreath also seems on a linguistic "stage," where disembodied minds recount sensations without feelings. Neither story destabilizes the mind-body split. Instead, the narrators' invulnerable minds seem always already detached from their disintegrating bodies.

But what about that nose-pulling? In his wonderful essay "The Nose, the Lie, and the Duel," Kenneth Greenberg argues that nose-pulling became central to gentry rituals of honor in the Old South. For men who would be masters, appearing anywhere in public required strutting and self-display, and the nose was the ultimate physical symbol of self-projection, at least for men without beards. To pull someone's nose was to accuse him of lying, and more profoundly to show contempt for the man's mask of masterly appearance.[7] But Greenberg's astute analysis of the public symbolic implications of nose-pulling too quickly dismisses the relevance of sexual interpretations. As Poe's story extravagantly suggests, private anxieties about male physical lacks, sexual and otherwise, helped to spur public contentions about honor.

During the early 1830s, Poe continued to satirize the South's preoccupation with manliness, noses, and dueling, sometimes to expose sexual implications, sometimes to play with the mind-body split. In "The Duc de l'Omelette" (1832), a satire of N. P. Willis's effeminate and "queenly" persona, the Duc dies because he sees an unfeathered bird, then challenges the Devil to a duel when the Devil tells him to strip (*PT,* 143–44). In "Bon-Bon" (also 1832), the eyeless Devil observes that men expel bad ideas by sneezing (*PT,* 174). When Pierre Bon-Bon, a metaphysical cook proud of his food for thought, begins to bargain with the Devil for his soul, the Devil sneezes, implicitly rejecting Bon-Bon's soul as a bad idea.

In "Lionizing" (1835), Poe satirizes nose-pulling more directly, to eroticize as well as mock the culture of literary lions. After writing a pamphlet on the science of noses, the narrator gains his fifteen minutes of fame. At parties "I turned up my nose, and I spoke of myself." "'He is coming!'" everyone exclaims. Finally, even the duchess exclaims with delight, "'He is come, the little love!'—and, seizing me firmly by both hands, she kissed me thrice upon the nose." Her nose-kiss creates an ambiguously "marked sensation" in his rivals, and no doubt in himself as well. In the ensuing duel, the narrator shoots off his challenger's nose, only to learn from his father that "'there is no competing with a lion who has no proboscis at all'" (*PT,* 216–17).

Overtly, these stories feature depersonalized body parts to mock rituals of honor and celebrity. But Poe's hapless narrators or protagonists use body detachment to restore their sense of control. Fetishizing may defend against castration anxiety, in the traditional Freudian view, but fetishizing also reflects what Scott Derrick calls "the ongoing work of patriarchy," which "defensively maintains male identity" in part by manipulating feminization and self-fragmentation as disguises for preserving narrative agency. Poe's satirical uses of public body parts, especially noses, to expose private lacks finally reinforce the ways that such cultural fetishizing functions, in Louise Kaplan's terms, "to provide individuals relief from troubling affects and emotions."[8]

From the start, however, Poe yearned for cosmopolitan recognition, not membership in a provincial literary coterie. He wanted to make a cross-cultural impact, create a buzz. His poems and his satires were not doing that. So he ambivalently embraced the new literary market for sensationalism, while raising the stakes in his contentious reviews. If mad Ireland hurt Yeats into poetry, as Auden claims in his elegy for Yeats, then antebellum readers' avidity for sensationalism hurt Poe into writing great short fiction. To satisfy his own craving for literary distinction, Poe turned from homosocial burlesques to heterosexual horror tales.

2

As Karen Halttunen notes, the first use of sensation to signify an excited or violent feeling came in 1779. Linking the rise of humanitarian sympathies to the rise of sadistic and masochistic narrative spectacles, Halttunen argues that representing pain gained a new shock value because middle-class spectators felt safely distant. Pain became not an inescapable fact but an alluring taboo, to be experienced through vicarious sympathy by reading Gothic fiction or newspaper accounts of murder trials. At one such murder trial, in 1830, Daniel Webster closed with a rumination that makes him sound like the narrator of "The Man of the Crowd": "So strangely was the mind of man constructed, that pleasure could be gathered from the elements of pain, and beauty seen in the Gorgon head of horror" ("Humanitarianism," 311).

From its inception, sensationalism joined contrary constituencies as well as contrary modes of experience—not simply pleasure and pain, but elite and popular audiences. "The horror tale in *Blackwood's*," as Daniel Hoffman notes, drawing on Michael Allen, "developed as an effort to attract the sensation-loving vulgar readers into the same tent as the loftier reviews and articles." Allen argues that Poe used sensationalism to appeal to a mass audience, while he used the pose of gentleman-writer to consolidate gentry Virginia's aristocratic code against Northern pretensions.[9]

In the second volume of *Democracy in America* (1840), Alexis de Tocqueville explains the desire of American readers for short, novel sensations: "Accustomed to the struggle, the crosses, and the monotony of practical life, they require strong and rapid emotions, startling passages, truths or errors brilliant enough to rouse them up and to plunge them at once, as if by violence, into the midst of the subject" (62; bk. 1, chap. 13). While one might question the fantasy aspects of Tocqueville's claim that readers want to be roused and plunged by simulated violence, recent historians tend to agree about the "struggle" and "crosses" afflicting ordinary antebellum American lives. Where Tocqueville saw only "monotony," historians have found pervasive instability and ideological tensions.

In *Murder Most Foul*, Karen Halttunen emphasizes a variety of factors stimulating the rise of tabloid journalism in the 1820s and 1830s, from "the new shock value of pain" to technological innovations such as steam printing and stereotyping. Halttunen intriguingly speculates that sensational journalism and Gothic fiction about bodies in pain helped to articulate the "fault lines" (168) in several social transformations. First, until the early 1840s, public hangings were common spectacles, with twelve, thirty, or even fifty thousand attending (69–72). Second, while states slowly privatized public punishment, complementary transformations in the home began to turn the traditional patriarchal family toward new middle-class norms of sentimental privacy and new disciplining practices of moral persuasion rather than physical force. Like newspaper accounts of grisly murders, Gothic narratives "may be read as cultural nightmares of the new sentimental domesticity" (160), ostensibly reinforcing idealized norms by offering didactic "cautionary tales" of "patriarchal violence, female depravity, and child abuse."[10]

Halttunen neglects one of the most paradoxical causes for the rise of tabloid journalism: the active patronage of the federal government, which aggressively subsidized newspapers and magazines from 1790 on through very low postal rates. The government's goal of an informed citizenry succeeded. Within a few decades the United States was by far the most literate country in the world.[11] As with the public's thirst for knowledge, federal subvention stimulated the public's thirst for guilty pleasures, especially after the penny press took off in the 1830s.

Two instances can illustrate the variety of social transformations refracted in sensational journalism. In the 1828 "Robards affair," charges of adultery and bigamy threatened Andrew Jackson's election, since Jackson had not realized his wife's first marriage had never been legally terminated. Norma Basch's analysis of newspaper accounts shows how sensational journalism gained popularity by exploiting the deepening disjunctions between public and private life, particularly the transformation of marriage from public contract to private domesticity. The new private model of marriage no longer had the same symbolic resonance with national union, though the ideal of man as protector persisted and the woman's public identity remained "a threadbare abstraction" (916).

In 1836, the murder of Helen Jewett, a high-priced New York prostitute, propelled James Gordon Bennett's recently founded *Herald* to fame and fortune. Bennett took every opportunity to describe Jewett's near-naked, mutilated body, while defending the young middle-class suspect—the actual killer, as it turned out, though never convicted. One of the most bizarre aspects of Bennett's marketing strategy was his relish for reporting how he himself was frequently beaten on the streets. As David Anthony points out, Bennett seems oddly playful about it. Like Jewett, he uses his body as "bait" for profit (496). To stabilize his tabloid's position and class status, Anthony concludes, Bennett deliberately destabilizes his gendered identity, substituting a fluid rhetoric of masculine submission for traditional conventions of male dominance or self-possession.

By 1836, Poe, too, had discovered there was a market for stories of male abjection as well as female corpses. With "Berenice" and "Morella" (both 1835), Poe inaugurates his stories about shameful men obsessed with the corpses of beautiful women. No one can forget the thirty-two teeth that the narrator of "Berenice" discovers he has extracted from his almost-dead cousin's mouth. As Poe wrote to the editor of the *Southern Literary Messenger*, perhaps with punning complacency, the ending might have been "on the very verge of bad-taste." On the other hand, "To be appreciated you must be *read*, and these things are invariably sought after with avidity."[12]

Poe's stories challenge the new spectatorial distance from pain that Halttunen describes. It is as if he dares his readers: Can you take your sympathies this far? His narrations seek to obliterate the middle-class boundaries between civilized and savage, public and private, normal and alien, rational and insane. Yet Poe's uncanny effects depend on the tug between his controlling if deconstructive language play and his out-of-control body shocks. If psychoanalytic invocations of a vagina dentata or phallic woman stabilize the horror in one way, the narrator himself controls it in another, by repeatedly punning on how change threatens "iden-tity" (*PT,* 226, 229; emphasis added). After his mind-body split collapses into the narrator's delusive obsession that somehow Berenice's teeth would restore his reason, since *"tous ses dents étaient des idées"* (*PT,* 231; emphasis in original), the horrific finale excavates and resuscitates not only her dead-undead body but also the dead-undead pun on identity. As the narrator used "in-struments of dental surgery" on her mouth, her nails "in*dented*" his own hand (*PT,* 233; emphasis added). Poe's unnervingly deper-sonalizing wit augments the oppositely unnerving depersonaliza-tion of Berenice's body.

In "Morella," too, an intellectualized discussion of the prob-lem of "identity," defined in Lockean terms as "the sameness of a rational being" (*PT,* 235), quickly becomes the narrator's patho-logical "alienation" not from his own identity but from his loathed wife. She dies yet lives on in her identical yet changeable daughter, who dies with Morella's voice saying, "'I am here!'" (*PT,* 238). The narrator's loathing of the elder Morella ostensibly reflects his philosophical concern to preserve identity as rational consistency, not his feelingful responses to either woman. Yet to him as to the narrator of "Berenice," the changeable female body represents a fascinating, terrifying site of crossing between life and death, mind and body. Who speaks the "I"? And whose "I" speaks? Seemingly naked loathing and yearning cohabit with bilingual puns; in "Berenice," as Joan Dayan points out, "Egeaus pursues his *I/dents/idées*" while Morella's name joins "Mort" with "Elle," as in "Mort/elle/à."[13] Such linguistic and physical in-betweenness arouses the narrators to malevolence, perhaps because its paradoxical vitality seems more real than their own disembodied claims to linguistic continuity and logical abstraction.

Much of Poe's uncanniness in these and later horror stories comes from techniques that work at cross-purposes. As sensational crossings whip male subjectivities into a momentary agony of life, destabilizing modes of narrative control preserve their mind-body splits in an abstracted linguistic limbo. While bodies become depersonalized fragments, identities become alphabet soup. No interpretive stabilization stays put, and that's a goodly part of how Poe keeps creating a buzz.

In "Ligeia" (1838), for instance: psychologically, the secret heart of Gothic narrative is the return of the dead-undead mother, as Claire Kahane has argued. That return helps to explain the narrator's mourning and yearning, if one adds his inner child's reciprocally secret doubling of "I can't live without her" and "Did I kill her?" Cynthia Jordan has speculated that the narrator in fact did kill Ligeia as well as Rowena—"I saw that she must die" (*PT*, 267).[14] But what if one then adds Toni Morrison's insight that the secret heart of the slave narrative is the mother's wish to kill her child? Whose subjectivity centers "Ligeia"—the enthralled narrator or the "will" of his dark beloved? And what if Ligeia is secretly a mulatta, as Joan Dayan has suggested, and the narrator's terror also reflects the specter of a black woman on top?[15] And still deeper the meaning of that story of Narcissus, who because he could not grasp the tormenting, mild image he saw in the foun—oops, sorry. Wrong text.

There, *that's* the Poe-jolt.

3

Occasionally Poe tries to critique tabloid journalism directly, especially in "The Mystery of Marie Rogêt" (1842–43). This narrative forfeits its sensational possibilities by simply parroting popular culture while pretending to intellectual superiority. Dupin's tedious close readings of various nominally Parisian journals continuously betray Poe's anxious dependence on the tabloids, since the narrator's notes ostentatiously supply parallels with

New York newspaper stories about the case of Mary Rogers, whose body was found in the Hudson River in 1841. Poe presumes readers know the intimate ongoing details of this unsolved murder, and the many quotations from tabloid journalism serve as a pre-text to show how Dupin is a better close reader than either the journalists or the sensation-seeking public. In fact, as John Walsh notes in *Poe the Detective*, Poe tried to peddle his story to newspaper editors by saying he had solved the Mary Rogers murder and that this story would "'give renewed impetus to the investigation'" (47).

By endlessly deferring the sensational climax, Dupin's detection becomes an annoying tease. The story has three mysteries: (1) Who killed her? (2) Where and how? (3) Did she or didn't she? (The patriarchal translation: Was she a virgin or a slut?)[16] After proliferating indeterminacies for all three, at length, the narrative leaves all three unsolved. As if displacing and duplicating the fixation of Poe's narrators on women they love and loathe, Dupin avidly reads and critiques tabloid sensationalism, but only to deny his dependence while maintaining an inscrutable superiority.

The better tales subvert such impotent poses. Poe was fascinated with doublings and reciprocal convertibility, which he used to destabilize Lockean notions of personal identity. To extend Joan Dayan's insight in *Fables of Mind* about Poe's skepticism, only at moments of destabilizing convertibility does sensation erupt. Barbaric hordes of sensations chain male narrators to their bodies, or a single demonic "imp" chains them to a "perverse" identity. Either way, having embodied subjectivity means losing your mind, which means losing your claim to mastery and transsubjective aristocracy. The self feels real, comes into existence, only at the moment that the mind crosses from the honored impersonality of what John Irwin calls Poe's godlike Master Mind to the shameful depersonalization of the body's mortal otherness.[17] Poe's hyperrational male narrators experience this crossing as both self-creation and self-torture.

To conflate Dayan and Irwin, the binary states of womblike, undifferentiated, Neoplatonic Master Mind or Mortal Mechanical Body become the class-linked binary poles by which narrators evade subjectivity. Through reasoning, a "double Dupin" ("Murders in the Rue Morgue," *PT,* 402) can display cosmopolitan distinction and impersonate other identities without ever losing control or being afflicted with a body's passionate interests. Sensations, and the sensational, erupt at the moment of crossing, from living to dead or back again, or from omnipotent mind to vulnerable body, from godlike reason to brutal perversity, from manly control to feminized victim, or from white mastery to black servitude. Skepticism deregulates intellectual mastery, but in an intellectual way; sensation records the mastermind's irrevocable fall. As the mind's reasoning capacity becomes obscurely linked to its shameful or guilty or suppressed passions, narrators are reduced from explanation to a helpless witnessing of the crossing. The narrator of "Murders in the Rue Morgue" feels obscurely terrified at the "half-formed" possibility of crossing from human to animal agency (*PT,* 421). Then Dupin confirms a more sensational reverse crossing, when the Ourang-Outang's mutilation of Madame L'Espanaye with a razor follows its "imitation of the motions of a barber" (*PT,* 430).

What, for instance, does the narrator of "Usher" witness? Madeline returns from her coffin, falls "heavily *inward* upon the *person* of her brother," and "*bore* him to the floor a corpse, and a victim" (*PT,* 335; emphasis added). Here Roderick's "person" is his body, which develops life and inwardness only as Madeline births his death: she "*bore* him to the floor a corpse" (emphasis added). Self-birthing becomes self-murder. Besides, whose inwardness is it, Roderick's or Madeline's? Roderick's previous lack of inwardness, or feelingful subjectivity, has depended on suppressing both Madeline and his unacknowledged desires for her, just as his leisured pursuit of pure thought has depended more conventionally on invisible servant hands.

A closer look at "The Premature Burial" (1844) can expose the covert social destabilizations impelling Poe's ostentatious narrative play with boundaries between life and death. To create fictional sensations, the narrator begins, a writer has to evoke a "thrill" of "'pleasurable pain,'" without giving offense or evoking "disgust" (*PT,* 666). Whereas the mass horrors of earthquakes or massacres can be represented with "propriety" only through the authority of "Truth," the fiction writer's inventions have to excite the reader by representing individual, solitary agonies. "To be buried while alive, is, beyond question, the most terrific of these extremes," because that experience exposes how "shadowy and vague" are "[t]he boundaries that divide Life from Death" (*PT,* 666).

The narrator then lures readers toward the abyss, but only to tease. After telling various stories of being buried alive, he climaxes his account of his own premature burial with the discovery that he had simply been sleeping in a cramped ship's cabin with his jaw bandaged. The horror story becomes a tall tale. Those terrifying sensations didn't come from his buried body at all, the narrator realizes; they were all in his head. The discovery promptly cures his body of its hypochondria.

Despite the jokey double cross, the narrator's initial claim has become something of a paradigm for critical approaches to Poe's sensationalism, and for good reason. In story after story, Poe obsessively returns to the drama of being buried alive, ostensibly to expose the tenuousness of the boundary between life and death. As the opening paragraphs of "The Premature Burial" suggest, the trope may also serve as a devious maneuver. First, the narrator hints, perhaps a "romanticist" such as Poe turns to the buried-alive motif because readers would be disgusted or offended by more repulsive horrors of social trauma. Second, though the narrator announces his narrative as fiction, he presents his instances of premature burial as historical or journalistic facts. Fragile individual boundaries between life and death oddly have more "propriety" in fiction than do fragile social boundaries between fact and fiction, mass and singular horror.

Though the ending restores both the narrator's control of the fiction and the mind's mastery of the body, what lingers in the reader's mind are the sensations erupting at moments of intensely embodied helplessness: "the stifling fumes from the damp earth—the clinging of the death garments—the rigid embrace of the narrow house—the blackness of the absolute Night—the silence like a sea that overwhelms" (*PT,* 672). By implication, Poe's covertly social meanings emerge as and through sensations of pleasurable pain, at the intersections where the body's facts meet the mind's fictions. Through personal dramas of life-in-death, forms of "blackness" and "silence" that would otherwise horrify or disgust genteel white antebellum readers can be put into words.

A more well-known example can amplify my claim that social conflicts as well as linguistic alienation loom in what looks like psychological and philosophical preoccupations. Midway through "The Fall of the House of Usher" (1839), another of Poe's many anonymous white male narrators muses on his friend's artistic productions. Soon he, too, begins to sense the thrill of "pleasurable pain." One of Roderick's improvised musical compositions, for instance, lingers "painfully in mind" (324). As if his mind has stepped onto a linguistic roller coaster, that "pain" reminds him of Roderick's "paintings," which also sought to embody "pure abstractions." Yet when faced with Roderick's abstracted canvases, the narrator shudders—"shuddered the more thrillingly, because I shuddered knowing not why."

Like his well-educated contemporaries, the narrator believes the mind can use common sense and rational explanation to keep sensations from getting sensational. Now, when he witnesses Roderick's attempts to give physical embodiment to pure "ideality," that faith grows shaky. The narrator experiences both thrill and pain, without being able to explain either state of mind. Moreover, Roderick's artistic vitality seems obscurely twinned with death, much as Roderick later links himself to his twin sister, Madeline, by "sympathies of a scarcely intelligible nature" (*PT,* 329). His mysteriously haunting music sounds like "dirges." The one picture capable of being reduced from "the spirit of abstraction" to mere words anticipates Madeline's underground burial vault. Somehow, the narrator senses, putting pure thought into paint or music is like being buried alive.

Then the world's first abstract expressionist becomes the world's first rhap artist. Roderick sings or chants one of his improvised "rhapsodies," "The Haunted Palace." Like the house of Usher itself, as many critics have noted, the poem represents a once-lordly mind about to crack. The palace is the head of "monarch Thought," the "two luminous windows" are his eyes, the "pearl and ruby glowing" at the palace door are his teeth and lips. Formerly this allegorical royal skull has resounded with dancing "Spirits" and "Echoes" who sing "[t]he wit and wisdom of their king." But Thought has been overthrown, and now "[v]ast forms" instead of spirits move behind "the red-litten windows." As the narrator fancies, the poem implies "for the first time, a full consciousness on the part of Usher, of the tottering of his lofty reason upon her throne" (*PT,* 325).

All this seems rather formulaic, except perhaps for the blurring of "his" and "her." Then, in the last stanza, as the meter accelerates, a strange self-alienation deepens and disconcerts the allegory:

> While, like a rapid ghastly river,
> Through the pale door,
> A hideous throng rush out forever,
> And laugh—but smile no more. (*PT,* 327)

At the simplest level of strangeness, why does the throng rush *out* of the head and not *into* it, from outside? By implication, these forces were always present in the palace of King Thought, passionate, vulgar, suppressed but seething. Now, ungovernable at last, they erupt to give the palace hideous life.

The mob's laughter transforms subjects into diverse subjectivities that can not be acknowledged, at least not within the depersonalized realm of Reason. The "pale door" suggests that Reason's palace is white, while the throng are people of color, "red" and "ghastly," though without any discernible individuality. All those people are vulgar; they all look alike. Their collective usurpation prefigures the "buried-alive" climax, as Madeline returns from her coffin with "blood upon her white robes" to enact a woman-on-top revenge (*PT,* 335). Beyond anticipating Madeline's return from her premature burial, the usurpation also suggests a slave revolt, suitably distanced in chivalric abstractions. These are the bad spirits, wearing black ("in robes of sorrow"), moving "fantastically" to "discordant" music, as if they were boogying at the birth of jazz or dancing in voodoo rituals.

Here Poe's allegorizing works in at least a fourfold way. Psychologically, it anticipates how Roderick's unconfessable, incestuous desire for Madeline overwhelms his reason. Politically, it sketches the fall of gentry Federalism to the Jacksonian democratic rabble. Socially, it hints at slave or Indian revolts. And philosophically, it suggests the triumph of an unacknowledged third term, the return of repressed passions in the mind-body split. Gone are the "good angels" who deferentially "tenanted" the king's happy valleys at the start of the poem. Gone, in short, is the rule of a Jeffersonian gentry elite, "men of letters" for whom Reason served as a kind of eighteenth-century cosmopolitan Internet to govern the body politic, while servants or slaves attended to their bodies' needs.

But such allegorizing does not wholly explain Poe's uncanny effects. The "hideous throng" rushing out through the castle-skull's "door" are *words*, the same ones now rushing out of Roderick's mouth. The art form that used to dance so harmoniously in the mind as pure abstraction now speaks its own ugly, botched, embodied otherness from within, in the act of birthing itself as material sounds. Who is the Fissure King's "I," at this moment? Who sings his throng-song?

Once again, contradictory depersonalizations destabilize any and all attempts to gain intellectual control, whether by Roderick, the narrator, or the reader. Contra-dictions become whipsaws. The poem's slow-motion uncanniness culminates in Roderick's half-consciousness that his rhapsodic words may be spoken from below his consciousness, perhaps by a gathering of unspeakable tribes, or by an unspeaking sister whom he has not quite been able to bury alive.

4

Mixing it up with tabloid journalism liberated Poe from Virginia gentry constraints. By indirections he found directions out; in reaching for a national audience, he risked exploring rather than mocking his own inward crossings, doublings, and abjections. Not coincidentally, fathers and patrilineal identities quickly become vestigial or nonexistent. As paternalistic controls disintegrate in Poe's stories, mind-body crossings intensify. The father who instructs his son in "Lionizing" (1835) becomes a dramatic absence only three years later in "Ligeia" (1838). As the narrator says at the start, he can not even remember Ligeia's "paternal name," though he easily remembers the family and last name of Rowena. To him, paternal identity seems irrelevantly external to the transcendental intensities of the "spirit which is entitled *Romance*" (*PT*, 262). A year later, Roderick Usher's "deficiency" reflects his status as the last of his paternal line (*PT*, 318–19).

In a later story, "The Imp of the Perverse" (1845), the most subtle crossing or doubling comes not in the parallel sensations of jumping from a precipice at the middle and the end but in the murder itself. It takes work to figure out that the narrator has killed his father. Only the fact of his inheritance provides the clue that the narrator has secured his mental and physical stability by erasing his father's identity as well as body. He has made his father a nobody in his narrative, as well as in life. Moreover, he kills his father through the air, with a poisoned candle. J. Gerald Kennedy has suggested that the murder represents the narrator's attempt to destroy that part of the self which suffers mortal anxiety, the embodied self that experiences all sensations as death in the offing (137–38). Yet that repressed self returns in the narrator's sensations of rushing annihilation, which uncannily replicate his father's gasping final moments. Once again, self-birthing is self-murder.

If the attenuation of provincial paternal controls precipitates Poe's most creative fiction, the protracted sickness of his wife, Virginia, who died in early 1847 at the age of twenty-four, precipitated inward chaos. Poe died only two years later. During the mid-1840s, his play with sensationalism's subversive crossings becomes a more chaotic unsettling of the white-black binary underpinning ideals of manly honor. The doublings of white mastermind and black brute bodies begin as racist farce but end in a black hole of rage.

Blackness or black characters appear in Poe's early satires as incidental figures of entertainment or signifiers of social ridicule. In "Loss of Breath," the narrator betrays his haplessness at the start when he affirms Anaxagoras's belief "that snow is black" (153). More centrally, several tales use the trope of the slave on top much as Renaissance writers used the trope of the woman on top, to mock white characters who assent to an unnatural social order. In "A Predicament," the second half of "How to Write a Blackwood Article," Poe clearly thinks it's very funny that Psyche Zenobia's black servant Pompey is only three feet tall, about seventy years old, and without a neck (*PT,* 289).

It's also intrinsically funny to Poe that a white woman works. It's still more hilarious that this self-described "Signora," who pretentiously calls herself by an inflated name to evade her ordinary name of "Suky Snobbs," throws herself into involuntary sexual intimacy with her black servant, who has an equally inflated name. Pompey wears only an old overcoat, which drops away from him as he falls toward her, his head "striking me full in the——in the breast" (*PT,* 291). After his head presumably encounters her groin, they tumble together on the belfry floor, until she tears out "a vast quantity" of his woolly hair (*PT,* 291). Thereafter, at least until her head rolls into the street and her eyes literally start from their sockets, she sits on Pompey's shoulders. Wondering whether her head or her body constitutes her "proper identity," she "candidly" inventories her literalized sensations (*PT,* 295). The original meaning of "candid" is "white." In the most racist finale to any of Poe's stories, Psyche Zenobia concludes, "Dogless, niggerless, headless . . . I have done" (*PT,* 297).

A more masterful yet similarly self-effacing Pompey appears in "The Man That Was Used Up" (1839). While most of the narrative uses this Pompey for laughs, its end suddenly presents a chiasmatic crossing as the black servant composes the body and voice of his eminent white master out of various mechanical parts and prostheses. Who is the master? Who is the slave? The racial crossing unsettles the story's specific satire of Martin Van Buren's vice president, a much decorated and wounded veteran of military campaigns against the Indians, and its more "general" satire of manliness and celebrity sound bites.

In the early 1840s, Poe's white-black doublings and crossings intensify their ambiguous destabilizations of the master-slave relation. At the beginning of "The Gold-Bug" (1843), the old farcical tropes still seem serviceable. William Legrand looks so down-and-out that the narrator suspects Legrand's family has instructed a faithful old Negro servant, a manumitted former slave called Jupiter, to be his supervisor and guardian (PT, 561). Worse, Jupiter is entitled "'to gib him a d——d good beating'" if Legrand misbehaves (*PT,* 565). Yet once the white man's mind has secured its proper mastery, Jupiter's uncanny doubling provides the story's one semisensational moment. When the narrator, Legrand, and Jupiter discover the buried treasure through Legrand's reasoning, Jupiter's body and voice dramatize the ecstatic sensations the two white men also feel but suppress.

First Jupiter turns white, with "as deadly a pallor" as any black man's face can "assume." Then he enacts the sensations.

> He seemed stupified—thunderstricken. Presently he fell upon his knees in the pit, and, burying his naked arms up to the elbows in gold, let them there remain, as if enjoying the luxury of a bath. At length, with a deep sigh, he exclaimed, as if in a soliloquy,
>
> "And dis all cum ob de goole-bug! De putty goole-bug! De poor little goole-bug, what I boosed in dat sabage kind ob style! Aint you shamed ob yourself, nigger?—answer me dat!"
> (*PT,* 578)

The passage exploits blackface minstrel dialect to ridicule Jupiter's explanation, since he says the bug rather than Legrand caused their discovery. Yet his language undermines the props for such ridicule, the white binaries of civilized and savage, honor and shame, even human and animal, as well as white and black. As his body sensuously luxuriates in a gold "bath," he distinguishes his present honor from his previous shame by saying he was savage ("'sabage'") to have abused ("'boosed'") the bug. Similarly, Legrand's sudden upward mobility rescues him from his former buglike degradation, just as his mastery is now secured from the danger of being "'boosed'" by a black servant. In pretentiously soliloquizing about his former "'shamed'" state, Jupiter gives external voice to Legrand's inward state of mind. Stagily admonishing his former self, he duplicates the self-doubling thoughts, if not the diction, of his master. Legrand's story ends with a more ominous reverse crossing: the implication that the mastermind could brutally kill his two associates, mirroring Captain Kidd (*PT*, 595–96).[18]

More disturbingly, black-white crossovers in "The Facts in the Case of M. Valdemar" (1845) give an underspin of racial amalgamation to overt sensations of being alive yet dead. Valdemar is particularly "noticeable for the extreme spareness of his person . . . and also for the whiteness of his whiskers, in violent contrast to the blackness of his hair" (*PT*, 833). The confusion of "person" with body and the "violent" juxtaposition of black with white leap into noticeability again just as Valdemar seems to die. His skin resembles "white paper," while his jaw falls open, "disclosing in full view the swollen and blackened tongue" (*PT*, 839). After almost seven months in a comatose state, Valdemar's final sensation sexualizes the eruption of this black tongue into dead-undead white man's speech. Now "ejaculations of 'dead! Dead!' absolutely *bursting* from the tongue and not from the lips" (*PT*, 842) ink the reader's white page, before Valdemar's "whole frame . . . shrunk—crumbled—absolutely *rotted* away beneath my hands. Upon the bed, before that whole company, there lay a nearly liquid mass of loathsome—of detestable putridity."

At one level this climax is simply a truly grotesque masturbation fantasy. Or, at a more unsettling level of homoerotic self-alienation, a white man discovers he has been masturbating with a black man's penis.[19] At yet another level, the undecidable in-betweenness of dying becomes charged with racialized oppositions and mixings. At a fourth level, in Jonathan Elmer's fine reading (*Reading at the Social Limit*, 122–25), the story becomes Poe's most radical literalization of sentimental tropes, as the scientific narrator fails to "recompose the patient" (*PT*, 841). At a fifth level, the "whole frame" of the mind-body split, like that of white mastery and black abjection, rots into indistinguishably mixed and disgusting liquidity. At a sixth level, speech itself becomes a prisoner of a detached body part in the body's suspended death, beyond any mental controls. And beyond all that, the story plays with an implied pun on the quick and the dead.

It is only a step from there to "Hop-Frog" (1849), where few readers can identify with anyone except perhaps Trippetta. There, as the dwarf vindictively torches the king and his courtiers, their "blackened mass" vies with the grinding of Hop-Frog's "fang-like teeth" (PT, 907) to shock readers beyond any stabilizing gestures of sympathy.

The most complex of Poe's sensational black-white crossings occurs in "The Black Cat" (1843). Here the narrator interprets his experience of sensations as a fall from godlike Reason into perverse impulses. Defining himself as "a man, fashioned in the image of the High God" (PT, 603), he ends as a brute, not only by brutally killing his cats and wife but also by being afflicted with "the *rabid* desire to say something" (PT, 605; emphasis added). As his high white mind falls to black deeds, the black cat rises from a naturally loving animal to a supernatural avenger who embodies the narrator's lost manliness as well as his punitive conscience. The head of the household in effect becomes not the narrator but the second black cat, first discovered reposing upon the head of one of the immense hogsheads of gin, and finally sitting with its phallic eye atop the head of the wife's erect corpse.

The sensations, and the sensationalism, come not at the beginning and end points of the status and gender reversals but at the moments of crossing. Consider the transformations of the noose, which passes from the first cat's neck to its image on the one remaining plaster wall. Then it becomes an increasingly visible emblem on the neck of the second cat. At the end, while the narrator blames the beast for having seduced him into murder, he declares that its "informing voice had consigned me to the hangman" (PT, 606). The noose will be his last sensation. Moreover, since "informing" connotes both shaping identity and giving information, the beast's voice now seems the narrator's maker, witness, and judge, a three-in-one God, as well as the witch suggested earlier by his wife (PT, 598). The cat's instability of identity is really the narrator's.

At the end, the cat's voice has a similarly disorienting instability of identity, again exchangeable with the narrator's. It begins as "a cry, at first muffled and broken, like the sobbing of a child" (PT, 606). That sound evokes an abused, loveless, already broken child-self, but it quickly swells into "a scream, utterly anomalous and inhuman," as if from hell, conjointly "from the throats of the damned in their agony and of the demons that exult in the damnation." The story gives readers no other access to the abused child. After Stanley Cavell's analysis, however, one can easily interpret this narrator as a serial killer, so far on only a domestic scale. As with most serial killers, his sadism acts out abusive self-splitting, from both sides. To exorcise haunting memories of childhood abuse, he sadistically kills his own vulnerable self, displaced and disowned as feminized, to invite the eternal abuse or damnation he thinks he deserves. Yet that interpretive stabilization, too, lets me disown the story's sensational power, which depends on racialized moments where self-protective binary splittings become self-destabilizing doublings and crossings of white and black.

5

I have been arguing that mind-body crossings expose and displace cultural tensions between disembodied white mastery and embodied, alienated forms of servitude. A differently gendered political context, provided by Jonathan Elmer, emphasizes the complex relations of Poe's sensationalism to sentimentalism, particularly his literalizing mimicry of sentimental conventions for representing loss and mourning. A recent essay by Joanne Dobson argues that we should take sentimental conventions seriously in formalist terms, since they articulate the complex ways all affective relationality is steeped in love and loss. Sentimental conventions and tropes convey the primary vision of human connection in a dehumanized world. Dobson is particularly good on the sentimental keepsake, which constitutes a vivid symbolic embodiment of the primacy of human connection and the inevitability of human loss.[20] For the middle class, in mid-nineteenth-century America, this was women's work.

In that context, Poe's sensationalism turns the potential danger of feelingful relations into narcissistic paranoia about the loss of solipsistic genius. Sensation in Poe becomes a male defense against the danger of sentiment. Like sentimentalism, sensations make a gendered male self feel real, in conditions of unreality. But sensation in Poe becomes a narcissistic way of feeling real, by magnifying the mind-body split while reducing intimate relations—with the wife in "The Black Cat," the father in "Imp of the Perverse"—to nobodyhood. The onset of embodied individuality is experienced as a kind of paranoid narcissism, in which sensations signify the loss of the controlling womb-mind and the "I" becomes someone else's speech.

Better a self grandiosely damned to eternal abuse and punishment, goes this male logic, than the experience of real pain, the experience of loss inseparable from subjectivity. To minds preoccupied with mastery, sensations may function as hidden signifiers of loss, if only of a consciously yearned-for loss of damnable self. Sensations might be considered a kind of token, like Little Eva's hair, twining around the mind's solitary dreams of omnipotence. These sentimental keepsakes turn malevolent, as if Eva's hair had become Berenice's teeth. If the mastermind now feels like bullet-headed Simon Legree, then sensations record the pleasurable pain of becoming unmanly, by shamefully exposing the master's vulnerability and his passionate malice.

Ironically, the Poe text that made the most sensational splash was not a horror story but a poem, "The Raven" (1845), which transforms the sentimental trope of a house pet into an omen of never-ending loss. A depressed but highly educated speaker becomes another of Poe's abjected males, prostrate in the shadow of a black brute. Like the narrator at the end of "The Black Cat," he ends enslaved to a godlike "ebony bird." Moreover, after this bird permanently perches "on the pallid bust of Pallas," its black body boldly displays mastery over a classical symbol of elite education as well as white-mindedness.

Yet the Raven also seems curiously androgynous. It struts in "with many a flirt and flutter," though with a "stately" or even "saintly" manner. The gender irresolution persists: "with mien of lord or lady"? The narrator cannot decide. The Raven seems both comic and tragic. Moreover, though its countenance wears a "grave and stern decorum" and makes no "obeisance" to the narrator, it beguiles him out of sadness "into smiling." All these inversions and instabilities tease, baffle, and fascinate the speaker, before the bird's one relentlessly repeated word reduces him to helpless prostration.

Simultaneously and contradictorily, the speaker and his readers revel in displaying the poem's astonishing technical control, which Poe himself relished celebrating and inflating in "The Philosophy of Composition." There in a nutshell is the doubled source of Poe's sensationism: the technical virtuosity and the shameful subjection, crossing and recrossing between white mastermind and abjected black body, in control and out of control at the same time. Forever flirting and fluttering between these two contradictory sites of Poe's enduring appeal, neither his narrators nor his readers can make up their minds.

It was no accident, then, that "The Raven" created Poe's greatest sensation, since its form takes "white" literary control and "black" emotional abjection to their contrary extremes. Plunged from mastery into terror, the speaker yields to the bird's speech with his last word—"'Nevermore!'"—while his "soul" merges with the bird's "shadow that lies floating on the floor." Yet throughout his descent, his metrics hold to their rigidly patterned and even grandiloquent literariness, and his voice preserves an exaggerated literary decorum.

To return once more to the epigraph from Jessica Benjamin, Poe's poem gained him the literary recognition he craved by depicting a symbiosis of power and powerlessness. Once again, Poe's sensational effects depict a state of in-betweenness, in which a man's fall from mind to body, reason to brute, control to helplessness, evokes a more threatening social crossing of master and slave. As with so many of Poe's white male narrators, the speaker remains alien from any subjective state except two grandiose extremes of narcissistic desire: the yearning to be one with God's controlling Master Mind, and the equal and opposite craving to be scourged into hell by a black, bestial manifestation of God's righteous wrath. In Poe's most memorable linguistic turn, the black beast scourges the narrator out of his mind not with a whip but with a word.

NOTES

1. See Dayan, "Amorous Bondage"; Nelson, *National Manhood*, esp. 206–16 on "Some Words with a Mummy"; Goddu, *Gothic America*, esp. 73–93 on Poe criticism and *Pym*.

2. On Poe's aping and undermining of honor-shame codes, see my "Poe and Gentry Virginia." On gentry fears of "the passions and the interests," see Hirschman, *The Passions and the Interests.*

3. Cavell, "Being Odd, Getting Even," esp. 29–35 on "Imp" and "Black Cat"; also Cavell, "The Avoidance of Love," on King Lear's terror of being loved and therefore known.

4. Elmer, *Reading at the Social Limit,* 93: "the sensational—the moment of shock, or horror, or revulsion—erupts from within the sentimental." I prefer Elmer's alternative formulation of this sentence, that "the sensational . . . vampirizes the sentimental" ("Terminate or Liquidate," 91).

5. Waller makes a similar argument that male writers in early nineteenth-century France, facing a crisis of paternal authority, used fictions of impotence to restore male power; see *The Male Malady,* esp. 1–24, 179–83.

6. Auerbach, *Romance of Failure,* 21.

7. Greenberg, *Honor and Slavery,* 3–23. See also Gorn, "'Gouge and Bite,'" for an analysis of lower-class white rituals of fighting in the antebellum South, particularly the use of thumbs to gouge out eyes and teeth to bite off ears. "'Saving face' was not just a metaphor" (28). Emphasizing honor, male status insecurity, and the unpredictability of violence, Gorn suggests that these sadistic rough-and-tumble fights flamboyantly exalted male toughness while inverting the self-control displayed in gentry dueling practices and distancing poor white men from black submissiveness (41). Perhaps in "Loss of Breath" and other early stories, Poe appropriates this "folklore of exaggeration" (29–30) to blur white hierarchies of high (dueling) and low (body disfigurement).

8. Derrick, *Monumental Anxieties,* 74–75, on "The Purloined Letter"; Kaplan, *Female Perversions,* 512 and passim. Kaplan and Derrick both emphasize gendered and psychological aspects of fetishism and perversion.

9. Hoffman, *Poe Poe Poe Poe Poe Poe Poe,* 84, drawing on Allen's *Poe and the British Magazine Tradition,* 133. Allen emphasizes Poe's elitist British poses, as well as his self-divisions (e.g., 192).

10. On changing norms of discipline, see also Brodhead, "Sparing the Rod."

11. Reynolds notes that the antebellum United States had more newspapers than there are now, and that newspapers were more

competitive, with smaller circulations (*Beneath the American Re-naissance*, 169–70). See also Stevens, *Sensationalism and the New York Press*.

12. Quoted by Reynolds, *Beneath the American Renaissance*, 226, also 225–48 on Poe's complex relation to tabloid sensationalism and popular science.

13. Dayan, *Fables of Mind*, 145, 162; also see Elmer, *Reading at the Social Limit*, 102–8.

14. Jordan, *Second Stories*, 135–39. A student once said in class that he thought the narrator killed Ligeia "with garden tools," though he could not support that intuition. It took me a few days to realize he was probably just laying it on with a trowel.

15. Dayan, "Amorous Bondage," 199–202. My next sentence cribs from the first chapter of Melville's *Moby Dick*.

16. On the possibility that the secret in "The Mystery of Marie Rogêt" is abortion, see Saltz, "Recovering the Body of Marie Rogêt."

17. Irwin, *Mystery to a Solution*, 123, 108. Emphasizing Poe's yearning for a "mastermind" state of Neoplatonic undifferentiation, Irwin explores Poe's uses of Lockean sensations as an interface between "godlike pure spirit (a simple intellectual substance) and the complex bodily mechanism which that substance inhabits and directs but to which it is essentially alien" (114). As Kennedy has argued in *Poe, Death, and the Life of Writing*, Poe's tales of self-destruction spring from the compulsive need to destroy the counterpart who incarnates our human frailty (143–44).

18. Daniel Hoffman suggests this possibility in *Poe Poe Poe*, 128.

19. I am indebted to several students in my spring 1999 graduate class for pointing out the racial and homoerotic possibilities here.

20. Elmer, *Reading at the Social Limit*, 93–125; Dobson, "Reclaiming Sentimental Literature," 268, 273.

WORKS CITED

Allen, Michael. *Poe and the British Magazine Tradition*. New York: Oxford University Press, 1969.

Anthony, David. "The Helen Jewett Panic: Tabloids, Men, and the Sensational Public Sphere in Antebellum New York." *American Literature* 69 (1997): 487–514.

Auerbach, Jonathan. *The Romance of Failure: First-Person Fictions of*

Poe, Hawthorne, and James. New York: Oxford University Press, 1989.

Basch, Norma. "Marriage, Morals, and Politics in the Election of 1828." *Journal of American History* 80 (1993): 890–918.

Benjamin, Jessica. *The Bonds of Love: Psychoanalysis, Feminism, and the Problem of Domination.* New York: Pantheon, 1988.

Brodhead, Richard H. "Sparing the Rod: Discipline and Fiction in Antebellum America." In *Cultures of Letters: Scenes of Reading and Writing in Nineteenth-Century America,* 13–47. Chicago: University of Chicago Press, 1993.

Cavell, Stanley. "The Avoidance of Love: A Reading of *King Lear.*" In *Must We Mean What We Say? A Book of Essays,* 267-353. New York: Scribner, 1969.

———. "Being Odd, Getting Even (Descartes, Emerson, Poe)." In Rosenheim and Rachman, 3–36.

Dayan, Joan. "Amorous Bondage: Poe, Ladies, and Slaves." In Rosenheim and Rachman, 179–209.

———. *Fables of Mind: An Inquiry into Poe's Fiction.* New York: Oxford University Press, 1987.

Derrick, Scott S. *Monumental Anxieties: Homoerotic Desire and Feminine Influence in Nineteenth-Century U.S. Literature.* New Brunswick, N.J.: Rutgers University Press, 1997.

Dobson, Joanne. "Reclaiming Sentimental Literature." *American Literature* 69 (1997): 263–89.

Elmer, Jonathan. *Reading at the Social Limit: Affect, Mass Culture, and Edgar Allan Poe.* Stanford, Calif.: Stanford University Press, 1995.

———. "Terminate or Liquidate? Poe, Sensationalism, and the Sentimental Tradition." In Rosenheim and Rachman, 91–120.

Goddu, Teresa. *Gothic America: Narrative, History, and Nation.* New York: Columbia University Press, 1997.

Gorn, Elliot J. "'Gouge and Bite, Pull Hair and Scratch': The Social Significance of Fighting in the Southern Backcountry." *American Historical Review* 90 (1985): 18–43.

Greenberg, Kenneth S. *Honor and Slavery.* Princeton, N.J.: Princeton University Press, 1996.

Halttunen, Karen. "Humanitarianism and the Pornography of Pain in Anglo-American Culture." *American Historical Review* 100 (1995): 303–34.

————. *Murder Most Foul: The Killer and the American Gothic Imagination.* Cambridge, Mass.: Harvard University Press, 1998.

Hirschman, Albert O. *The Passions and the Interests: Political Arguments for Capitalism before Its Triumph.* Princeton, N.J.: Princeton University Press, 1977.

Hoffman, Daniel. *Poe Poe Poe Poe Poe Poe Poe.* Garden City, N.Y.: Anchor, 1973.

Irwin, John T. *The Mystery to a Solution: Poe, Borges, and the Analytic Detective Story.* Baltimore: Johns Hopkins University Press, 1996.

Jordan, Cynthia S. *Second Stories: The Politics of Language, Form, and Gender in Early American Fictions.* Chapel Hill: University of North Carolina Press, 1989.

Kahane, Claire. "The Gothic Mirror." In *The (M)other Tongue: Essays in Feminist Psychoanalytic Interpretation,* ed. Shirley Nelson Garner, Claire Kahane, and Madelon Sprengnether, 334–51. Ithaca, N.Y.: Cornell University Press, 1985.

Kaplan, Louise J. *Female Perversions: The Temptations of Emma Bovary.* New York: Doubleday, 1991.

Kennedy, J. Gerald. *Poe, Death, and the Life of Writing.* New Haven, Conn.: Yale University Press, 1987.

Leverenz, David. "Poe and Gentry Virginia." In Rosenheim and Rachman, 210–36.

Nelson, Dana D. *National Manhood: Capitalist Citizenship and the Imagined Fraternity of White Men.* Durham, N.C.: Duke University Press, 1998.

Reynolds, David S. *Beneath the American Renaissance: The Subversive Imagination in the Age of Emerson and Melville.* New York: Knopf, 1988.

Rosenheim, Shawn, and Stephen Rachman, eds. *The American Face of Edgar Allan Poe.* Baltimore: Johns Hopkins University Press, 1995.

Saltz, Laura. "'(Horrible to Relate!)': Recovering the Body of Marie Rogêt." In Rosenheim and Rachman, 237–70.

Stevens, John D. *Sensationalism and the New York Press.* New York: Columbia University Press, 1991.

Tocqueville, Alexis de. *Democracy in America.* Vol. 2. Trans. Henry Reeve and Francis Bowen. Ed. Phillips Bradley. 1840. New York: Vintage, 1945.

Waller, Margaret. *The Male Malady: Fictions of Impotence in the French*

Romantic Novel. New Brunswick, N.J.: Rutgers University Press, 1993.

Walsh, John. *Poe the Detective.* New Brunswick, N.J.: Rutgers University Press, 1968.

Whalen, Terence. "The Code for Gold: Edgar Allan Poe and Cryptography." *Representations* 46 (1994): 35–58.

———. "Edgar Allan Poe and the Horrid Laws of Political Economy." *American Quarterly* 44 (1992): 381–417.

Poe and Nineteenth-Century Gender Constructions

Leland S. Person

Recent biographical assessments of Poe seem to be reaching a consensus, in J. Gerald Kennedy's words, on the "compulsions—intellectual and imaginative—that shaped his work" ("Violence," 534). Because these compulsions and the object relations they entail divide along gender lines, they represent a useful paradigm for beginning an overview of Poe and nineteenth-century gender constructions. Like Kennedy, Kenneth Silverman emphasizes the importance of Eliza Poe's death (as well as the deaths of Fanny Allan and Jane Stanard) on the youthful Poe, especially the way his mother's death causes a life-long fixation on women's deaths and returns from the grave. Silverman accounts for the "peculiar cluster of dead-alive persons" in the poetry and fiction by appealing to modern theories of childhood bereavement. Adults "learn to live with the death of someone they have loved by gradually and painfully withdrawing their deep investment of feeling in the person. But children who lose a parent at an early age, as Edgar lost Eliza Poe, instead invest more feeling in and magnify the parent's image" (76). The grieving child, in other words, invests desire in the parent's return from the dead.

On the male side, Poe's contentious relationship with John Allan, who took him in after his parents' deaths without ever legally adopting him or giving him his name, significantly influenced Poe's conception of male identity. The young Poe seemed determined to fulfill an ideal of genteel patriarchy and to define himself as a Southern gentleman—initially, by trading on the reputation of his paternal grandfather, General David Poe, and by portraying himself as the son of the genteel John Allan and then, after Allan's death, by establishing an alternative model of gentility through the medium of his writing. As he would tell John Pendleton Kennedy in an 1834 letter, early in his life he had "looked forward to the inheritance of a large fortune." Now, with John Allan dead and himself disinherited, Poe says, "I am thrown entirely upon my own resources with no profession, and very few friends. Worse than this, I am at length penniless" (*L*, 54). If his mother's early death forever fixated Poe's attention on idealized women who die and then return from the grave, Poe's relationship with Allan, in which he continually sought Allan's approval and money, cast him squarely between genteel and self-made models of manhood.

According to Michael Kimmel, definitions of nineteenth-century manhood existed in a state of tension, largely coincident with the separate spheres. "Women were not only domestic," Kimmel argues, "they were domesticators, expected to turn their sons into virtuous Christian gentlemen—dutiful, well-mannered, and feminized." At the same time, part of the definition of American manhood became "the repudiation of the feminine, a resistance to mothers' and wives' efforts to civilize men" (*Manhood in America*, 60). Men were expected to make themselves by competing with other men in the marketplace but to throw off that self-made mantle when they entered the domestic sphere. Anne Lynch, who hosted New York's premier literary salon during the mid-1840s, found Poe an "ideal guest for the polite atmosphere of her salon" (Silverman, 279). He "'had always the bearing and manners of a gentleman,' she wrote later, 'interesting in conversation, but not monopolising; polite and engaging. . . . quiet and unaffected, unpretentious, in his manner'" (Silverman, 279). Caught between domestic expectations of gentility that he would associate with a dying Angel in the House and market expectations that emphasized self- and money-making, Poe wrote sharp gender differences into his letters and his fictions. As Kennedy puts it, Poe's circumstances entailed a "rigidly gendered mode of behavior acted out in the author's personal life and staged repeatedly in his poetry and fiction, in which Poe/the male protagonist/the I-narrator either falls into abjectly dependent relationships with dead or dying women (who become objects of uncontrollable fascination) or engages in hostile encounters with men (who evoke mistrust, deceit, or violence)" ("Violence," 539).

Scholars have recently begun to question the notion of "separate spheres" as an interpretive strategy for understanding nineteenth-century American life. In Cathy Davidson's words, "[I]t is simply too crude an instrument—too rigid and totalizing—for understanding the different, complicated ways that nineteenth-century American society or literary production functioned" (445). Poe's writing is remarkably resistant to categories of all sorts; he seemed to have an instinctive grasp of deconstruction before there was such a term. In examining Poe's "gendered mode of behavior" in both his life and his writing, therefore, I want to be careful not to reinforce its rigid outlines but to interrogate the gender identifications he represents. "Alas, my whole existence has been the merest Romance," he would tell Jane Locke a year before his death, "in the sense of the most utter unworldliness" (L, 267), but here I want to examine the "worldliness" of Poe's existence—biographical and fictional—by analyzing his representation of gender in its nineteenth-century context. "I mean to say," Poe commented, in critiquing Margaret Fuller's *Woman in the Nineteenth Century* (1845), "that the intention of the Deity as regards sexual differences—an intention which can be distinctly comprehended only by throwing the exterior (more sensitive) portions of the mental retina *casually* over the wide field of universal *analogy*—I mean to say that this *intention* has not been sufficiently considered." Poe's verbal stuttering and especially his appeal to a notion of "super-naturalized" differences warranted by a divine intentional fallacy suggest his discomfort with the way Fuller unsettles conventional gender boundaries. Indeed, he goes on to criticize Fuller for generalizing about women and their capabilities from her own individual example. "She judges *woman*," he concludes, "by the heart and intellect of Miss Fuller, but there are not more than one or two dozen Miss Fullers on the whole face of the earth" (*ER*, 1173). Making Margaret Fuller an anomaly leaves conventional models of womanhood intact; appealing to the "Deity" as the source of "sexual differences" makes gender and gender differences natural rather than social constructs.

Poe's Portraits of Women

Poe had many personal and professional relationships with women. He encouraged, promoted, or reviewed many women writers. His poetic "affair" with Frances ("Fanny") Osgood in the pages of the *Broadway Journal* in 1845 captivated New York literati (see DeJong). He reviewed works by Anna Lewis, Lydia Sigourney, and Elizabeth Oakes Smith. In 1846, under the title "The Literati of New York City," he published essays on many contemporary writers, including a dozen women, for *Godey's Lady's Book* (*ER*, 1118–222). He wrote review essays on Anna Cora Mowatt, Ann S. Stephens, Mary Gove, Margaret Fuller, Caroline Kirkland, Emma C. Embury, Francis Osgood, Lydia Maria Child, Elizabeth Bogart, Catharine Maria Sedgwick, Anne C. Lynch, and Mary E. Hewitt—a veritable Who's Who of women writers whom twentieth-century scholars have rediscovered and republished during the past twenty years. In his relations with literary women in particular, Poe aspired to be what Susan Coultrap-McQuin calls a "Gentleman Publisher." Although she does not mention Poe, whose difficulties in keeping editorial positions, much less becoming an entrepreneur-publisher, would hardly qualify him as a gentleman publisher, Poe did exhibit many of the same characteristics in his professional relationships with women. According to Coultrap-McQuin, gentlemen publishers shared three aims: "[T]hey sought to develop trusting, paternalistic, personal relationships with their authors; they claimed to have goals beyond commercial ones to advance culture and/or provide a public service; and they assumed the role of moral guardian for their society" (34). Poe's promotion of women writers, his fervent desire to found a new literary magazine that would appeal to elevated tastes, and particularly the moralistic tone of his literary criticism bear many similarities to the gentleman publisher type Coultrap-McQuin describes. Poe's construction of a male persona, about which I shall have more to say in the second part of this chapter, depended upon his gentlemanly treatment of women, but it also depended upon exercising verbal control over women as literary constructs.

Poe could be brutal as a critic, and his assessments of women writers anticipate both the negative (arguably patriarchal) criticisms that relegated them to the margins of literary history during the first half of the twentieth century and the positive, gynocentric criticisms that have recently led to their resurrection. He detects "not a particle of originality" in Anna Mowatt's fiction, for example (*ER*, 1138), but he praises Mary Gove's "truly imaginative" subjects and her "luminous" and "precise" style, although qualifying that praise by noting its rarity "with her sex" (*ER*, 1163). His evaluation of Ann Stephens seems balanced, as he praises her "quick appreciation of the picturesque" while criticizing her "turgid" style (*ER*, 1160). He praises Caroline Kirkland extravagantly for her lucid, terse, "faultlessly pure," and bold style (*ER*, 1183). He lauds her frontier narrative, *A New Home, Who'll Follow?* (1839), for its depiction of women's spaces, using terms very similar to those employed by recent feminist critics such as Annette Kolodny. To Mrs. Kirkland "alone," he enthuses, we are "indebted for our acquaintance with the *home* and home-life of the backwoodsman" (*ER*, 1181).

Poe knew and respected women writers, and his many personal and professional relationships with women certainly provided him with models on which he could have based complex female characters. It is difficult to think of another body of fiction by a nineteenth-century male writer, on the other hand, that contains so many otherworldly women characters. For Poe "separate spheres" more often meant this and some other world than domestic and workaday worlds. Poe's women especially seem exempt from the material conditions of the cultural moment in which they are embedded. Measuring Poe's female characters against the standard of True Womanhood, for example, reveals as many differences from the ideal as similarities to it. A "hostage in the home," the True Woman features four "cardinal virtues"—piety, purity, submissiveness, and domesticity (Welter, 21). Poe's female characters (Morella, Berenice, Ligeia, Eleonora, the wives in "The Black Cat" and "The Oval Portrait") do seem confined to the domestic sphere, but Poe's tales about women parody the intended effects of separate sphere ideology. While some of these female characters are little more than passive victims—"invalid" women, in the double sense in which Diane Herndl uses the term—others more nearly resemble the "New Woman" that Frances Cogan has posited as a legitimate alternative to True Womanhood.[1]

Nancy F. Cott points out that the "values of domesticity" underwrote the separate sphere of "comfort and compensation, instilling a morality that would encourage self-control, and fostering the idea that preservation of home and family sentiment was an ultimate goal" (69). Poe's domestic tales, on the other hand, depict the home as the nightmarish site of barely repressed hostility between men and women. As a "most wild, yet most homely narrative" (*PT,* 597), "The Black Cat," for example, features a childless couple and an intemperate narrator whose drinking leads him to beat and finally kill his wife, as well as mutilate the black cat itself. "Authors of domestic literature, especially the female authors," Cott points out, "denigrated business and politics as arenas of selfishness, exertion, embarrassment, and degradation of soul" (67), but this narrator's metamorphosis not only occurs within the domestic sphere but also seems a product of that sphere and its claustrophobic limitations. His wife, moreover, seems utterly powerless to prevent his "degradation of soul." "The moodiness of my usual temper increased to hatred of all things and of all mankind," the narrator confesses; "while, from the sudden, frequent, and ungovernable outbursts of a fury to which I now blindly abandoned myself, my uncomplaining wife, alas! was the most usual and the most patient of sufferers" (*PT,* 603). As if mocking the reforming power of piety and other domestic values, Poe transforms this particular domestic "angel" into an uncomplaining victim and then, finally, into a corpse. The Angel in the House becomes the Dead Wife in the Basement.

"Ligeia" also might be read as a parody of domestic values and the positive influences of separate spheres. Cynthia Jordan has argued that the closed room in "Ligeia" is the narrator's mind, but she also notes the struggle between Ligeia and the narrator for authority over that separate sphere (136). Positing Ligeia as an alternative source of authority within a confined domestic space seems to fulfill the Angel in the House requirements of True Womanhood, as well as reinforce the idea that a woman's separate sphere is circumscribed by male ideology, but the qualities that constitute Ligeia's authority and power subvert more than they reinforce domestic values. Jordan notes, for example, that Ligeia "usurps the traditional male prerogative" in the story (137). Whereas True Women "were warned not to let their literary or intellectual pursuits take them away from God" (Welter, 23), Ligeia possesses "immense" learning and guides the narrator, whom she reduces to "child-like" dependence, "through the chaotic world of metaphysical investigation" (*PT,* 266). Poe did not know Margaret Fuller when he published "Ligeia" in 1838, but it is tempting to add Ligeia's name to the short list of exceptional women Poe associated with Fuller. Like the powerful Fuller, Ligeia reverses the conventional power imbalance between husband and wife. Whereas a True Woman was supposed to be submissive and "completely dependent" upon her husband—"an empty vessel, without legal or emotional existence of her own" (Welter, 24)—Ligeia remands the narrator to a feminine place within the domestic sphere. He will be home-schooled by a mother-wife. In her erudition and intellectual power Ligeia has her origins in the "Ideal of Real Womanhood" that Cogan has gleaned from nineteenth-century sources:

> Whatever genre they used—short story, domestic novel, advice book, magazine article, or editorial—writers supporting the Ideal of Real Womanhood all seem to demand that young women have a rounded, fully developed liberal education with which to realize their feminine obligations. To a great extent, the stress on academic knowledge stretched the normal dimensions of the traditional woman's sphere considerably beyond anything the name now implies. (Cogan, 74)

Biographically considered, representing an erudite woman and emphasizing her power to reduce the narrator to a state of "child-like" dependence would have fulfilled the needs of the identity theme that Silverman, Kennedy, and others have marked out for Poe himself.

By 1838, when he published "Ligeia," Poe had long since established himself and his child bride, Virginia, in a household presided over by her mother, Maria Clemm—a caricature in many respects of the ideal nineteenth-century household supported by a male breadwinner. When Poe learned in 1835 that Maria Clemm and Virginia were considering an offer from Neilson Poe to live with him and his family, he wrote a wildly impassioned and pathetic letter to Mrs. Clemm, professing his love for Virginia, begging her to reconsider the move, and claiming (as he often did) that her refusal would drive him to the grave. Poe also noted that he "had procured a sweet little house in a retired situation" for the three of them and had been "dreaming every day & night since of the rapture I should feel in having my only friends—all I love on Earth with me there" (*L*, 70). The scenario anticipates the "retired situations" in which the narrator of "Ligeia" places himself and his two wives; and although neither Virginia nor Maria Clemm bears any resemblance to Ligeia herself, certainly the deaths of both Ligeia and Rowena (as well as Morella and Berenice) uncannily anticipate Virginia's agonizing death in 1847.

Unlike the angelic Virginia, Ligeia resists a conventional female role even in her death. "The death of a beautiful woman, cherished in fiction, represented woman as the innocent victim, suffering without sin, too pure and good for this world but too weak and passive to resist its evil forces," Welter comments (31). But Ligeia is notable for her force of will and, arguably, her ability to overcome death and the narrator's murderous designs. She wills herself back to life—significantly, by displacing the much more conventional Rowena, whose utter passivity fulfills a common nineteenth-century stereotype of "invalid" womanhood. Herndl argues that "Ligeia" "sets out the difficulties of understanding what man's relation to the 'new woman' could be and uses the conventions of gothic horror to explore the woman's new power" (91). Ligeia's resurrection may not represent the triumph of feminist self-sufficiency, but her real womanhood, at least in the area of her superior knowledge, underwrites a misandrous power of will that turns the tables on male misogyny.

Although Poe obviously attracted women and enjoyed their company, he clearly understood misogyny and the male psychology in which it was rooted. "Thou wretch!—thou vixen!—thou shrew!" the narrator of "Loss of Breath" (1832) exclaims to his wife on the morning after their wedding, and he continues this misogynistic tirade in such extravagant terms that he literally runs out of breath: "thou witch!—thou hag!—thou whippersnapper!—thou sink of iniquity!—thou fiery-faced quintessence of all that is abominable!" (*PT*, 151). He stops the assault, which even includes seizing her by the throat, only when he loses the ability to speak. Poe's claim in "The Philosophy of Composition" (1846) that the death of a beautiful woman is "the most poetical topic in the world" seems to follow logically from the vituperations voiced by this earlier male character. Women, if the tissue of body parts that composes so many of his female characters can be called "women," almost always die in Poe's tales. Their deaths, furthermore, rarely mean anything in and of themselves. They become meaningful only as they are interpolated into male experience. Poe seldom grants female characters subjectivity or a voice, while he repeatedly emphasizes his male characters' verbal control over them. In "How to Write a Blackwood Article" (1838), in fact, Poe even employs a female narrator to describe her own dismemberment. In the embedded tale ("A Predicament") Psyche Zenobia describes losing her eyes (one at a time) and finally her head. She ends up divided from herself in grotesquely comic, but culturally appropriate terms. "My senses were here and there at one and the same moment," she observes. "With my head I imagined, at one time, that I the head, was the real Signora Psyche Zenobia—at another I felt convinced that myself, the body, was the proper identity" (*PT*, 295). At a time when women were being divided from their bodies by authors of advice books and the medical establishment, Poe parodies that microcosmic separation of spheres in the process of satirizing the sensational tastes of popular magazines.

Although Cynthia Jordan and I have both attempted to recover a woman's story from many of Poe's tales, Poe's representation of female characters reveals much more about nineteenth-century male psychology and a patriarchal ideology that objectifies women as objects of beauty and pleasure than it does about women's subjective experience. Nathaniel Hawthorne's story "The Birthmark," according to Judith Fetterley in *The Resisting Reader*, "provides a brilliant analysis of the sexual politics of idealization and a brilliant exposure of the mechanisms whereby hatred can be disguised as love, neurosis can be disguised as science, murder can be disguised as idealization, and success can be disguised as failure" (22–23). Poe's tales about women reveal a very similar sexual politics at work—a sexual politics that may be mapped upon the nineteenth-century separate spheres model of gender differences. The death of a beautiful woman, Poe seemed to recognize, is not only the most poetical topic in the world; it is a logical outcome of woman's separation and idealization. The Truest Woman, in effect, is a dead woman—an object, not a subject.

The Marchesa Aphrodite in "The Assignation" (1834), for example, is indistinguishable from her portrait, which represents the "same ethereal figure" whom the narrator has seen in the flesh. Her key features are one "small, fairy foot" that "barely touched the earth" and a "pair of the most delicately imagined wings" that "encircle and enshrine her loveliness" (*PT*, 210). Aphrodite has no subjective life of her own. She does not represent herself. She is an angel, or fairy, in a sphere of her own. In the other tales that feature women, Poe's narrators commonly act like verbal Pygmalions, creating female characters by anatomizing and idealizing parts of their bodies.

The most bizarre example, in "Berenice" (1835), turns on the narrator's fixation on his fiancée's teeth, which he fetishizes to the point that they eclipse the rest of her identity. Egaeus admits that, despite Berenice's "unparalleled beauty," he never loved her. His feelings "*had never been* of the heart"; his "passions *always were* of the mind." "I had seen her—not as the living and breathing Berenice, but as the Berenice of a dream—not as a being of the earth, earthy, but as the abstraction of such a being—not as a thing to admire, but to analyze—not as an object of love, but as the theme of the most abstruse although desultory speculation" (*PT,* 229). As verbal constructs, Poe's female characters typically decompose; their diseases reflect their creators' dis-ease with their embodied beings. Berenice's body becomes excessively emaciated; "not one vestige of the former being, lurked in any single line of the contour." "The eyes were lifeless," and the narrator shrinks from their "glassy stare to the contemplation of the thin and shrunken lips," which part, and in a "smile of peculiar meaning, *the teeth* of the changed Berenice disclosed themselves slowly to my view" (*PT,* 230). Several critics have noted the suggestive language of this description and concluded that the narrator particularly fears Berenice's sexuality, which he represents as a *vagina dentata* (e.g., Porte, 83). In fact, the narrator spontaneously develops a love-hate, attraction-repulsion relationship with Berenice's teeth, which become the "essence" of his "mental life" (*PT,* 231). The psycho-logical result of intellectualizing and abstracting Berenice is the narrator's surgical removal of her teeth after she has been buried prematurely. The implications for the nineteenth-century reader, as in Hawthorne's "The Birthmark," involve a surgical intervention into a woman's sexual being—analogous in its violation to a clitoridectomy or oophorectomy (female castration), surgical practices introduced into American medicine in the late 1850s and 1860s (Barker-Benfield, 120–21). For this very reason Sandra Gilbert and Susan Gubar consider Poe's premature burial theme paradigmatic of nineteenth-century women's "plight" within a patriarchal culture: her identity rendered coincident with her womb, her "cave-shaped anatomy is her destiny" (94). Michael Kimmel notes that the doctrine of separate spheres was a male creation, first promoted by male writers of advice books to serve men's needs (*Manhood in America,* 52), and Egaeus's equation of Berenice's teeth with ideas (*PT,* 231) reflects the psychological underpinnings of this separation. Disembodied and transformed into ideas in men's minds, women are separated from themselves in the process of being separated from the world of men's work.

Although the narrator of "Morella" (1835) evokes John Locke's theory of personal identity ("the *principium individuationis*—the notion of that identity *which at death is or is not lost forever*, was to me—at all times, a consideration of intense interest" [*PT*, 235]) he pays little narrative attention to Morella's identity. More a collection of attributes subsumed by a name, Morella does speak more words than most of Poe's female characters—albeit ventriloquistically, with a male-identified voice that announces her approaching death to the narrator, who has already acknowledged that he "longed with an earnest and consuming desire for the moment of Morella's decease" (*PT*, 236). Although the narrator notes that Morella's "erudition was profound" and "her powers of mind were gigantic" (*PT*, 234), he soon grows unable to "bear the touch of her wan fingers, nor the low tone of her musical language, nor the lustre of her melancholy eyes" (*PT*, 235). Morella's strength of character, her individuality and learning, seems to inspire the narrator's hatred. In Joan Dayan's words, "Morella's deathbed scene becomes a struggle for domination through utterance" (*Fables*, 160)—literally, a power struggle over the right to name a woman. Morella gives birth to a daughter on her deathbed, and the narrator repeats the same attraction-repulsion with the unnamed child. With faint undertones of incestuous desire—he gazes, "day after day," upon the child's "holy, and mild, and eloquent face, and pored over her maturing form" (*PT*, 237)—he waits until his daughter's belated baptismal day to give her the name, "Morella," whereupon she abruptly dies. While it might be tempting to consider this matrilineal action a feminist triumph—a denial of patriarchal authority—Poe represents the narrator's nominal authority quite differently. "I snatched from the scrutiny of the world a being whom destiny compelled me to adore," the narrator confesses, "and in the rigorous seclusion of my home, watched with an agonizing anxiety over all which concerned the beloved" (*PT*, 237). Inverting the ideal of separate spheres and gender roles, in which mothers assumed responsibility for their children's education within the home, Poe represents a father who experiences "terrible" and "tumultuous thoughts" as he watches the development of his daughter's "mental being" (*PT*, 237). And instead of encouraging his daughter's independent identity, the narrator kills her (kills her individuality) by forging a "too perfect *identity*" between mother and child. He has only room enough in his consciousness for one idea of woman. All women look and are alike.

Tales such as "Berenice" and "Morella" argue strongly for Poe's subjection of women to the objectifying, even murderous, powers of the male gaze. "The Oval Portrait" (1842) epitomizes such objectifying tendencies, as the tale reverses the story of Pygmalion and Galatea. Instead of bringing an aesthetic replica of a woman to life, the husband-painter in Poe's tale kills a woman into art by transferring his wife's vital energy into a painting. Literalizing the metaphor that the painter had a "bride in his Art," Poe describes him as "grown wild with the ardor of his work." "And he *would* not see that the tints which he spread upon the canvas were drawn from the cheeks of her who sate beside him" (*PT,* 483). At the very moment that the painter triumphantly succeeds in creating "*Life* itself," he confronts the fact that his wife is dead (*PT,* 484). Except as an object, the woman in "The Oval Portrait" has no life. She does not speak, for example, so that the tale might actually be considered a parody of male objectifying tendencies—Poe's representation of the dire consequences of male gazing.

Poe could parody story ideas he also took seriously, as G. R. Thompson points out in his study of Poe's romantic irony, and he clearly parodies the objectifying power of the male gaze in "The Spectacles" (1844). In the process he parodies the very obsessive-compulsive behavior he would exhibit in his relationships with Helen Whitman and Annie Richmond toward the end of his life. So vain that he refuses to wears glasses to correct his serious myopia, Poe's narrator falls in love at first sight with Eugenie Lalande when he sees her one evening at the opera. For one reason or another in this rather silly tale, the narrator never gets a good look at Madame Lalande, who turns out to be his eighty-two-year-old great-great-grandmother. It is only after their wedding (which is actually a practical joke arranged by his friend Talbot), when the narrator has fulfilled his promise to wear glasses, that he discovers the truth about his bride—the truth about the physical reality and mortality of a woman's body. Poe makes myopia a function of male vanity and egotism in this tale. The narrator refuses to wear glasses because he is "youthful and good-looking," in his own words, and because glasses have a "savor of downright foppery and affectation" (*PT,* 619). He falls instantly in love with Madame Lalande, furthermore, and his rapture mocks the obsessive idealizations of other male narrators who identify female beauty with the feelings in themselves that it produces. "I can never forget the intense emotion with which I regarded this figure," the narrator recalls. "It was that of a female, the most exquisite I had ever beheld." He goes on comically to anatomize the woman he can barely see—her Greek head, her thrilling left arm, particularly its "upper portion," and the "admirable roundness of the wrist" (*PT,* 620). "I saw—I felt— I knew that I was deeply, madly, irrevocably in love," he exclaims, "and this even before seeing the face of the person beloved" (*PT,* 621). Poe's narrator is more in love with the idea of love than he is with Madame Lalande or her daughter Stephanie, whom he eventually marries. "Infirm, homely, old, woman is horrifying," Simone de Beauvoir observed. "It is upon woman's body . . . that man really encounters the deterioration of the flesh" (180–81). As Eugenie Lalande deteriorates before his "corrected" vision, the narrator discovers a "villainous old hag" without hair and teeth (*PT,* 638). In its comical fashion the tale expresses a male fear of carnality—the flip side of the idealizations Poe represents in his better-known tales about women characters.

Poe called "Ligeia" (1838) his best tale (*L,* 309, 329), and his relationships with women late in his life suggest that "Ligeia" served him imaginatively and emotionally as a master narrative. As we have already seen, Poe and his narrators typically anatomize women, inventorying their bodies, often reducing them to a single, fetishized body part or a single word. In his essay on Margaret Fuller Poe would claim that the "supposition that the book of an author is a thing apart from the author's self is, I think, ill-founded. The soul is a cypher, in the sense of a cryptograph; and the shorter a cryptograph is, the more difficulty there is in its comprehension" (*ER,* 1178). He went on to claim that Fuller's "personal character and her book [*Woman in the Nineteenth Century*] are merely one and the same thing. We get access to her soul *as* directly from the one as from the other" (*ER,* 1179). Equating the soul with the book—the woman with her words—

Poe laid the foundation for male control over both. He prided himself on being able to solve puzzles and on several occasions invited readers of the literary magazines he was editing to try to stump him with cryptograms (see Silverman, 152–53). He would tell Helen Whitman that, in the presence of her letter to him, he had lost the "power of words," but his fictional narrators and the narrating voice we can hear in his letters suggest the important coincidence of power over words and verbal power over women. A Pygmalion with words, as I have elsewhere termed the narrator of "Ligeia" (*Aesthetic Headaches,* 30), Poe enjoyed what might be called a cryptographic relationship with women. He sent women acrostic poems (e.g., the "Valentine" [*P,* 388–89] he sent to Fanny Osgood in 1846), and he even changed women's names. He renamed Nancy Richmond "Annie" and even convinced her to call herself "Annie" (Silverman, 370). He told Helen Whitman that he wrote the first "To Helen" (1831) in honor of *Jane* Stanard, the deceased mother of a childhood friend, and he sent that poem to Whitman late in his life, claiming that those lines expressed *"all* that I would have said to you—so fully—so accurately and so exclusively, that a thrill of intense superstition ran at once throughout my frame." "To accomplish, *as* I wished it, precisely *what* I wished, seemed impossible," he wrote Whitman, "and I was on the point of abandoning the idea, when my eyes fell upon a volume of my own poems; and then the lines I had written, in my passionate boyhood, to the first, purely ideal love of my soul—to the Helen Stannard [*sic*] of whom I told you— flashed upon my recollection" (*L,* 385). Through the medium of the single word "Helen" (which he had invented for *Jane* Stanard), Poe confused two women, subsuming them under a single name and interpolating them into a poem. He had done much the same thing in "Ligeia," and when he sent Helen Whitman a new poem entitled "To Helen," he explicitly made a link to that tale. In *Edgar Poe and His Critics* (1860), Whitman indicated that Poe included a marginal note with the poem, comparing the "mental condition which gave rise to 'Ligeia'" with the origin of his poem to her (*P,* 444).

Ligeia herself, as Kennedy has noted, had her origins in Poe's early poem "Al Aaraaf," which includes the lines, "Ligeia! Ligeia! /

My beautiful one!" (*Poe*, 82). Disengaging Ligeia from her familial and cultural origins and making her a pure product of imagination, the narrator remembers almost nothing about her that would situate her in the world of history and culture. He recalls nothing about her family or when he first met her; he does not even remember her last name (*PT*, 262). Ligeia, then, represents a clear field, or blank page, on which the narrator can stage his verbal construction of a woman. It is "by that sweet word alone—by Ligeia—that I bring before mine eyes in fancy the image of her who is no more," says the narrator of "Ligeia" (*PT*, 262). He goes on to inventory in meticulous detail her attractive "features": "the skin rivalling the purest ivory," "the raven-black, the glossy, the luxuriant and naturally-curling tresses," "the delicate outlines of the nose," "the magnificent turn of the short upper lip—the soft, voluptuous slumber of the under," "the teeth glancing back, with a brilliancy almost startling," and of course the eyes, "those large, those shining, those divine orbs" (*PT*, 264–65). In his later sketches of "The Literati of New York City," Poe always included a thumbnail sketch of the writer, male or female, and he often provided a trait-by-trait anatomy of which this lengthy inventory of Ligeia's features is an exaggeration. He noted Anna Mowatt's face, forehead, hair, eyes, nose, chin, mouth, teeth, and lips, for example (*ER*, 1140).[2] Joan Dayan has convincingly examined connections between this process of anatomization and nineteenth-century obsessions with racial traits and identities: "Poe signals the same physiognomic traits as did taxonomists of color in the Caribbean and the South: hair, eyes, and skin" ("Amorous Bondage," 200). She carefully notes how Ligeia's features suggest ambiguous racial identity. One of the reasons for the ambiguity is Ligeia's silencing. She is an object of the narrator's fixation but only once, despite her reputedly "immense" learning (*PT*, 266), a speaking subject. Even though the narrator emphasizes his fascination with the "expression" of her eyes, he seems far more interested, narcissistically, in the feelings and thoughts they cause in him than he does in anything they might truly express about her. In a lengthy paragraph he describes a "circle of analogies"—a list of the many other "existences in the material world" that have produced the same feeling as Ligeia's eyes. The list, which includes a "rapidly-growing vine," "one or two stars in heaven," passages from books, a moth, and the "glances of unusually aged people," seems a parody of romantic discourse—a Hallmark card list of verse ideas. This "circle of analogies," moreover, does not express Ligeia's subjectivity; the expression of her eyes instead is made equivalent to the feelings and meaning evoked in the narrator. Ligeia becomes a kind of hypertext—with each body part (and especially her eyes) linked to some classical or mythological site (e.g., the "Homeric epithet, 'hyacinthine,'" "the graceful medallions of the Hebrews," the "fabulous Houri of the Turk" [*PT*, 263, 264]).

When Ligeia dies and the narrator marries the fair-haired and blue-eyed Rowena, whom he unaccountably loathes "with a hatred belonging more to demon than to man" (*PT*, 272), Ligeia's restoration, or transubstantiation, entails a relatively simple process—a reconstruction project involving the body parts the narrator has already inventoried. Hating Rowena, he notes immediately that his memory "flew back" to Ligeia, and he revels in "recollections of her purity" (*PT*, 272). I have argued elsewhere that in coming back to life Ligeia resists "objectification, death, and denial" by the narrator and thus demonstrates the failure of this particular male effort to control the "dehumanizing imaginative process" by which a woman is reduced to the status of a harmless object (*Aesthetic Headaches*, 32, 33). Ligeia's resurrection also explodes the Angel in the House ideology. Kennedy notes that the scene of Ligeia's resurrection "exposes a cultural and historical anxiety: divested of sentimental illusion, the dead body has become a potentially revolting sight" (*Poe*, 85). The scene might also be read from a woman's point of view for its depiction of the domestic Angel's revenge. Virtually imprisoning the Lady Rowena in the bridal chamber within his isolated abbey, the narrator ends up as a madman in the attic—the captive not only of his own imagination but also of the two women in his life, who effectively conspire or cooperate with one another to produce a "hideous drama of revivification" (*PT*, 276) and to reconstruct themselves in the form of a single, terrifying female body with the power to paralyze and chill him into stone (*PT*, 277).

This catastrophic return-from-the-dead of Poe's female characters (Morella, Berenice, Madeline Usher, as well as Ligeia) might be compared to the liberation of the figure behind the wallpaper in Charlotte Perkins Gilman's later work "The Yellow Wallpaper" (1892). The situation of female imprisonment Gilman describes resembles the situations in many of Poe's tales about women—tales that similarly exaggerate the "Angel in the House" paradigm of female confinement. Much as the narrator of Gilman's story cooperates with the woman behind the wallpaper to tear down the barriers that patriarchy erects between women and female empowerment—whether conceived psychologically or politically—Ligeia and Rowena cooperate to confuse the categories (Dark and Light) into which Poe's male imagination consigns women. Their strategy—to produce a unified and powerful female body through transubstantiation— resembles the transubstantiation that occurs when the woman behind the wallpaper switches places with the narrator, "Jane." In both cases, a more powerful female figure replaces a weaker one, rendering the male observer (Poe's narrator, Gilman's John) either paralyzed with fear or unconscious.

The paradigm of anatomization and the rhythm of death and resurrection originated deep within Poe's psyche, it seems to me, because he repeats these patterns almost obsessively in other stories and also in the relationships he had with women toward the end of his life. In describing Virginia's death to George Eveleth in an 1848 letter that demonstrates, in Kennedy's words, a "bizarre intermingling of life and writing" (*Poe*, 104), Poe adapts his narrative to the pattern he had used at the end of "Ligeia":

> Six years ago, a wife, whom I loved as no man ever loved before, ruptured a blood-vessel in singing. Her life was despaired of. I took leave of her forever & underwent all the agonies of her death. She recovered partially and I again hoped. At the end of a year the vessel broke again—I went through precisely the same scene. Again in about a year afterward. Then again—again—again & even once again at varying intervals. Each time I felt all the agonies of her death—and at each accession of the disorder I loved her more dearly & clung to her

life with more desperate pertinacity. But I am constitutionally
sensitive—nervous in a very unusual degree. I became insane,
with long intervals of horrible sanity. (*L*, 356)

Although Poe goes on to claim that "it was the horrible never-
ending oscillation between hope & despair" that he "could *not*
longer have endured without the total loss of reason" (*L*, 356), his
fiction and letters both suggest that Poe and his male narrators
tease out a sado-masochistic pleasure, what Kennedy calls a
"metafiction of personal suffering" (*Poe*, 105), for themselves by
identifying imaginatively with the rhythm of a woman's "oscillation" between life and death. Poe employs a similar strategy in a
pleading letter to Marie Louise Shew in 1848. Are "you to vanish
like all I love, or desire, from my darkened and 'lost Soul'?" he
asks (*L*, 372). As in "Ligeia" or the other revenant tales, Poe
resurrects Louise Shew, or at least her influence. "Is it possible
your influence is lost to me?" he asks rhetorically. "Such tender
and true natures are ever loyal until death, but you are not dead,
you are full of life and beauty!" He goes on, in fact, to craft
a bizarre narrative in which Louise Shew enters the house in
a "floating white robe" to say, "Good morning Edgar" (*L*, 73).
This fantasy makes a woman's appearance much more benign
than Ligeia's or Madeline Usher's horrifying entries at the end of
those tales, but the pattern of loss or death and then resurrection
is still present.

The most striking example of adaptation occurs in Poe's letters to Sarah Helen Whitman, the Providence, Rhode Island,
poet to whom he was briefly engaged in 1848. About the length
of one of his shorter tales, Poe's letter of October 1, 1848, for example, includes many story elements from "Ligeia," including
the emphasis on the verbal nature of love relationships, the inventory of idealized body parts, and the fascination with mortality, death, and resurrection. In falling in love with Helen Whitman, Poe fell in love with a verbal construct. "It is by that sweet
word alone—by Ligeia—that I bring before mine eyes in fancy
the image of her who is no more," Poe's narrator had begun his
story (*PT*, 262). "Some few casual words" spoken by Anne C.
Lynch caused him to fall in love, Poe told Whitman. "Since that

period I have never seen nor heard your name without a shiver half of delight, half of anxiety" (*L*, 384). Poe's narrator takes inventory of Ligeia's features. In describing how Helen Whitman's "personal presence" makes her "*Helen—my* Helen—the Helen of a thousand dreams—she whose visionary lips had so often lingered upon my own in the divine trance of passion," Poe notes that he grows faint with the "luxury" of Helen Whitman's voice and blind with the "voluptuous lustre" of her eyes (*L*, 387). Responding to Whitman's concern about being several years older than he (an ironic echo of Madame Lalande's concern in "The Spectacles"), Poe assures her that, even if she were everything that her "enfeebled and perverted" fancy supposed, he would still love her. Indeed, he says, "if illness and sorrow have made you seem older than you are—is not this the best reason for my loving you the more? (*L*, 388). Like Ligeia and the other "beautiful women" who die in Poe's fiction, Helen Whitman takes on the properties of a fictional character, and her body registers both the attractions and the anxieties of physical deterioration, old age, and mortality.

Despite intense, even desperate relationships with Whitman, Annie Richmond, and Elmira Royster Shelton after Virginia's death in January 1847, Poe did not succeed in remarrying—in finding a Rowena to replace the Ligeia who had died. This is not surprising, for Poe did not write happy endings to his stories of male-female relationships, except in the anomalous case of "Eleonora" (1841). In that tale the narrator falls in love with his younger cousin, dwelling idyllically with her for fifteen years in an Edenic Valley of the Many-Colored Grass before she takes ill and dies. Although she extracts from the narrator a vow that he will never transfer his love to "some maiden of the outer and every-day world" (*PT*, 471), he does finally leave the Valley and eventually becomes "bewildered and intoxicated" by the "radiant loveliness of woman." "What indeed was my passion for the young girl of the valley," he apostrophizes, "in comparison with the fervor, and the delirium, and the spirit-lifting ecstasy of adoration with which I poured out my whole soul in tears at the feet of the ethereal Ermengarde?" (*PT*, 473). Not surprisingly, Eleonora returns from the grave after the narrator's wedding to

Ermengarde, but instead of exacting revenge for his betrayal of his vow, she blesses his marriage in the "Spirit of Love" (*PT,* 473). Although both Eleonora and Ermengarde resemble other ethereal female characters in Poe's fiction, the story stands out for the unusual way Poe resolves the tension between unworldly and worldly love.

"Eleonora" is not a prophetic story for Poe himself, however, as the last two years of his life reflect a fruitless search for an Ermengarde. "At your feet—if you so willed it," he would tell Helen Whitman in 1848, "I would cast from me, forever, all merely human desire, and clothe myself in the glory of a pure, calm, and *unexacting* affection." If she died, he vowed, "then at least would I clasp your dear hand in death, and willingly—*oh, joyfully—joyfully—joyfully*—go down *with* you into the night of the Grave" (*L,* 390). In effect, Poe was imagining himself as one of his heroines—becoming a purer male self, clothed in a pure love that would disembody him. Similarly, he would tell Annie Richmond in a letter of February 19, 1849, that she was "purer & nobler, at all points, than any woman" he had ever known, "*or could have imagined to exist upon the earth.*" "God knows dear *dear* Annie, with what horror I would have shrunk from insulting a nature so *divine* as yours, with any impure or earthly love" (*L,* 431). In effect, Poe had placed himself under the vow that Eleonora had exacted from the narrator of that earlier tale. In the process, he illustrates the reflexive power of his ideal characterizations of women—the power he creates for even his "real-life" female characters to make him a better man.

Poe's Portraits of Gentlemen

Poe's male characters seem more substantial than his female characters, if only because they typically narrate his tales in the first person and thus allow us to infer much about their gendered identities. With the exception of David Leverenz, who examines how the "Southern ideal of the gentleman plays a crucial role in his writings as well as in his life" ("Poe," 211), scholars have devoted little attention to Poe's male characters. Even though Poe's

men, like his women, seem tenuously connected to the culture
and material conditions of their literary origins, Poe did engage
contemporaneous issues surrounding nineteenth-century manhood in his writing. He represented and often satirized many
male character types. Just as his portraits of women deviate
weirdly from nineteenth-century models of ideal womanhood,
his depictions of men and male behavior reveal extraordinary
tensions between a gentlemanly surface and volatile, even violent depths.

As Helen Whitman remembered Poe (in an 1874 letter to John
Ingram), "*No* person could be long near him in his healthier
moods, without loving him & putting faith in the sweetness &
goodness of his nature & feeling that he had a reserved power of
self-control that needed only favoring circumstances to bring his
fine qualities of heart & mind into perfect equipoise" (Miller, 88).
In emphasizing Poe's self-control, Whitman was citing one of
the key building blocks of nineteenth-century gentlemanly behavior. As genteel patriarchy grounded in landownership gave
way to the "self-possession of the independent artisan, shop-
keeper, or farmer (the Heroic Artisan)" and then in turn to the
self-made manhood of the early nineteenth century (Kimmel,
Manhood in America, 9), manhood increasingly became a construction of particular circumstances. David Leverenz notes
"three ideologies of manhood in the antebellum Northeast: pa-
trician, artisan, and entrepreneurial." Like Kimmel, he observes
that the "older ideologies of genteel patriarch and artisan independence were being challenged by a new middle-class ideology
of competitive individualism" (*Manhood*, 3). Indeed, the century
featured several competing models of manhood and manly behavior, usually turning on the question of men's self-control.
"Control was the basic building block of personality," Charles
Rosenberg concludes (137), and the all-American "athlete of con-
tinence" was the Christian gentleman—a man who "eschewed
excess in all things" (139), including sexual expression. In contrast, the masculine achiever articulated an "archaic male ethos"
in which "physical vigor" and "aggressive sexual behavior" were
the central components (144). Paradoxically, as Kimmel points
out, "the self-control required of marketplace success required

the sexual control of a disciplined body, a body controlled by the will" ("Consuming Manhood," 15).

Even though Poe rarely situates his male characters in the social and economic sphere of the nineteenth-century marketplace, he often builds these same tensions between aggressive behavior and self-control into his portraits of gentlemen. As she remembered Poe for Ingram's benefit, in her very next sentence, Whitman acknowledged the darker side of Poe's personality: "But after seeing the morbid sensitiveness of his nature & finding how slight a wound could disturb his serenity, how trivial a disappointment could unbalance his whole being, no one could feel assured of his perseverance in the thorny paths of self-denial & endurance" (Miller, 88). Silverman concludes that in "wanting to excel and command, Edgar resembled many other orphans, in whom a feeling of nonexistence and the need to master changeable surroundings often produce a will to power" (25). Poe's letters reflect such a will to power even as they often show Poe in abject relation to others, particularly men from whom he was asking money or some other favor.

For most of his life, in fact, Poe struggled to find the terms in which he could identify himself as a man. As his letter to J. P. Kennedy suggests, he wanted to see himself as an aristocratic heir, a gentleman by adoption, but his relationship with John Allan was always troubled, as Poe alternately begged for forgiveness and money and complained about his stepfather's lack of attention and love. J. Gerald Kennedy has brilliantly analyzed Poe's twenty-seven extant letters to Allan, emphasizing Poe's efforts to prevent the reenactment of his parents' deaths by keeping his parental bond with Allan intact (*Poe*, 95). In the process Poe made a concerted effort to represent himself as the man he knew Allan wanted him to be. Ironically, Allan's persistent refusal to send Poe the money for which he begged prevented Poe's fulfilling the gentlemanly ideal that Allan himself defined by his example. Indeed, Poe maintained an anxious, even angry, relationship to nineteenth-century gentlemanly ideals. Leverenz argues that "Poe inhabits and undermines gentry fictions of mastery, not least by exposing the gentleman as a fiction. Typically, he displays cultivated narrators unable to master themselves." Poe "constructs, then deconstructs," the private lives of gentlemen, Leverenz says, "by transgressing the great social divide between public displays of mastery and an inwardness felt as alien to oneself" ("Poe," 212). Poe's portraits of men display the same, often violent tensions we discover in his portraits of women. Although Poe rarely sets a tale in the world of work or social interaction, he incorporates the values of the nineteenth-century marketplace into the enclosed spaces of his fictions. From tales of genteel one-upmanship ("Mystification") and intellectual competition between men ("The Purloined Letter") to tales of more violent vengeance ("The Cask of Amontillado," "Hop-Frog") to parodies of military manhood ("The Man Who Was Used Up") or business manhood ("The Business Man"), Poe waged a kind of rhetorical war upon nineteenth-century manhood. Forgoing the aggressive marketplace behavior of the masculine achiever, Poe competed with other men intellectually—in effect, domesticating competition and bringing it into the world of art.

"As the strong man exults in his physical ability, delighting in such exercises as call his muscles into action," remarks the narrator of "The Murders in the Rue Morgue" (1841), "so glories the analyst in that moral activity which *disentangles*" (*PT*, 397). Having chosen to construct a male self through literature, Poe incorporated literary competitions into his fiction, thus conflating the marketplace values he ostensibly eschewed and the genteel values he tried to emulate. The early tale "Mystification" (1837), for example, involves the noble Baron Ritzner Von Jung in a conflict with Johann Hermann (whose name, "Her-Man," suggests his feminization) over the "etiquette of the *duello*," on which both men claim expertise (*PT*, 256). The aristocratic Von Jung serves Poe as a trickster, a powerful literary mystifier who can avenge the sorts of slights that Poe no doubt experienced at the University of Virginia and at West Point. From the "first moment of his setting foot within the limits of the university," Poe's narrator recalls, "he began to exercise over the habits, manners, persons, purses, and propensities of the whole community which surrounded him, an influence the most extensive and despotic" (*PT*, 253). Not unlike Poe as he was beginning to identify himself through his writing, Von Jung has made the "science of *mystifica-*

tion" the "study and the business" of his life (*PT*, 254), and he has become particularly adroit at escaping the "natural consequence of his manoeuvres" (*PT*, 255). Thus, when Hermann indulges himself in a long monologue upon the etiquette of the duel, Von Jung concocts an ingenious plot to expose him for the coward and ignoramus that he is. The narrator, "Mr. P——," serves as go-between, carrying notes from one man to the other, and thus bears witness to Von Jung's triumph, which involves referring Hermann to a nonsensical treatise on the art of the duel and so playing upon his unwillingness to admit that he cannot understand it. The passage actually presents a "most horribly absurd account of a duel between two baboons," and the "language was ingeniously framed so as to present to the ear the outward signs of intelligibility, and even of profundity, while in fact not a shadow of meaning existed" (*PT*, 260–61).

It is tempting to see Poe's literary career prophesied in that concluding statement. Certainly he went on to mystify readers and to play with the possibility of creating "outward signs of intelligibility, and even of profundity, while in fact not a shadow of meaning existed." Poe tried to make a living and a self through his writing—to "invent a public image as a man of letters" (Kennedy, *Poe*, 97)—and the last twenty years of his life register the difficulty in nineteenth-century America of making meaning, even the appearance of meaning, as a writer and a man. As Leverenz puts it, Poe tried to make "textuality itself the source of true aristocracy" ("Poe," 220). Publication of *Al Aaraaf, Tamerlane, and Minor Poems* in 1829 (when Poe was twenty) seemed to mark the first turning point in his sense of his male identity. In a well-known letter of introduction to writer John Neal, Poe identified himself confidently. "I am young—not yet twenty," he begins, "*am* a poet—if deep worship of all beauty can make me *one*—and wish to be so in the common meaning of the word" (*L*, 32). Career choice was "above all, a decision about what *sort* of a man one wished to be," observes Anthony Rotundo, and Americans "viewed different professions as more or less manly." A career in the arts was clearly marked "female" (170), so that Poe's embrace of poetry—his love of the beautiful and his literary intimacy with women—relegated him to a woman's sphere, threat-

ening him with the sort of terrible alteration that renders Roderick Usher a male neurasthenic who suffers from a "morbid acute-
ness of the senses" (*PT,* 322).[3] Committing himself to the literary
profession, moreover, was a risky way of trying to make a living,
and Poe found himself continually dependent upon others for
notice and for success. At the age of twenty, in a letter to John
Allan of February 4, 1829, Poe tried to convince his stepfather to
subvent publication of a volume of poetry. "At my time of life
there is much in being *before the eye of the world*—if once noticed I
can easily cut out a path to reputation," Poe claims, but he goes
on to ask Allan to give him a letter for publishers Carey, Lea, and
Carey "saying that if in publishing the poem 'Al Aaraaf' they shall
incur any *loss*—you will make it good to them" (*L,* 20).

In a society that increasingly defined manliness in economic
terms, Poe's solution to career anxiety was to found a literary
journal, to capitalize writing, and he spent much of his adult life
soliciting contributions for the *Penn* and then the *Stylus*—in effect, repeating the independent-dependent scenario he had performed with John Allan in 1829. Kennedy concludes, in fact, that
"ownership of a literary periodical became the dominant compensatory fantasy of Poe's adult life, a dream engendered by
separation anxiety and dread of death, which saw Poe winning
public admiration, asserting his self-worth, establishing a 'name'
(that is, supplanting the father by becoming his own creator),
and, in the face of his personal mortality, insuring the survival of
his writerly identity" (*Poe,* 98). In addition to fulfilling such exis-
tential goals, journal ownership would provide the money to
ensure social status, and editorial power would enable Poe to pa-
tronize other writers, especially admiring female writers. Owning and editing a periodical would enable Poe to be a genteel patriarch. "I am actuated by an ambition which I believe to be an
honourable one," he would comment in an 1840 letter, "the ambition of serving the great cause of truth, while endeavouring to
forward the literature of the country." Poe had to acknowledge
that his "exertions" had so far only enhanced his "literary reputation" and only benefited "*others* so far as money was concerned,"
but he felt determined to make "fame & fortune" go "hand in
hand"—literally to capitalize on his literary reputation. "My

chances of establishing a magazine depend upon my getting a certain number of subscribers previously to the first of December," he concluded. "This is rendered necessary by my having no other capital to begin with than whatever reputation I may have acquired as a literary man" (*L*, 143). Furthermore, Poe consistently associated his editorial plans with class status. Writing itself could confer that status. "As a man of the world," he flattered Robert T. Conrad in 1841, "you will at once understand that what I most need for my work in its commencement (since I am comparatively a stranger in Philadelphia) is *caste*. I need the countenance of those who stand well not less in the social than in the literary world" (*L*, 154). Two years later, in a letter to Frederick Thomas, Poe repeated his concern in the process of asking Thomas to solicit an article from Judge Abel Parker Upshur (shortly to become U.S. secretary of state) for the magazine he was planning. If "I could get him interested in the scheme he *might*, by good management, be induced to give me an article, I care not how brief, or on what subject, *with his name*. It would be worth to me at least $500, and give me *caste* at once" (*L*, 224). In this letter we see all of Poe's concerns come together. The planned literary magazine, supported by a superior male patron and blessed with his "name" (much as Poe longed for John Allan to give him his name), will bring him money and "caste" at one and the same time.

Poe could also caricature such entrepreneurial efforts, as he did in "The Literary Life of Thingum Bob, Esq." (1844), a first-person narrative aimed at detailing "those important, yet feeble and tottering first steps" by which the literary lion Thingum Bob has "attained the high road to the pinnacle of human renown" (*PT*, 766). Inspired by his barber father, who has earned some fame by publishing a poem, "Oil-of-Bob," memorializing a hair oil he has invented, the narrator resolves "at once to become a great man and to commence by becoming a great poet" (*PT*, 767). On the strength of an egregious two-line poem, "To pen an Ode upon the 'Oil-of-Bob' / Is all sorts of a job" (*PT*, 772), and the pen name "Snob," the narrator is able to promote himself to the literary magazine establishment, to buy his own journal, and finally to take over his competitors.

One obvious way for Poe to rise above the low station into which he felt himself born and from which John Allan persistently refused to raise him was the military, and Poe's letters illustrate the emotional stake he felt in this form of making a name and place for himself. Even as he sought his discharge from the service, he insisted upon the metamorphosis that had occurred. "You need not fear for my future prosperity," he assured Allan. "I am altered from what you knew me, & am no longer a boy tossing about on the world without aim or consistency." "You will perceive that I speak confidently," he continues, "but when did ever Ambition exist or Talent prosper without prior conviction of success? I have thrown myself on the world, like the Norman conqueror on the shores of Britain &, by my avowed assurance of victory, have destroyed the fleet which could alone cover my retreat—I must either conquer or die— succeed or be disgraced" (*L*, 10). Ironically, Poe's inflated sense of self and power flies in the face of his rhetorical purpose— convincing John Allan to write the army on his behalf and thereby secure his discharge. Although he had imbibed the rhetoric of military conquest—he could write like a soldier— Poe must have felt his dependency even as he insisted upon his independence.

Poe could parody male construction efforts, and he did so in very efficient fashion in "The Man That Was Used Up" (1839), a critique of male military identity. Surveying Brigadier General John A. B. C. Smith with a transparently desiring male gaze, Poe's narrator describes the usual body parts, each of which he idealizes in the manner of an infatuated lover.[4] The general's "jetty black" hair "would have done honor to a Brutus," and he sports the "handsomest pair of whiskers under the sun." His mouth is "utterly unequalled" (*PT*, 307). His teeth are the "most brilliantly white of all conceivable teeth." His "deep hazel" eyes are "exceedingly large and lustrous" (*PT*, 308). "I have a passion for fine shoulders," the narrator acknowledges, and the General has the most perfect pair he has ever beheld—as well as the "*ne plus ultra* of good legs." "I could not imagine a more graceful curve than that of the *os femoris*, and there was just that gentle prominence in the rear of the *fibula* which goes to the conforma-

tion of a properly proportioned calf" (*PT*, 308). A "perfect desper-
ado" and "down-right fire-eater" (*PT*, 309), General Smith epitomizes the military male that Poe himself briefly aspired to be
during his erstwhile sojourn at West Point, and his literal deconstruction in this tale helps Poe de-compose the military model of
manhood that his culture had carefully constructed out of the Indian removal campaigns of the 1830s. The general, it turns out,
lost many parts of his body during the Bugaboo and Kickapoo
Indian campaign, and he has been mechanically and prostheti-
cally reconstructed part by part— proof that he does indeed live,
as he puts it, in a "wonderful age of invention" (*PT*, 313). Michael
Williams notes that his "condition literalizes the fate of all assumed independent unified identities in Poe's fiction as narrators
strive to recuperate them in language that necessarily marks their
dis-unity" (24), but the general's particular identity derives directly from his cultural moment. Constructed on a foundation of
racism (Indian removal) and racial revenge (he has been taken
apart by the Indians), the general must be reconstructed every
morning with the help of his "old negro valet," Pompey, whom
he calls "nigger" (*PT*, 315) and "black rascal" (*PT*, 316). As Dayan
puts it, with "each successive body part replaced, the general re-
gains the voice of the consummate southern gentleman while remaining utterly dependent on the 'old negro' he debases"
("Amorous Bondage," 197). Ingeniously, Poe conflates military
power and racist ideology, constructing his "man that was used
up" out of artificial materials manufactured by the capitalist and
industrial inventions that white racism made possible. The general's situation contrasts sharply with the one Poe experienced in
John Allan's household. In a March 19, 1827, letter to Allan, for example, he complained, "You suffer me to be subjected to the
whims & caprice, not only of your white family, but the complete authority of the blacks—these grievances I could not sub-
mit to; and I am gone" (*L*, 8). Poe feels doubly abused and
disadvantaged—according to both class and race hierarchies.
What he calls Allan's "delight" in "exposing" him (*L*, 8) remands
him to a second-class position within the family, making him feel
his Cinderella-like status as a stepchild, but Allan humiliates him
even more by preferring his black slaves above his stepson.

Of all the markers of successful manhood that Poe lacked, however, he felt his lack of a secure job most acutely. "In the nineteenth century, middle-class men's work was vital to their sense of who they were," observes Rotundo. "If a man was without 'business,' he was less than a man" (168). Poe himself continually struggled to make a living, and very few of his male characters seem to work outside the home. The married narrators of "Berenice," "Morella," and "Ligeia" do not seem to be breadwinners, although they appear to have independent means. C. Auguste Dupin lives upon a "small remnant of his patrimony" but still manages, "by means of a rigorous economy" that would have resonated for the impoverished Poe, to "procure the necessaries of life" (*PT,* 400). Poe observed the business world from a distance, epitomized in his fiction by the condescending perspective shown by the narrator of "The Man of the Crowd," who amuses himself, with a cigar in his mouth and a newspaper on his lap, by cataloging the "tides of population" that stream by on the streets of London (*PT,* 388). Before fixing his attention on the stranger whom he follows for more than twenty-four hours, Poe's narrator surveys London working people in much the same way that Walt Whitman would later do in "Song of Myself" (1855). Poe's narrator lacks Whitman's celebratory spirit, however, preferring to descend "in the scale of what is termed gentility" and to emphasize the nighttime squalor of the city streets and its people (*PT,* 393).

More directly, Poe parodied business values and business manhood in "The Business Man" (1840). Ostensibly an apostrophe to that "positive appetite for system and regularity which has made me the distinguished man of business that I am" (*PT,* 373), the sketch devolves into an account of connivance and scavenging as the narrator climbs down the ladder of success, all the while extolling his business methods. "In my case," says the narrator, "it was method—not money—which made the man: at least all of him that was not made by the tailor whom I served" (*PT,* 375). The tale deconstructs self-made manhood as effectively as "The Man That Was Used Up," for the narrator has literally transformed himself into a "Walking-Advertisement" for his tailor, whom he serves by promenading about and bringing customers back to the store. Like Brigadier General John A. B. C. Smith, he is a shell of a man. When he has a falling-out with the tailor over his fee, the business man turns to the "Eye-Sore line": he buys property near buildings under construction and builds an "ornamental mud hovel" so that the owners will pay him to remove it (*PT,* 388). He turns to the "Assault and Battery business," picking fights on the streets and then suing the men who "assault" him. After finding the "exactions of the profession" too much for his "delicate state of body" (*PT,* 378), the businessman resorts to "Mud-Dabbling" and "Cur-Spattering"—in both cases blackmailing "customers" into paying him for not splashing them with mud. He tries organ-grinding not because he has musical talent but because he doesn't; people pay him *not* to play. Finally, he achieves a good income by cutting the tails off cats—after the legislature passes a bill designed to rid the area of cats. Because he has discovered a way to re-generate the cat tails that he severs in order to earn the reward they signify, the narrator has cornered the market in dead cats. By means of a little "Macassar oil," he brags, "I can force three crops a year. . . . I consider myself, therefore, a made man, and am bargaining for a country seat on the Hudson" (*PT,* 381).

David Leverenz has argued that Poe "negates a progressive ideology of individualism by emptying out the meaningfulness of the self as a social construct," and he notes Poe's "profoundly skeptical play with social fictions of self-making" ("Poe," 212, 218). Stories such as "The Man That Was Used Up" and "The Business Man" clearly suggest such skepticism and negation, as Poe exposes both title characters as empty forms of successful manhood. Of course, Poe would have gained some consolation for himself by creating those empty forms—by discovering a self-creating power as the maker of even hollow men. "Literature is the most noble of professions," he would tell Frederick Thomas just eight months before his death. "In fact, it is about the only one fit for a man. For my own part, there is no seducing me from the path. I shall be a *littérateur,* at least, all my life; nor would I abandon the hopes which still lead me on for all the gold in California." Deliberately setting himself off from the gold-driven frenzy of the age, Poe retreats confidently to the world of litera-

ture. "Talking of gold, and of the temptations at present held out
to 'poor-devil authors,' he continues in the letter to Thomas, "did
it ever strike you that all which is really valuable to a man of
letters—to a poet in especial—is absolutely unpurchaseable?
Love, fame, the dominion of the intellect, the consciousness of
power, the thrilling sense of beauty, the free air of Heaven, exercise of body & mind, with the physical and moral health which
result—these and such as these are really all that a poet cares for"
(*L*, 427).

This heartfelt statement, a valedictory and eulogy for his own
career, offers a catalog of terms that can help us understand the
relationship between Poe's construction of gender and his literary selfhood. Poe's life as a litterateur hardly seemed to grant
him the priceless pleasures he had listed. Moreover, he was imagining a powerful, self-fulfilling form of manhood that does not
appear to exist in his fiction. But in marking off a separate sphere
for literature and litterateurs, Poe revealed many of the wishes
he tried to fulfill in his literary practices. In linking "dominion of
the intellect, the consciousness of power, the thrilling sense of
beauty," for example, Poe sketched a blueprint for the psychological underpinnings of many of his fictions. In his tales about
the lives of beautiful women, he regularly brings female characters within the dominion of the male intellect, inventorying the
beautiful parts of their bodies, often reducing them to a single
fetishized part or a single word, and thus representing male
achievement of spectacular verbal power. Poe's tales about men
also seem to depend upon verbal power relations and intellectual
domination, if not a "thrilling sense of beauty." Baron Von Jung's
literary triumph over Johann Hermann, Dupin's intellectual mastery of Prefect G——, the sadistically playful vengeance of characters such as Montresor and Hop-Frog, not to mention the verbal power Poe's narrators wield over the "business man" and
General John A. B. C. Smith—all enable enjoyment of power
over other men.

"Thou art the man!" utters the corpse of Barnabas Shuttleworthy at the climax of Poe's "Thou Art the Man" (1844), a little-
known murder mystery written in the same year as "The Purloined Letter." While suspicion for Shuttleworthy's murder falls

immediately upon his nephew, Mr. Pennifeather, the narrator's elaborately orchestrated expose entraps the real murderer, Charley Goodfellow, causing a spontaneous confession and then his death. "Thou Art the Man" does not equal "The Murders in the Rue Morgue" or "The Purloined Letter" as a detective story, in part because the detective-narrator is so absorbed with exposing Charley Goodfellow's "miserable soul" that he eliminates most of the mystery. With obvious sarcasm, he has introduced Goodfellow as an "open, manly, honest, good-natured, and frank-hearted fellow, with a rich, clear voice, that did you good to hear it, and an eye that looked you always straight in the face, as much as to say, 'I have a clear conscience myself; am afraid of no man, and am altogether above doing a mean action'" (*PT,* 728–29). Much like "The Man That Was Used Up" and "The Business Man," in other words, "Thou Art the Man" is designed to expose this "walking gentleman" (*PT,* 729) as a fraud. "For the words which I intended the corpse to speak," the narrator boasts at the end of the story, "I confidently depended upon my ventriloquial abilities" (*PT,* 742). Poe loved to stage scenes of corpses coming back to life—as much as anything else for the effect such returns-from-the-dead could have upon the living. Whether in this case or in the more common case of a woman's returning catastrophically from the dead to force a male character to confess his crime ("The Black Cat"), to "chill" a male narrator into stone ("Ligeia"), or to scare a male character to death ("The Fall of the House of Usher"), exercising the "ventriloquial" power that enabled corpses to terrify the living enabled Poe to enjoy a godlike "consciousness of power." The death of a beautiful woman may have been the most poetical topic in the world for Poe, but the exercise of verbal power over fictional life and death was better, as he indicated to Thomas, than gold. Poe may not have enjoyed such power in his personal and professional life, but in the separate sphere of his fiction Poe could be "the Man."

NOTES

1. Invalidism in the nineteenth century "referred to a lack of power as well as a tendency toward illness," Herndl says. *Invalid* car-

ries "traces of its etymology and suggests the not-valid" (1). In contrast, according to Cogan, the "ideal of Real Womanhood based its
advice not, as did the Cult of True Womanhood, on the physiologi-
cal and biological interpretations of female inferiority offered by
heroic medicine, but rather on the triple bases of absolute necessity,
health reform precepts, and observable clinical reality. Far from assuming that women were nervous, hysterical, and biologically weak
specimens from birth, easily subdued and dominated by male force,
strong emotion, and male rationality, the Real Womanhood ideal offered American women a vision of themselves as biologically equal
(rationally as well as emotionally) and in many cases markedly superior in intellect to what passed for male business sense, scholarship,
and theological understanding" (4–5).

2. Poe anatomized male writers in much the same way. His
lengthy review of Fitz-Greene Halleck, for example, concludes with
the following description: "His age is about fifty. In height he is probably five feet seven. He *has been* stout, but may now be called well-
proportioned. His forehead is a noble one, broad, massive, and intellectual, a little bald about the temples; eyes dark and brilliant, but
not large; nose Grecian; chin prominent; mouth finely chiseled and
full of expression, although the lips are thin;—his smile is peculiarly
sweet" (*ER*, 1159).

3. Roderick Usher seems to fit the pattern that Anthony Rotundo identifies with "male neurasthenia"—what today we would
popularly call "burnout." Male neurasthenia "contained a profound
element of gender meaning," Rotundo points out. "A man who
steered away from the middle-class work-world was avoiding a
man's proper place" and was "retreating into the feminine realm. By
going home to rest, he was seeking out the domestic space of
women" (191).

4. As I have noted, Poe included physical descriptions of male as
well as female writers in his "Literati of New York" review essays.
He offers an extended description of N. P. Willis, for example, that is
both adoring and undercutting. "He is yet young, and, without
being handsome, in the ordinary sense, is a remarkably well-looking
man," Poe begins. "In height he is, perhaps, five feet eleven, and
justly proportioned. His figure is put in the best light by the ease and
assured grace of his carriage." As soon as Poe identifies Willis in
terms of his upper-class characteristics, however, his assessment

turns more negative. "His whole person and personal demeanour bear about them the traces of 'good society,'" Poe continues. "His face is somewhat too full, or rather heavy, in its lower portions. Neither his nose nor his forehead can be defended; the latter would puzzle phrenology. His eyes are a dull bluish gray, and small." Poe goes on, under the guise of praising Willis, to feminize him. "His hair is of a rich brown, curling naturally and luxuriantly," he concludes. "His mouth is well cut; the teeth fine; the expression of the smile intellectual and winning" (*ER*, 1130).

WORKS CITED

Barker-Benfield, G. J. *The Horrors of the Half-Known Life: Male Attitudes toward Women and Sexuality in Nineteenth-Century America*. New York: Harper and Row, 1976.

Beauvoir, Simone de. *The Second Sex*. Trans. H. M. Parshley. New York: Knopf, 1952.

Cogan, Frances B. *All-American Girl: The Ideal of Real Womanhood in Mid-Nineteenth-Century America*. Athens: University of Georgia Press, 1989.

Cott, Nancy F. *The Bonds of Womanhood: "Woman's Sphere" in New England, 1780–1835*. New Haven, Conn.: Yale University Press, 1977.

Coultrap-McQuin, Susan. *Doing Literary Business: American Women Writers in the Nineteenth Century*. Chapel Hill: University of North Carolina Press, 1990.

Davidson, Cathy N. "Preface." *No More Separate Spheres!* a Special issue of *American Literature* 70 (1998): 443–63.

Dayan, Joan. "Amorous Bondage: Poe, Ladies, and Slaves." In *The American Face of Edgar Allan Poe*, ed. Shawn Rosenheim and Stephen Rachman, 179–209. Baltimore: Johns Hopkins University Press, 1995.

———. *Fables of Mind: An Inquiry into Poe's Fiction*. New York: Oxford University Press, 1987.

DeJong, Mary. "Lines from a Partly Published Drama: The Romance of Frances Sargent Osgood and Edgar Allan Poe." In *Patrons and Protégées: Gender, Friendship, and Writing in Nineteenth-Century America*, ed. Shirley Marchalonis. 31–58. New Brunswick, N.J.: Rutgers University Press, 1988.

Derrick, Scott S. *Monumental Anxieties: Homoerotic Desire and Feminine Influence in Nineteenth-Century U.S. Literature.* New Brunswick, N.J.: Rutgers University Press, 1997.

Fetterley, Judith. *The Resisting Reader: A Feminist Approach to American Fiction.* Bloomington, Ind.: Indiana University Press, 1978.

Gilbert, Sandra M., and Susan Gubar. *The Madwoman in the Attic: The Woman Writer and the Nineteenth-Century Literary Imagination.* New Haven, Conn.: Yale University Press, 1979.

Herndl, Diane Price. *Invalid Women: Figuring Feminine Illness in American Fiction and Culture, 1840–1940.* Chapel Hill: University of North Carolina Press, 1993.

Jordan, Cynthia. *Second Stories: The Politics of Language, Form, and Gender in Early American Fictions.* Chapel Hill: University of North Carolina Press, 1989.

Kennedy, J. Gerald. *Poe, Death, and the Life of Writing.* New Haven, Conn.: Yale University Press, 1987.

———. "Poe, 'Ligeia,' and the Problem of Dying Women." In *New Essays on Poe's Major Tales*, ed. Kenneth Silverman, 113–29. New York: Cambridge University Press, 1993.

———. "The Violence of Melancholy: Poe against Himself." *American Literary History* 8 (1996): 533–51.

Kimmel, Michael S. "Consuming Manhood: The Feminization of American Culture and the Recreation of the Male Body, 1832–1920." In *The Male Body: Features, Destinies, Exposures*, ed. Laurence Goldstein. 12–41. Ann Arbor: University of Michigan Press, 1994.

Kimmel, Michael S. *Manhood in America: A Cultural History.* New York: Free Press, 1996.

Kolodny, Annette. *The Land before Her: Fantasy and Experience of the American Frontiers, 1630–1860.* Chapel Hill: University of North Carolina Press, 1984.

Leverenz, David. *Manhood and the American Renaissance.* Ithaca, N.Y.: Cornell University Press, 1989.

———. "Poe and Gentry Virginia." In *The American Face of Edgar Allan Poe*, ed. Shawn Rosenheim and Stephen Rachman, 210–36. Baltimore: Johns Hopkins University Press, 1995.

Miller, John Carl, ed. *Poe's Helen Remembers.* Charlottesville: University Press of Virginia, 1979.

Person, Leland S. *Aesthetic Headaches: Women and a Masculine Poetics* in *Poe, Melville, and Hawthorne*. Athens: University of Georgia Press, 1988.

Porte, Joel. *The Romance in America: Studies in Cooper, Poe, Hawthorne, Melville, and James*. Middletown, Conn.: Wesleyan University Press, 1969.

Rosenberg, Charles E. "Sexuality, Class, and Role in Nineteenth-Century America." *American Quarterly* 25 (1973): 131–53.

Rotundo, E. Anthony. *American Manhood: Transformations in Masculinity from the Revolution to the Modern Era*. New York: Basic Books, 1993.

Silverman, Kenneth. *Edgar A. Poe: Mournful and Never-Ending Remembrance*. New York: HarperCollins, 1991.

Thompson, G. R. *Poe's Fiction: Romantic Irony in the Gothic Tales*. Madison: University of Wisconsin Press, 1973.

Welter, Barbara. *Dimity Convictions: The American Woman in the Nineteenth Century*. Athens: Ohio University Press, 1976.

Williams, Michael J. S. *A World of Words: Language and Displacement in the Fiction of Edgar Allan Poe*. Durham, N.C.: Duke University Press, 1988.

Poe and the Issue of
American Privacy

Louis A. Renza

> . . . in this country, which has set the
> world an example of physical liberty,
> the inquisition of popular sentiment
> overrules in practice the freedom as-
> serted in theory by the laws.
> —Edgar Allan Poe, "The Literati of
> New York City" (1846)[1]

I

At first glance, few readers would identify Poe as a socially representative writer. But at least in one important social area, the increasingly critical issue of American private freedoms becoming
threatened by "the inquisition of popular sentiment," one could
make precisely this case. Tocqueville gave special notice to this
problem in mid-nineteenth-century democratic culture: "[T]he
power exercised by the mass upon the mind of each individual is
extremely great. . . . Wherever social conditions are equal,
public opinion presses with enormous weight upon the minds
of each individual. . . . As men grow more alike, each man
feels himself weaker in regard to all the rest" (2:275). This way
of formulating the issue tends to reduce it to the sociological

shibboleth of an ideological ethos—American individualism—contradicted by the very mass society to which it gives rise. If only in his fiction, however, Poe stages the crisis besetting individual freedom in terms of a compromised private sphere, which, inextricably bound to its particular, social construction, permits one to entertain the notion of such freedom in the first place.

This no doubt appears a strange claim to make in the face of evidence to the contrary. Poe, after all, wrote his tales and essays primarily in terms of a public literary stage. At bottom, simply by writing works that have afforded him a certain, if also continually vexed, canonization within American literary history, he manifests a desire to go public with them. In his 1836 Drake-Halleck review, he writes "that *the world* is the true theatre of the biblical histrio" (*ER,* 506; emphasis in originial). Poe undoubtedly desired literary fame, recognition, and, at the minimum, economic subsistence from his works. This fact certainly seems to characterize the way many of his tales cater to the baser interests of the American literary public in the macabre-Gothic-sensational, the dark side, as it were, of the period's coequal taste for sentimental literature.[2] And for the most part, Poe's works are eminently accessible. They play to, even when they spoof or hoax, the American literary-public marketplace. For that matter, on occasion Poe was not above appealing to mass public taste, if only to contest that of the period's publishing industry and those literary cliques with which he frequently carried on his well-known literary battles[3]

On the other hand, Poe plays fast and loose with his mass literary public, especially when deploying for no immediately appreciable reason subtly concealed, rhetorical gambits, each occuring in concussive fashion depending on a reader's level of interpretive awareness. For instance, what to make of the anagrammatic pun, "E.A.P.," marking the "ape" killer in "The Murders in the Rue Morgue" (1841), to which Poe passingly refers (*PT,* 430) as a casual synonym for the tale's famous "Ourang-Outang"? A suspicion, moreover, always lurks that a Poe tale constitutes an encoded cryptogram. This is all the more the case since, as Shawn Rosenheim has pointed out, Poe could even write about "secret writing" in cryptographic fashion, thus enacting privately his already privacy-oriented "defence of cryptography as a means of preserving the self-in-writing from a destructive world by locking it with the key of a private code" (35).[4] Suggestively occurring as if to elude detection by others altogether, such concealments transcend their possible deployment for journalistic or fictional effect, even with regard to an individualist-minded, American reading public.

But if these cryptorhetorical gambits at first appear an idiopathic mutation or consequence of "American individualism," in another sense might they not dramatize, and precisely for manifesting the desire to remain concealed or private, a socially representative, critical response to the very public environment this individualist ethos had helped bring about? This surmise gains more credence if one keeps in mind the upsurge in Poe's time of an amorphous public sphere resulting from multiple social factors— economic, political, demographic, cultural, technological—the composite force of which framed the conventionally understood private sphere in distinctly defensive if critically restive terms.

In the United States during the early nineteenth century, "private" and "public" had referred to different realms of social experience, but less as oppositional than complementary, if uneasily coexisting, ones. Federalist and Republican leaders acknowledged the attraction of private domestic life, although as "gentlemen" they conceded the compelling importance of, and thus felt obliged to give their greater attention to, constructing a new, post-Revolutionary public sphere.[5] Writing in 1835, Tocqueville even implied that the country's geopolitical isolation in itself comprised a kind of macroprivate figure: "The policy of Americans in relation to the whole world is exceedingly simple; and it may almost be said that nobody [i.e., no other nation] stands in need of them, nor do they stand in need of anybody" (1:136).

Unthreatened by other countries on its borders, the Union government's structure further underwrote American citizens' pursuits of private affairs. For example, the country's location, size, and constitutional government each and together worked to preclude the kind of invasive surveillance exercised by small nation-states like those in Europe where "the watchfulness of society penetrates everywhere, and a desire for improvement pervades the smallest details" (Tocqueville, 1:165). Indeed, such local-institutional settings had also defined early American-Puritan communities in which social privacy, already obstructed by physical living arrangements, was severely limited in action and thought by a sociotheological ethos prone to similar surveillance practices.[6] To a certain extent, even early, nineteenth-century domestic ideology purveyed a similarly restricted and ambivalent definition of privacy, for example, by establishing social norms that effectively "proscribed" single persons from "living alone," which during this period "was customarily seen as a sign of eccentricity or even madness" (Larkin, 11).

Yet if privacy was no uncomplicated social desideratum in the early American republic, the geographic circumstances of the United States, especially rural settlers' encounter with the "frontier," had all along engendered an assumption of privacy rights as part of the country's very constitutional fabric. Richard Hixson maintains that "the case of access to ownership or possession of land in the New World furnished a secure base for the enjoyment of privacy. Because of the increasing distance between homes, particularly farm homes, physical privacy became a characteristic of everyday life" (9). For Hixson, this sociobehavioristic pattern helps explain why "American courts and legislatures had for some time recognized the home, confidential communications, and public records as private domains" (35).[7] Nor was this more positive valuation of privacy impeded by the steady growth of urban-commercial centers during the preindustrial period of United States culture; for these, too, "provided the 'protective anonymity' that could less readily be found in smaller towns," which additionally contributed to the notion of "personal privacy at least, if not spatial seclusion" (9). Such urbanization, that is, in effect internalized the rural propagation of privacy. Transposing Richard Sennett's characterization of eighteenth-century London city squares, one might even surmise that early nineteenth-century American urban settings, most notably in the Northeastern corridor, doubled "as a free zone of crowds" that allowed people to act out different public roles without exposing their private selves (Sennett, 54).

By the time Poe began writing his tales, however, privacy was becoming anything but what Hixson terms "taken for granted" or "not seriously threatened" (18). The competitive market economy, with its abstract inflection of things and people, made moot would-be urban maskers, not to mention any cooperative construction of a person-oriented, public sphere. This impersonal public filtered what privacy now meant. On one hand, the marketplace bred suspicions about strangers' private motivations; on the other, to alleviate the anxiety aroused by such suspicion, it inversely promoted the ethos of "sincerity"—a kind of quarantined zone, especially associated with the domestic realm, where one could think to know the other's true motivations.[8] Privacy, in short, became a reactionary category of social experience. Milette Shamir argues that American privacy concerns during this period set the stage for the later 1890 Warren-Brandeis legal defense of "the right to privacy," and did so "precisely in order to counter the problem of the alienability of personhood that emerged with modern capitalism, in order to keep stories about the self from circulating in the market and hence to resist the risk of appropriation by the market" (Shamir, 748).

But the market economy represented just one aspect of an increasingly invasive public realm. Even the infrastructural connections between cities and rural communities, sponsored by the U.S. government, were invading previously assumed private spaces: "The process of building public thruways, bridges, wharfs, and even parks involved the public expropriation and extinguishment of preexisting rights, usages, and expectations. The invention of public space was contested terrain in the early nineteenth century, requiring a full deployment of the rhetorics and techniques of the well-regulated society" (Novak, 117). Transportational changes, most notably railroad expansion after 1830, along with telegraph linkages between cities begun around 1844, further shrunk the sense of privacy formerly promoted by American geographic space; conversely, bureaucratic and "industrial innovations" that had become available for commercial use diluted entrepreneurial dependence on the putatively private family for their execution (Beniger, 17, 128).[9] Moreover, the large American city developed sectored microcommunities, each subject to organizational networks, and for the most part based on class and ethnic identity. Social groups thus in effect appeared private to each other. But at the same time, the mass-market economy and its infrastructural support systems at once increased and promised relief from certain social problems (epidemics of disease, for example) that required common urban solutions. This situation further helped induce the sense of an abstract "public," an aspect of which Poe took notice, for instance, in his allusion to the public waterworks system and public parks of Philadelphia around the time he wrote his 1844 article "Morning on the Wissahiccon" (*PT,* 943).[10]

In cultural areas as well, the public was assuming a dominant if inchoate social presence. For example, mass political participation became a distinctive feature of American life in the Jacksonian era (Schudson, 149). In the name of an egalitarian ethos, public opinion, fostered by the mass press, exercised, as we have seen Tocqueville note, an "enormous weight upon the minds of each individual." The press itself appeared dedicated to uncovering the private lives of public figures—of transforming public opinion into a new species of publicity. In Tocqueville's words, contemporary American journalists coarsely "appeal [ed] to the passion of [their] readers" and "abandon [ed] principles to assail the characters of individuals, to track them into private life and disclose all their weaknesses and vices" (1:194).[11]

Most relevant to Poe's situation, all this occurred alongside the more rapid dissemination of information through technological innovations in printing and cheaper postal rates for newspapers as well as personal letters. Such infrastructural changes inevitably affected how people construed writing per se: more as a public flow of information and less as a medium virtually instantiating personal interaction. Even letter writing by private as opposed to public or political figures accrued a privative (i.e., secondary) ambience in this context. Letters, as Richard Brown notes, had "been vital sources of information on events beyond one's locality" in early America. But now assuming a kind of "quasi-public quality"—all the more so "since they might be opened and read as they passed from hand to hand"—they became a medium "almost exclusively devoted to personal concerns," yet at the same time sufficiently haunted by a sense of unwanted public scrutiny that they required legal protection by federal law (Brown, 230).[12]

Poe's resistance to his encroaching public complex, then, could easily account for his interest in and general fictional enactments of "secret writing," particularly as he expressly broached this topic in a popular run of articles for *Alexander's Weekly Messenger* in 1841. If nothing else, this popularity testifies to their striking a social nerve and registering contemporary American concerns about keeping personal letters private: the "desire," as he states in his initial article, "of transmitting information from one individual to another, in such manner as to elude general comprehension" (*ER*, 1277).

2

Yet one cannot summarily dismiss Poe's exploitative motives even regarding this social privacy issue. On the contrary, a full-fledged participant in the period's mass-cultural milieu, Poe engaged in journalistic practices that frequently verged on outright violations of literary privacy. This is the tenor, for instance, of his notorious allegations of Longfellow's plagiarisms in the "Outis" articles, or of his conveying the purportedly actual opinions of "private [literary] society" about contemporary writers in his "Literati" pieces (*ER*, 1120). Reducible to mere literary politics, such detections nonetheless dovetail with the period's newly invested social interest in actual criminal detections. With Dupin as their social hero, Poe's three "ratiocinative" tales at once exploit this interest and advertise methods to ferret out secrets dangerous to the public order. These tales all occur in Paris, an impersonal urban setting that figures an abstract public sphere characterized by anonymous and suspicious strangers or potential carriers of such secrets: "[I]t thus arose that during the 19th Century in both Paris and London the detective and the mystery novel became a popular genre. Detectives are what every man and woman must be when they want to make sense of the street" (Sennett, 168).

Poe's possible allegiance to "public" ideology occurs in more allusive ways as well. In devolving on theatricalized visual scenes, many Poe tales figuratively mimic an increasingly popular mode of entertainment for middle-class European and American audiences during his period. Presented with technological inventions as well as post-Revolutionary access to art previously reserved for the private viewing of social elites, Poe's democratic contemporaries experienced new visual stimuli afforded by the diorama and panorama, stereoscopes, the phantasmagoria (ghostly illusions via magic lanterns), and most notably the daguerreotype. As Terry Castle argues, the Poe tale frequently stages phantasmagoric effects, a common feature of which was a "spectacle," complete with "bizarre, claustrophobic surroundings, the mood of Gothic strangeness and terror, the rapid phantom-train of images, the disorientation and powerlessness of the spectator" or reader (43).

Indeed, middle-class tastes would come to prefer such technotheatrical media over pictorial art. Even by 1840, Poe himself would undercut the value of painting by considering the daguerreotype "perhaps the most extraordinary triumph of modern science," terming it "*infinitely* more accurate in its representation than any painting by human hands" and surmising that its "consequences" would "exceed, by very much, the wildest expectations of the most imaginative" (*PT,* 37, 38, emphasis in original). Nor is this all, for both the phantasmagoria and the daguerreotype possess more than mere entertainment, mimetic, or scientific value for their viewers. Among other things, they propagate the notion of anyone's quasi-private viewing of anyone else's "real," as opposed to artistically imagined, sensory experience of nature or people. The legerdemain of such media projects such experience as if it were already occurring or simply *could* occur before other viewers. Put another way, the new visual media induce a sociobehavioristic habit of seeing double where one formerly observed not only other persons and events but also one's personal, spatiotemporal experience of them sans their technological reproducibility. As with the narrator Wilson's eponymous double in Poe's 1839 tale "William Wilson," the public now features the capacity to witness one's heretofore designated "private" actions.

In short, the private stage of self here becomes conditioned by an imaginary, internalized public capable of visualizing it. The visual media available by Poe's time help inaugurate the illusion of access by "almost anyone" to "people at an inaccessible distance," even those "long dead," as in fact became the case for Poe's biographers deploying his most well-known "Ultimate Thule" daguerreotype to get at his real "character" (Pannapacker, 18). This viewpoint somewhat complicates Richard Sennett's observation about "the fall of public man" in nineteenth-century Western urban cultures: "There grew up the notion that strangers had no right to speak to each other, that each man possessed as a public right an invisible shield, a right to be left alone. Public behavior was a matter of observation, of passive participation, of a certain kind of voyeurism" (Sennett, 27). For Sennett, this situation promotes a sociopolitical reactionary or voyeuristic mode of privacy. But the period's visual ethos ends up haunting even such voyeurism by intimating its own vulnerability to other voyeurs. That is, anyone's sense of a privileged privacy can no longer escape and in fact is predicated on the possibility of its reversible public observation: I regard strangers without their knowledge, but this only means that they could do the same with me.

It is exactly this predicament that happens to define "The Man of the Crowd" (1840). Of all Poe's tales, this one appears most explicitly to represent "his generation's shock at realizing that the urban stranger cannot be known" (Halttunen, 36). From evening until daybreak, the tale's narrator pursues an old man rushing through the crowds of London, and whom he finally associates with a book that "does not permit itself to be read" (*PT*, 388). Focusing on the old man's apparently aimless, urban meanderings, the reader initially tends to agree with this judgement, having become infected with the narrator's sense of the man's inscrutable motives and their contradictory manifestation of "solitude and sociality" (Elmer, 172).

But of course the narrator resembles a little too much the typical bourgeois voyeur. Before his pursuit, he sits in a hotel after having been "ill in health. . . . amusing myself . . . in poring over advertisements, now in observing the promiscuous company in the room and now in peering through the smoky panes into the street" (*PT,* 388). He regards others, that is, "through a glass darkly," which given his apparently secular rather than spiritual concerns constitutes a hyperbolic biblical connotation similar to the one he again later unwittingly invokes when he complains of being "wearied unto death" by the old man's interminable peregrinations (*PT,* 396). The narrator, in any case, naively thinks he can know others by categorizing them in terms of class stereotypes that "[d]escend[]" from higher to lower readable groups (*PT,* 391)—to gamblers, "Jew pedlars," beggars, prostitutes, the indigent. But he eventually comes upon a figure who fits no known type, and whose therefore "absolute idiosyncracy [*sic*]" he cannot read (*PT,* 392). This old man's urban rambles amid the crowds of people "without apparent object" finally exhaust the narrator, leading him to judge that the man possesses "'the genius of deep crime,'" someone who, in his alienated solitude, "'refuses to be alone. *He is the man of the crowd*'" (*PT,* 396; emphasis in original).

It becomes clear, however, that this "crime" is itself all too *un-*clear. Does the old man represent an impersonal, urban public realm gone amok, or does the narrator judge him criminal for his not being publicly transparent in what appears to be his purposeless and therefore mad street wanderings? Needless to say, the narrator's assessment also redounds to himself. He, too, is "the man of the crowd," and "The Man of the Crowd" thus easily lends itself to the sociocritical interpretations it has received. Far from reflecting the republican ideal of an interactive public sphere, the narrator and old man personify the alienation from public life identified with the capitalist marketplace. Despite the London setting, they together figure the "'double life' of community and privacy in America's republic," where "[t]he mutually isolating anonymity of the crowd, expressed in the exchange of gazes to which all seems equally and freely visible, conceals the privacy of self-interest" (Byer, 226, 227).

But Poe's narrator hardly represents an unequivocal figure harboring concealed notions of bourgeois self-interest. For one thing, the "crime" he imputes to the old man could just as easily signify his displaced guilt over his own obsessional voyeurism. Poe's scenario in fact underwrites this possibility, for if the old man's actions pointedly appear unusual to the narrator, *his* obsessive pursuit also does to us. Moreover, both its scenario and the tale itself hint at a familiar Poe "put-on." It remains perfectly feasible, for example, to regard the old man as a kind of agent provocateur of public ideology, his frenetic movements intended to stoke the curiosity of his conspicuous pursuer—as if he were entrapping the narrator himself into performing the role of voyeuristic *object*. And in depicting the narrator quite specifically as a reader of an unreadable text, Poe additionally positions us readers as analogous observational objects of the tale itself. Where does it all end? Hardly appearing content with this infinite publicity, Poe at best seems resigned to it, as if privacy were an entirely gutted alternative. No one, not even Poe as writer perforce constructing his tale in a mass-cultural public milieu, can escape possible public scrutiny for very long. His narrator's public malaise affects him too, preventing any imaginative response to the tale's epigraph from La Bruyère: "Ce grand malheur, de ne pouvoir être seul" (*PT*, 388).

So it at least makes sense to hold out for an ambivalent "public" Poe, whatever evidence exists to suggest that he practices certain modes of literary privacy within many of his fictional works. The old man's dashes to nowhere, the narrator's conspicuously abrupt judgment of them as criminal, ours of these Rorschach-like events—all would-be private gestures are fungibly recoverable by public regimes of knowledge. In retrospect, this massive, public configuration makes moot any hypothesis about Poe's paradoxically attempting to produce texts designed as if perpetually to release surcharged, semiotic aftereffects to their readers. The so-called private Poe, like his private William Wilson, can never quite kill his public double (here his mass readership) so that he might "être seul." From his or his imaginary reader's perspective, sooner or later the impersonal marketplace inevitably inflects and infects either his plotted, textual resurrections or his deploying them as ruses to elicit what one might otherwise construe as some private scene of writing.

For example, Poe's comedic surrogate at the beginning of *Eureka* (1848) explicitly invokes a Romantic sense of originality in his "remarkable letter, which appears to have been found corked

in a bottle" and "found . . . floating on the *Mare Tenebrarum.*"
As if endorsing its tenor, Poe emphatically quotes the letter
writer's quotation from Kepler: "*I care not whether my work be read
now or by posterity. I can afford to wait a century for readers when God
himself has waited six thousand years for an observer. I triumph. I have
stolen the golden secret of the Egyptians. I will indulge my sacred fury*"
(*PT*, 1263, 1270; emphasis in original). Occuring at *Eureka*'s beginning, this (literally) doubled insistence apparently frames the
work's ensuing cosmological disquisition as a whole. Poe here
imagines himself—not necessarily the text's actual reader—as
recognizing and thereby vindicating his canonical ("sacred") literary "triumph." Even if we second-guess his Romantic bravado
("I care not whether my work . . .") in relation to his imagined
contemporary audience, the fact remains that he banks on his
work's deferred "power of words," as he elsewhere terms it, to
justify its public literary value to which he alone is presently
privy. But this prophecy simultaneously indicates the power of
the period's impersonal economic marketplace to invade Poe's
thinking about an otherwise strictly literary matter. For if it
withholds its value from his contemporaries, would his work not
paradoxically accrue additional value for him, if only as a fantasy
of its scarce commodity status within this marketplace?

And it remains entirely plausible that this economic inflection
is no fantasy at all. Resembling his fictional use of cryptography
and even his putative detections of literary plagiarisms (the "secret writing," as it were, of other writers), Poe often emplots his
literary works, a quintessential medium of public communication, with a withheld or mystified message bound to inflate their
public interest, in the two senses of this word. The paradigm for
this practice occurs in one of his earliest tales, "MS. Found in a
Bottle" (1833), which also happens to stage a surrogate letter writer
and *his* deferred text. Here the narrator inseminates his narrative
with the idea of "some never-to-be-imparted secret" (*PT*, 198), or
the semiotic conundrum, we could say, that Poe himself wants all
present and future readers of his tales to encounter:

A feeling, for which I have no name, has taken possession of
my soul—a sensation which will admit of no analysis, to

which the lessons of by-gone time are inadequate, and for which I fear futurity itself will offer me no key. To a mind constituted like my own, the latter consideration is an evil. I shall never—I know that I shall never—be satisfied with regard to the nature of my conceptions. Yet it is not wonderful that these conceptions are indefinite, since they have their origins in sources so utterly novel. (*PT,* 195).

This last sentence could easily comprise a question: "Is it not wonderful . . . ?" suggesting that Poe's *tale,* here characterized by its own indefinite conception, would remain sealed, "[admitting] of no analysis," and not merely from a *certain* public but from *any* imaginable one. Yet if the private here consists of some "utterly novel" vision that in the tale literally possesses zero semantic value, this could mean that, far from asserting some Romantic aporia, it resists becoming a commonplace or "popular" literary commodity. The fact that the tale never stipulates its "novel" vision teases readers into ferreting it out, transforming it into a kind of Ur-commodity perpetually promising and frustrating ("never-to-be-imparted") possession by others at some future time. Here again, in other words, the Poe tale possibly plays the economic game of the scarcer the supply, the greater the demand.

But this reduction of Poe to a "confidence-man" artist, "diddling" (as he termed it in another tale) others in the public literary marketplace, suppresses an equally plausible interpretation of his private rhetorical moves in this tale and others. Such a reduction presupposes that he holds something in reserve, a secret vision he knows to be valueless but that the tale's readers will not. Yet this vision's literally empty content in "MS. Found in a Bottle" makes it mystery, that is, its putative status as a mystified if also rarefied literary commodity, itself the open mystery. Instead of equating secrecy with privacy, one might argue that Poe's tale transforms the former into a pretext for wishing for the latter.[13]

This is to say that one can additionally frame his "private" rhetorical gambits in more socially palatable terms. Indicating neither his complicity with nor his resignation to his mass-public milieu, these authorial manipulations also manifest less a wish to gain future recognition for his literary prowess than to discharge a general social anxiety endemic to the period. As noted previously, the commercial and mass-cultural environment of his time threatens even as it traffics in the American ideological shibboleth of "individualism," particularly the notion of a "coherent identity," which Poe's first-person narrators, according to Jonathan Auerbach, at once representatively desire yet in the end cannot sustain (40). How can "I" have such an identity without corroboration from others? In a tale like "The Man That Was Used Up" (1839), for instance, Poe at once exploits and feels threatened by the mass public that evacuates "every individual's particularity" by suggesting that it "is [the mass public's] precipitate, rather than the other way around" (Elmer, 56).

In short, this social contradiction could just as easily account for and effectively recast the Poe text's "private" intimations—along with their apparent figurations of his contingent self-interest, canonically ambitious *or* commercially exploitative—into signs of a culturally representative struggle. Otherwise rife with dead-end private jokes and metareferential themes, Poe's works deploy fugitive figures or tropes that instead disclose his grappling with the earlier sketched, American public-private issue, which would find its legal and liberal-ideological expression fifty or so years later in Samuel Warren and Louis Brandeis's article "The Right to Privacy" in the *Harvard Law Review* of 1890. Take, for instance, the recurring, claustrophobic interior settings that mark many of his tales: the room in "Ligeia," the house in "The Fall of the House of Usher," the abbey in "The Masque of the Red Death." Critics tend to interpret such settings as metaphors of Poe's psychobiographical obsessions, his mise-en-scène of Romantic-epistemological solipsism, or even, if one accepts Robert Byer's argument that the crowd in "The Man of the Crowd" reflects "the phantasmagoric interior of the [socially alienated] private citizen" (231), of ideological fault lines in mid-nineteenth-century American society.

But whatever else they indicate, Poe's interior settings also trace the emergence of the modern American private sphere as a distinct, self-conscious, and beleaguered category of social experience. In this context, his well-known bête noire, the "mob," commonly understood to reflect his antidemocratic, anti-Northern, as well as antiabolitionist biases, refers in overdetermined fashion to the pressures of mass public opinion, particularly noticeable in his time, concocted by business, political, and media machinery.[14] Self-identity always requires confirmation from one or another public, familial or social; but the more abstract or imaginary this public, the more privacy serves as a defense against self-identity's coterminous attenuation, if only to make room, like Roderick Usher's project (which this sort of public perforce judges "mad"), for at least being able to fantasize such confirmation.

Framed this way, Poe's metafictional moves begin to make *social* sense. For example, his insulated interior settings metaphorically double his formalist views of literary composition, which for some critics also masks or represses his antidemocratic politics. Poe's tightly designed plots and narrative conundrums purport wholly to confine readers within his tales for the comparatively short period of time it takes to apprehend their "unity of impression." In one sense, of course, this poetics makes a virtue out of his necessities as a journalist subject to temporal and economic constraints. But in another sense, it works to promote the reader's literary experience of privacy. In contrast to the novel, the length of which allows "[w]orldly interests" to interrupt one's act of reading and thus to "modify, annul, or counteract . . . the impression of the book," the "brief tale" effectively excludes such public distractions: "the author is enabled to carry out the fulness of his intention, be it what it may. During the hour of perusal the soul of the reader is at the writer's control. There are no external or extrinsic influences" (Hawthorne Review, 1842; *ER*, 572). Moreover, in producing short works, Poe, it could be said, himself exercises a poetics of privacy, especially when glossed against his period's attraction to "the most gigantic effects" (Johnson, 155) produced by public-theatrical panoramas and the like.

Indeed, Poe's well-known antipathetic view toward allegory possibly includes a similar "private" effect. Allegory etymologically refers to discourse veiled from (*allos*: other to) that spoken in the marketplace or before a public assembly (agora), but pre-

sumably accessible to a private ot initiated group of interlocu-
tors. A common literary practice by Poe's time, however, allegory could be seen as appealing to educated readers, the group
effect of which constitutes an amorphous, intellectual public.
Thus, in resisting their translation into conventionally accessible,
allegorical codifications, Poe's tales enact a socioliterary mode of
privacy in line with allegory's original meaning.[15] This enact-
ment arguably occurs even in "The Man of the Crowd." which as
we have seen lends itself to the thematization of mid-nineteenth-
century American ties to an inescapable, all-pervasive public
world. As I have noted, this tale precipitates a virtually infinite series of readings that tend to confirm this pervasiveness: the narrator judges the old man, we judge the narrator, the tale judges
us in judging, and so on—in short, no one escapes the public
gaze.

This allegorical concatenation, however, thrives on precipi-
tous judgments that in each instance overlook the tale's ongoing
resistance to its reader's ready-to-hand codes of public understanding. From its opening lines "The Man of the Crowd" frames
itself as a text that "does not permit itself to be read." Also per-
sonifying the tale's impulse (who else speaks?), the narrator's
frantic pursuit of the old man in fact manifests his unconscious
wish not to negate or judge but precisely *to find* a stranger or
someone who embodies "absolute idiosyncracy," which given his
virtually total public orientation constitutes a wish for absolute
privacy. The narrator's illness here consists of his having repressed his own private spirit, or his having surrendered it to
public categorizations and characterizations. From this perspective, the old man, to whom the narrator and tale arbitrarily (i.e.,
wishfully) impute a "'wild . . . history'" (*PT*, 392), represents a
figure of redemption, which thus accounts for the narrator's
aforementioned biblical locutions. But the narrator, the neuroti-
cally maimed all-public man, can acknowledge the embodiment
of his desired redemption (or his wish) only in demonic terms
(anxiety). His narrative therefore ends without resolution and intimates spiritual despair: "I grew wearied unto death" (*PT*, 396)

If nothing else, "The Man of the Crowd" gestures toward a
privacy that would elude the tale's simultaneously staged and al-

ways imminent co-option (e.g., in the form of the narrator's socially definable voyeurism) by the public's permeating gaze. Unlike Emerson in his essay "Self-Reliance," who believes that one can willfully assert "solitude . . . in the midst of the crowd" or in *fact* throw off with "eclat" conformity to public regimens (263, 261) Poe opts for momentary, literary-guerilla-like inscriptions of privacy that may or may not reach his tale's readers. From public lights, the tale inscribes what even for him will eventuate in nothing more than the sheer fantasy of privacy. And like fantasies in general, this one exists indeterminately and effervescently, or only in the fictional moment of withdrawing from the "real" (as it were, a composite social fantasy), the recurring force of which neither he nor anyone else can ultimately deny.

But at least this "private" fantasy exists, and all the more so for its appearing in a literary tale, which for Poe, given his well-known Keatsian credo of beauty as truth, constitutes the primary medium for expressing in public the truth-eschewing and therefore paradoxical truth of the wish. For this reason, he can express this wish for privacy only in the one mode of allegory he finds tolerable: where "the suggested meaning runs through the obvious one in a *very* profound under-current . . . so as never to show itself unless *called* to the surface, [and] there only, for the proper uses of fictitious narrative, is it available at all" (Hawthorne Review, 1847; ER, 582–83; emphasis in original). This is why he never provides reasons for the narrator's abruptly declared "criminal" judgment of the old man. For to make it self-evidently comprehensible to readers would negate its "*very* profound" or reserved significance, in other words its signifying nothing more than the aura of privacy per se.

To be sure, one can always persist in trying to determine this private "undercurrent," but according to Poe's stricture only by relating it to the "proper" confines of the "fictitious narrative." Here what first resembles a principle again testifying to his otherwise socially repressive, aesthetic formalism accrues the additional, sociosymbolic import of resisting encroachments on privacy posed by a conspicuously and increasingly pervasive American public realm. And it does so more tellingly than do Poe's overt critical reactions to this public in the various guises of the "mob," the "magazine prison-house" (the publishing industry's cohabitation with a growing mass culture), or literary-political cliques. These reactions, after all, could just as easily suggest his effort to reform, or else his frustrated desires to become part of, his public environment, rather than a more exemplary, private struggle to defend a measure of social privacy. In the end, however, his ever-elusive, fictional inscriptions of an American-inflected desire for privacy effectively neutralize the force, if not the existence, of such "public" motivations.

NOTES

1. I wish to thank J. Gerald Kennedy for his editorial insights and encouragement in bringing the present chapter to term. I also wish to thank Milette Shamir for her knowledgeable advice in helping sharpen my overall argument and sketch of the period's privacy issue.

2. Cf. Tocqueville's remarks about American tastes for sensationalist literary works in *Democracy in America*, 2:62. Also cf. Elmer, *Reading at the Social Limit*, 93–125.

3. See, for example, Poe's 1842 review of Griswold's anthology of American poets in *Essays*, 553. For discussions of Poe's predicament as a magazinist and an embattled litterateur, see Charvat, "Poe: Journalism and the Theory of Poetry"; Allen, *Poe and the British Magazine Tradition*; Jacobs, *Poe: Journalist and Critic*; and Moss, *Poe's Literary Battles*.

4. Regarding Poe's use of puns, I note some of them in my essay "Poe's Secret Autobiography." These range from the literally obvious ("Edgartown" in *The Narrative of Arthur Gordon Pym*, for instance) to the more trompe l'oeil variety such as the "just kidding" ending of "The Gold-Bug."

5. See Wood, *The Radicalism of the American Revolution*, 83.

6. Flaherty, in *Privacy in Colonial New England*, argues that while one aspect of early colonial Puritanism promoted privacy by its emphasis on private conscience, the Puritan community's "pervasive moralism" enforced "the concept of watchfulness, the encouragement of mutual surveillance, and the suppression of self to community goals" (15).

7. Cf. Shamir, "Hawthorne's Romance and the Right to Privacy," 754, where she notes how the "'penumbra' [of privacy rights in the Bill of Rights] defines the contours of a mental zone of privacy, in the First Amendment's freedom of thought and conscience and in the Fifth Amendment's self-incrimination clause. . . . But it defines a broader zone as well, one that encompasses the domestic sphere, in the Third Amendment's prohibition against the quartering of soldiers without the consent of the owner, and in the Fourth Amendment's prohibition of unreasonable searches and seizures."

8. Karen Halttunen describes the midcentury American middle-class "cult of sincerity" in *Confidence Men and Painted Women*, 51 and passim.

9. One can of course use a socioeconomic framework to discuss the mid-nineteenth-century American privacy issue. Cf. Gilmore, for example, in *American Romanticism and the Marketplace*, esp. 13.

10. With respect to the sectored aspect of American cities, cf. Halttunen, *Confidence Men and Painted Women*, 39.

11. Related to Tocqueville's observation, Janna Malamud Smith (*Private Matters*, 201–2) cites an 1836 newspaper article maintaining that in the past, American "public acts and measures were the only subjects of [political] discussion, and rigid examination of private life was deemed illiberal. . . . Now, the current and sounder doctrine is that private vice and public virtue are inconsistent."

12. Regarding the publicly threatened nature of private correspondence, cf. John Quincy Adams's comments during the 1828 presidential campaign: "I write few private letters. . . . I can never be sure of writing a line that will not someday be published by friend or foe." Quoted in Johnson, *The Birth of the Modern*, 932.

13. Among others, Janna Malamud Smith makes this general distinction between secrecy and privacy; see *Private Matters*, 96.

14. Cf. Ryan, "Gender and Public Access," 267: "The steady expansion of the franchise and rapid growth of urban population had significantly enlarged and diversified the American citizenry by the second quarter of the nineteenth century. This process agitated everyday public life with particular force in the 1830s. . . . By the 1840s the dailies labeled densely packed columns of newsprint with the words 'Public Meetings.'"

15. Poe doubtless had some acquaintance with ancient Greek. See Silverman, *Edgar A. Poe: Mournful and Never-Ending Remembrance*,

23, 29–30. Poe typically expresses his distaste for allegory in his 1841 review of Edward Lytton Bulwer's *Night and Morning*: "Pure allegory is at all times an abomination—a remnant of antique barbarism— appealing only to our faculties of comparison, without even a remote interest for our reason, or for our fancy" (*ER*, 159).

WORKS CITED

Allen, Michael. *Poe and the British Magazine Tradition*. New York: Oxford University Press, 1969.

Auerbach, Jonathan. *The Romance of Failure: First-Person Fictions of Poe, Hawthorne, and James*. New York: Oxford University Press, 1989.

Beniger, James R. *The Control Revolution: Technological and Economic Origins of the Information Society*. Cambridge, Mass.: Harvard University Press, 1986.

Brown, Richard D. *Knowledge Is Power: The Diffusion of Information in Early America, 1700–1865*. New York: Oxford University Press, 1989.

Byer, Robert H. "Mysteries of the City: A Reading of Poe's 'The Man of the Crowd.'" In *Ideology and Classic American Literature*, ed. Sacvan Bercovitch and Myra Jehlen, 221–46. New York: Cambridge University Press, 1986.

Castle, Terry. "Phantasmagoria: Spectral Technology and the Metaphorics of Modern Reverie." *Critical Inquiry* 15, no. 1 (1988): 26–61.

Charvat, William. "Poe: Journalism and the Theory of Poetry." In *The Profession of Authorship in America, 1800–1870: The Papers of William Charvat*, ed. Matthew J. Bruccoli, 84–99. Columbus: Ohio State University Press, 1968.

Elmer, Jonathan. *Reading at the Social Limit: Affect, Mass Culture, and Edgar Allan Poe*. Stanford, Calif.: Stanford University Press, 1995.

Emerson, Ralph Waldo. *Emerson: Essays and Lectures*. Ed. Joel Porte. New York: Library of America, 1983.

Flaherty, David H. *Privacy in Colonial New England*. Charlottesville: University Press of Virginia, 1972.

Gilmore, Michael T. *American Romanticism and the Marketplace*. Chicago: University of Chicago Press, 1985.

Halttunen, Karen. *Confidence Men and Painted Women: A Study of*

Middle-Class Culture in America, 1830–1870. New Haven, Conn.: Yale University Press, 1982.

Hixson, Richard F. *Privacy in a Public Society: Human Rights in Conflict*. New York: Oxford University Press, 1987.

Jacobs, Robert. *Poe: Journalist and Critic*. Baton Rouge: Louisiana State University Press, 1969.

Johnson, Paul. *The Birth of the Modern: World Society 1815–1830*. New York: HarperCollins, 1991.

Larkin, Jack. *The Reshaping of Everyday Life, 1790–1840*. New York: Harper and Row, 1988.

Moss, Sidney P. *Poe's Literary Battles: The Critic in the Context of His Literary Milieu*. Durham, N.C.: Duke University Press, 1963.

Novak, William J. *The People's Welfare: Law and Regulation in Nineteenth-Century America*. Chapel Hill: University of North Carolina Press, 1996.

Pannapacker, William A. "A Question of 'Character': Visual Images and the Nineteenth-Century Construction of Edgar Allan Poe." *Harvard Library Bulletin* 7 (fall 1996): 9–24.

Poe, Edgar Allan. "The Daguerreotype." In *Classic Essays in Photography*, ed. Alan Trachtenberg, 37–38. New Haven, Conn.: Yale University Press, 1980.

Renza, Louis A. "Poe's Secret Autobiography." In *The American Renaissance Reconsidered: Selected Papers from the English Institute, 1982–83*, ed. Walter Benn Michaels and Donald E. Pease, 58–89. Baltimore: Johns Hopkins University Press, 1985.

Rosenheim, Shawn. *The Cryptographic Imagination: Secret Writing from Edgar Poe to the Internet*. Baltimore: Johns Hopkins University Press, 1997.

Ryan, Mary P. "Gender and Public Access: Women's Politics in Nineteenth-Century America." In *Habermas and the Public Sphere*, ed. Craig Calhoun, 259–88. Cambridge, Mass.: MIT Press, 1992.

Schudson, Michael. "Was There Ever a Public Sphere? If So, When? Reflections on the American Case." In *Habermas and the Public Sphere*, ed. Craig Calhoun, 143–63. Cambridge, Mass.: MIT Press, 1992.

Sennett, Richard. *The Fall of Public Man*. 1974. Reprint, New York: Norton, 1992.

Shamir, Milette. "Hawthorne's Romance and the Right to Privacy." *American Quarterly* 49 (1997): 746–79.

Silverman, Kenneth. *Edgar A. Poe: Mournful and Never-ending Remembrance*. New York: HarperCollins, 1991.

Smith. Janna Malamud. *Private Matters: In Defense of the Personal Life*. Reading, Mass.: Addison-Wesley, 1997.

Tocqueville, Alexis, de. *Democracy in America*. Rev. ed. 2 vols. Trans. Henry Reeve. Ed. Phillips Bradley. New York: Vintage, 1945.

Wood, Gordon S. *The Radicalism of the American Revolution*. New York: Knopf, 1992.

ILLUSTRATED
CHRONOLOGY

Poe's Life	Historical Events
1809: Born in Boston, January 19, to Elizabeth and David Poe, itinerant actors.	**1809:** Madison inaugurated president; first steam-powered sea voyage, New York to Philadelphia.
1811: Father disappears; mother dies of consumption in Richmond; becomes ward of John and Frances Allan.	**1812:** Louisiana admitted to Union; United States declares war on Great Britain.
1815–1820: Crosses Atlantic with Allans; visits Scotland; lives in London; attends Rev. Bransby's school in Stoke Newington.	**1814:** British burn Washington, attack, retreat from Baltimore; Key composes "Star-Spangled Banner"; Peace of Ghent signed; France exiles Napoleon I.
1820: Returns to United States; enters Richmond Academy.	**1817:** Monroe becomes president; Mississippi steamboat travel opens; Erie Canal project begins.
1822: Composes early poems; future wife Virginia Eliza Clemm born in Baltimore.	**1819:** Spain cedes Florida to United States; *McCulloch v. Maryland* clarifies federal authority over banking.
	1820: Missouri Compromise on extension of slavery; Inquisition suppressed in Spain.
	1822: Vesey slave revolt thwarted in South Carolina; Lowell textile mills founded in Massachusetts.
	1823: Monroe Doctrine enunciated; Nicholas Biddle heads Bank of United States; Cooper publishes *The Pioneers*.

"The Mother's Grave," by Kellogs and Thayer, 1846 (engraving). From editor's collection.

1823: Meets Jane Stith Stanard, mother of friend.

1824: Mourns death of Mrs. Stanard; serves in honor guard for French hero, General Lafayette.

1825: John Allen inherits fortune on death of uncle William Galt and purchases mansion; Poe meets Sarah Elmira Royster; becomes engaged.

1826: Attends University of Virginia; excels in classical and modern languages; incurs gambling debts.

1824: Congress endorses Henry Clay's "American System" of internal improvements; John Quincy Adams elected sixth president; Lydia Maria Child publishes *Hobomok*.

1825: Congress formulates Indian removal policy; Adams implements civil service system; Erie Canal completed; *Don Giovanni* performed in New York.

1826: Simon Bolívar calls Panama Congress; John Adams, Thomas Jefferson die on July 4, fiftieth anniversary of Declaration of Independence.

"University of Virginia, Charlottesville," The Lady's Book (*July 1835*).

"A Shanty on Lake Chaudiere," Graham's Magazine, *April 1845.*

1827: Poe withdraws from university, leaves Richmond; sails to Boston, publishes *Tamerlane and Other Poems*; joins U.S. Army; arrives at Fort Moultrie, South Carolina, after near shipwreck en route.

1828: Possibly composes "Al Aaraaf" at Fort Moultrie; unit reassigned to Fortress Monroe, Virginia; Poe seeks release from duty.

1829: Frances Allan dies February 28; Poe hires military replacement, leaves army service; moves to Baltimore, publishes *Al Aaraaf, Tamerlane, and Minor Poems*.

1827: Railroads built in Massachusetts and Pennsylvania; great Irish and German migrations to United States begin; John J. Audubon introduces *Birds of America* series; Northern states demand protective tariff.

1828: "Tariff of Abominations" marks height of antebellum protectionism; John Calhoun leads Southern protest; Andrew Jackson elected seventh president.

1829: Jackson introduces "spoils system," forms "Kitchen Cabinet"; Workingman's party organized; anti-Catholic agitation led by Rev. Lyman Beecher and Samuel F. B. Morse.

1830: Receives appointment to West Point; Allan marries Louisa Patterson in October; Poe excels in French and mathematics; neglects required duties.

1830: Beginnings of Underground Railroad; Indian removal policy ratified and implemented; King Louis Philippe begins French "bourgeois monarchy."

1831: Undergoes court-martial, dismissed from West Point; in New York publishes *Poems*; moves to Baltimore, lives with grandmother Elizabeth Cairnes Poe, aunt Maria Clemm, cousin Virginia, and brother Henry; enters literary contest, writing satirical tales; Henry dies August 1.

1831: William Lloyd Garrison founds the *Liberator,* launches abolitionist movement; McCormick reaper invented; Jackson reorganizes cabinet; Nat Turner tried, executed after bloody Virginia slave revolt; Anti-Masons organize party, nominate William Wirt for president; national hymn "America" first performed.

1832: Loses literary contest; Philadelphia *Saturday Courier* publishes "Metzengerstein" and four subsequent tales; Poe seeks work in Baltimore; John Allan revises will, excludes Poe.

1832: Sac and Fox Indians resist removal, U.S. Army fights Black Hawk War; Tariff of 1832 sparks Nullification Controversy; Jackson vetoes recharter of national bank, wins reelection by landslide.

1833: Lives with aunt and cousin; continues writing mostly satirical "Folio Club" tales; wins Baltimore *Saturday Visiter* literary contest with "MS Found in a Bottle"; meets novelist John Pendleton Kennedy.

1833: Jackson removes federal deposits from Bank of United States; Lewis Tappan founds American Antislavery Society; penny newspapers appear; Oberlin becomes first coeducational college in United States.

1834: Visits ailing John Allan in Richmond; Allan dies March 27; Poe enlists Kennedy's help in finding publisher for "Folio Club" tales; endures poverty.

1834: Congress censures Jackson for Treasury meddling; anti-Jackson forces unite to form Whig Party; National Trades Union holds first convention.

"John Pendleton Kennedy," The Prose
Writers of America, *ed. Rufus W.
Griswold (London, 1847).*

1835: Kennedy urges Poe to contact
Thomas W. White, publisher of
Southern Literary Messenger; Poe
contributes reviews, tales; death of
Elizabeth Cairnes Poe; Poe
becomes White's assistant; suffers
suicidal crisis; perhaps weds
Virginia in private rites; Virginia,
Mrs. Clemm join Poe in
Richmond.

1836: Achieves fame as
unacknowledged editor of
Messenger, publishing his own
essays, reviews, and reprinted tales;
marries Virginia in public
ceremony; abandons "Folio Club"
project after rejection by Harper
and Brothers; begins novel
demanded by publisher;
occasionally indisposed by drinking.

1835: Jackson escapes assassination
attempt; Samuel Colt patents
revolver; second Seminole war
begins; radical Democrats
("Loco-Focos") form Equal Rights
Party, reject Jackson's bank policy;
James Gordon Bennett founds *New
York Morning Herald,* launches crime
reporting.

1836: Republic of Texas established,
defended at Alamo and San Jacinto;
Bank of United States federal
charter expires, Jackson issues
Specie Circular; Thomas Cole
paints *The Course of Empire;*
Congress adopts "gag resolution,"
suppresses abolition issue; Van
Buren elected president; Emerson
publishes *Nature.*

1837: Panic of 1837 triggers
depression; John Deere invents steel
plow; death of King William IV,
coronation of Queen Victoria in
England; Michigan joins Union;
John L. O'Sullivan launches
Democratic Review; W. Burton
founds *Gentleman's Magazine.*

1838: Border incidents stir
anti-British agitation; Aroostook
controversy in Maine; Emerson
addresses Harvard Divinity School;
Wilkes expedition departs for South
Seas; Frederick Douglass escapes
slavery, travels to New York;
Audubon completes *Birds of
America* series.

"Mrs. Meriwether Administering Bitters," by J. W. Orr, illustration for J. P. Kennedy, Swallow Barn: or A Sojourn in the Old Dominion *(1835; reprint, New York: G. P. Putnam, 1854).*

1837: White dismisses Poe January 3; *Messenger* features two installments of "The Narrative of Arthur Gordon Pym"; Poe and family move to New York; completes novel, secures contract with Harper and Brothers, publication postponed.

1838: Moves to Philadelphia with Virginia and Mrs. Clemm, endures hardship and poverty; publishes *The Narrative of Arthur Gordon Pym*; writes "Ligeia"; seeks literary connections in Philadelphia and Baltimore; allows Thomas Wyatt to identify him as author of *The Conchologist's First Book.*

1839: Becomes coeditor of *Burton's Gentleman's Magazine*; writes "The Fall of the House of Usher" and "William Wilson"; publishes first volume of stories, *Tales of the Grotesque and Arabesque*; begins cryptography series for *Alexander's Weekly Messenger.*

"Washington Irving," The Prose Writers of America, *ed. Rufus W. Griswold (London, 1847).*

1839: Antislavery Liberty Party organizes; Caroline Kirkland publishes *A New Home, Who'll Follow?*; slave mutiny aboard Spanish ship *Amistad*; Charles Goodyear discovers rubber vulcanization process; Transcendentalists found *Dial*, edited by Margaret Fuller; Theodore Weld publishes *Slavery As It Is.*

1840: Congress passes Independent Treasury Act, establishing federal subtreasuries; end of Rocky Mountain fur trade; A. C. Ross writes "Tippecanoe and Tyler, Too," Whig campaign song; William Henry Harrison defeats Van Buren, elected ninth president; Cooper publishes *The Pathfinder.*

1841: Harrison dies one month after inauguration, John Tyler assumes presidency; Horace Greeley founds *New York Tribune*; Transcendentalists establish Brook Farm commune; Supreme Court hears *Amistad* case; Whig Congress repeals Independent Treasury Act; Tyler's cabinet (excepting Daniel Webster) resigns; *Creole* slave mutiny.

1842: P. T. Barnum opens American Museum; anaesthesia introduced; "great migration" to Oregon begins; Webster-Ashburton Treaty ends Maine land dispute; Northern states pass "personal liberty" laws.

"The New Exchange, Philadelphia," Atkinson's Casket, *February 1833.*

1840: Publishes six installments of travel hoax "The Journal of Julius Rodman"; accuses Longfellow of plagiarism; prepares prospectus for *Penn Magazine*; dismissed as editor by Burton; contributes "The Man of the Crowd" to first issue of *Graham's Magazine*; postpones *Penn* due to ill health.

1841: Bank panic further delays *Penn*; Poe takes editorial job ot *Graham's*; contributes reviews, tales, including "The Murders in the Rue Morgue"; seeks government appointment; solicits contributions from leading writers for new magazine to be coedited with Graham; meets Rufus Griswold; launches new "Autography" series.

American iconography, Burton's Gentleman's Magazine, *January–July 1839.*

"Hunting Buffaloe," Graham's Magazine, *September 1844.*

"The Island of the Fay," Graham's Magazine, *June 1841 (plate illustration for* Poe's tale).

"*Olden Times,*" Graham's Magazine, *July 1849.*

1842: Virginia suffers pulmonary hemorrhage; Poe resorts to drink; interviews Charles Dickens; resigns from *Graham's*; renews efforts to obtain government post; seeks editorial work in New York.

"*The Young Poetess,*" Graham's Magazine, *July 1844.*

1843: Charles Thurber invents typewriter; "Nativists" oppose political rights for Catholics, foreigners; minstrel show popularized; T. A. Beckett composes "Columbia, the Gem of the Ocean"; Great Comet appears; U.S. depression reaches lowest point.

1844: Oregon boundary dispute, annexation of Texas become campaign issues; James K. Polk defeats Clay for presidency; George Lippard publishes satire later titled *The Quaker City*; U.S. economic recovery begins; Morse invents telegraph.

1845: Polk inaugurated eleventh president; Texas annexed, admitted to statehood; O'Sullivan coins phrase "Manifest Destiny"; Mexico prepares to resist Texas annexation; George Colton founds Whig *American Review*; Douglass publishes *Narrative of the Life of Frederick Douglass*; United States attempts to buy California from Mexico.

1846: United States and Britain establish Oregon border at forty-ninth parallel; Mexican army crosses Rio Grande, seeks to recapture disputed territory; Congress declares war on Mexico; rotary press invented; Smithsonian Institution established; Neptune discovered; *Scientific American* founded; Melville publishes *Typee*.

1843: Revives plans for magazine, renamed the *Stylus*; visits Washington in search of government position, drinks excessively; wins $100 prize for "The Gold-Bug"; postpones *Stylus*; becomes target of temperance satire; lectures on American poetry.

1844: Moves with family to New York; creates sensation with "The Balloon Hoax"; as roving correspondent, composes "Doings of Gotham" series; joins staff of *Evening Mirror*; publishes "The Purloined Letter."

1847: John C. Frémont conquers California, Stephen Kearny takes New Mexico, Zachary Taylor captures Monterrey; Wilmot Proviso, barring slavery from former Mexican territories, defeated by Calhoun forces; Maria Mitchell discovers comet; Havana Opera Company visits United States.

"Pic-nic on the Wissahickon," Graham's Magazine, *October 1844.*

"*Park Row, New York, with a View of the Park Theatre,*" The Lady's Book, *August 1835.*

1845: Achieves fame with "The Raven"; lectures on poetry, becomes habitué of literary salons; develops flirtation with Mrs. Osgood; becomes coeditor of *Broadway Journal*, renews attacks on Longfellow; assumes ownership of *Broadway Journal*; publishes new edition of *Tales* and volume of poetry; offends Boston Athenaeum audience with poetry reading.

"*Our Contributors: Edgar A. Poe,*" Graham's Magazine, *February 1845.*

"Latest Fashions," Graham's Lady's and Gentleman's Magazine, *July 1845.*

1846: Suspends publication of *Broadway Journal*; brawls with Thomas Dunn English; publishes "The Literati of New York City" sketches in *Godey's Lady's Book*; moves to Fordham cottage; publishes "The Cask of Amontillado"; falls desperately ill as Virginia's health declines.

1847: Virginia dies of tuberculosis January 30; Poe remains bedridden; attracts more satires, parodies; wins libel lawsuit, $225 damages from *Evening Mirror*; visits Washington and Philadelphia; composes poem "Ulalume."

"Caroline M. Kirkland," The Female Prose Writers of America, *ed. John Hart (Philadelphia, 1852).*

Virginia Clemm Poe, 1847 (watercolor on paper). Courtesy of the Harry Ransom Humanities Research Center, The University of Texas at Austin.

1848: Revives *Stylus* project; presents cosmological lecture, publishes *Eureka*; meets Annie Richmond in Lowell, Massachusetts; visits Richmond, Virginia; pursues courtship of Sarah Helen Whitman, proposes marriage; ingests overdose of laudanum; lectures in Providence on "The Poetic Principle," resumes drinking; Mrs. Whitman breaks off wedding plans; Poe returns to New York.

1848: Upheaval in Europe, revolutions in France, Germany, Italy; discovery of gold in California; Treaty of Guadalupe Hidalgo ends Mexican War; Stephen Foster writes "Oh! Susannah"; Seneca Falls Convention launches crusade for women's rights; Free-Soil Party organizes, nominates Van Buren for president; Mexican War hero Gen. Zachary Taylor (Whig) elected president.

(Left) *The funeral of a young woman,*
Sartain's Magazine, *August 1850*
(illustration for "Rosamund").

(Below) *The "Whitman" daguerreo-*
type, 1848, by Samuel W. Harshorn.
Courtesy of the Brown University
Library.

The "Stella" daguerreotype, probably 1849. Courtesy of the Ingram Poe Collection (no. 38-135), Special Collections Department, University of Virginia Library.

Note from E. A. Poe to A. G. Chester, April 1, 1849, with copy of "For Annie." Courtesy, the Lilly Library, Indiana University, Bloomington, Indiana.

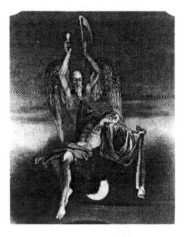

"Our Contributors: Rufus W. Griswold," Graham's Magazine, *June 1845.*

"The Death of the Year," Graham's Magazine, *November 1849.*

1849: Professes love for Annie Richmond, composes "For Annie"; contributes "Hop-Frog" to *Flag of Our Union*; receives proposal to publish the *Stylus* in Oquawka, Illinois; drinks excessively in Philadelphia, suffers hallucinations; sells poems "The Bells" and "Annabel Lee" to John Sartain; proposes to widow Sarah Elmira Royster Shelton in Richmond; lectures on poetry in Richmond and Norfolk; joins temperance group; receives acceptance from Mrs. Shelton, departs for New York; drinks heavily in Baltimore, lapses into coma; dies October 7.

1849: Gold rush begins; Asher Durand paints *Kindred Spirits*; Southerners in Congress oppose law prohibiting slave trade in District of Columbia; Whig Party splits along sectional lines; Californians ratify state constitution, prohibit slavery; Thoreau publishes *A Week on the Concord and Merrimack Rivers*; U.S. economy enters period of robust expansion; Walter Hunt invents the safety pin; Edwin Booth makes stage debut; Hawthorne loses job at Salem Custom House, writes *The Scarlet Letter*.

Bibliographical Essay

Major Editions and Landmarks of Poe Scholarship

Scott Peeples

Editions

Any discussion of book publications of Poe's work ought to begin with the observation that Poe really was not a writer of books; he complained that he was trapped in a "magazine prison-house," a common predicament of American writers who, especially after the Panic of 1837, faced a tight publishing market. Virtually everything Poe wrote for publication—with the notable exceptions of his early poems, most of *The Narrative of Arthur Gordon Pym*, and *Eureka: A Prose Poem*—was written for periodicals, ranging from weekly Baltimore papers to *Godey's Lady's Book*, the most widely circulated magazine of his time. And yet Poe's dream of controlling the content and design of his own magazine, his desperate attempt to keep the sinking *Broadway Journal* afloat, and his theory that brevity was an essential virtue in both poetry and fiction suggest his determination to make a respectable career for himself out of magazine writing.

Despite this half-voluntary commitment to the magazine prison house, Poe continually sought book publication and saw ten books into print under his name, including a textbook on seashells (that he did not write) and a pamphlet edition of two stories. Poe's first three books—*Tamerlane and Other Poems* (1827),

Al Aaraaf, Tamerlane, and Minor Poems (1829), and *Poems by Edgar A. Poe . . . .Second Edition* (1831)—sold poorly enough to convince the young poet to turn to the periodical market and the genre of short fiction. (Today copies of the 1827 *Tamerlane* are so rare that they command small fortunes at auction.) Harper and Brothers published Poe's only novel, *The Narrative of Arthur Gordon Pym*, in 1838. The following year Poe rented his name for $50 to scientist Thomas Wyatt for a reissue of Wyatt's text on conchology— Wyatt's publishers owned copyright, so Wyatt could not legally produce an abridged version, *The Conchologist's First Book* (1839), under his own name. In 1839 Poe convinced Lea and Blanchard of Philadelphia to publish his first collection of fiction, *Tales of the Grotesque and Arabesque*. Like all of Poe's books up to this point, it was a commercial failure: Lea and Blanchard claimed two years later that they had not recovered the costs of producing it. Poe's next attempt to publish his tales in a medium less ephemeral than magazines fared even worse: a projected series titled *The Prose Romances of Edgar A. Poe* (1843) generated only one issue, consisting of the oddly paired "The Murders in the Rue Morgue" and "The Man That Was Used Up." In 1845, riding the popularity of "The Raven," Poe brought out an updated collection of fiction titled simply *Tales,* and a few months later *The Raven and Other Poems*. Despite the popularity of "The Raven," *Tales* seems to have sold better—fifteen hundred copies in five months, according to Poe (although Poe's royalty earned him only about $120). Appropriately, his last publication during his lifetime was *Eureka* (1848), about which he wrote to Maria Clemm: "I have no desire to live since I have done 'Eureka.' I could accomplish nothing more."

This rather modest output has been collected, selected, edited, and repackaged hundreds of times since Poe's death. The first posthumous edition, *The Works of the Late Edgar Allan Poe* (1850–56), contains the infamous preface by its editor, Poe's literary executor Rufus Wilmot Griswold, which became a focus for nearly all published commentary on Poe for the rest of the nineteenth century. The year Griswold completed his edition of Poe, Charles Baudelaire published his first collection of French translations, *Histoires Extraordinaires*. This collection and the four that followed it (*Nouvelles Histoires Extraordinaires, Aventures d'Arthur Gordon Pym, Eureka,* and *Histoires Grotesques et Sérieuses*) made Poe more respected in France than in the United States, beginning a legacy of French appreciation of Poe analyzed by Patrick F. Quinn in *The French Face of Edgar Poe* (1957). Indeed, T. S. Eliot famously praised Baudelaire for "transform[ing] what is often slipshod . . . English into admirable French" (336).

James A. Harrison edited the first true scholarly edition of Poe, the seventeen-volume "Virginia Edition" of 1902–1903, *The Complete Works of Edgar Allan Poe.* Almost a century later, Poe scholars still find it valuable, despite a few false attributions. The Virginia Edition prevailed among scholars until Thomas Ollive Mabbott edited Poe's poetry and most of his short fiction in *The Collected Works of Edgar Allan Poe* (1969–78). Mabbott's prefaces to individual works as well as his erudite footnotes and listing of textual variants help make sense of Poe's often confusing early satires and shed much light on less context-bound tales as well. Unfortunately, although most college libraries purchased these books when they were new, the second and third volumes are long out of print, and so replacement and personal copies are hard to come by. Burton R. Pollin has taken on the task of completing Mabbott's series, thus far having edited *Pym* and the other "Imaginary Voyages" (in one volume) as well as "The Brevities," the *Broadway Journal* nonfiction, and *Southern Literary Messenger* writings as *The Collected Writings of Edgar Allan Poe* (1981–97). Poe scholars consider either Harrison or the recent Library of America volumes the standard texts for *Eureka* and the essays and reviews not yet edited by Pollin. The Library of America edition (1984) is reliable but light on notes and commentary. It has other virtues, though: attractive, easy-to-read (though small) typefaces and reasonable prices. The Library of America also offers a one-volume paperback edition of the fiction and poetry, with a few of Poe's major critical essays, for college use—the best single-volume Poe on the market (1996). Two other noteworthy paperback editions: Stuart Levine and Susan Levine's *The Short Fiction of Edgar Allan Poe: An Annotated Edition* (1976), for its insightful annotations; and the unfortunately out-of-print *Poe: Complete Poems*

(1959), for Richard Wilbur's groundbreaking introduction and notes. Facsimile editions of Poe's earliest tales (*Edgar Allan Poe and the Philadelphia Saturday Courier*, ed. John Grier Varner, 1933) and *Eureka* (ed. Richard P. Benton, 1974) have also been published but are out of print and not widely available. Poe's letters are available in a fine scholarly edition by John Ward Ostrom, *The Letters of Edgar Allan Poe* (1966), though as one would expect there have been quite a few discoveries since the time this edition was published.

BIOGRAPHY

Poe biography has been clouded and complicated by, among other obstacles, the fact that there is little evidence of Poe's whereabouts and activities during some crucial periods (the early 1830s, spent mostly in Baltimore, a period from early 1837 to early 1838 spent mostly in New York, and the week immediately preceding his death); Poe's own fictionalized biographical sketches (in *The Poets and Poetry of America* and the *Saturday Museum* in 1842), taken as fact by some later biographers; and, most notoriously, Griswold's defamatory characterization of Poe in his obituary for the *New York Tribune* and his preface to Poe's collected works. Although his accounts of Poe's life are brief, Griswold's influence on Poe biography is enormous: he exaggerated some of Poe's character defects and invented or enhanced certain key incidents (as well as parts of letters from Poe) to make Poe appear thoroughly depraved. Several friends came to Poe's defense in magazine articles, but Griswold's characterization stuck. Among the early book-length defenses of Poe's character are Sarah Helen Whitman's brief memoir *Edgar Poe and His Critics* (1860) and John H. Ingram's full-length biography *Edgar Allan Poe: His Life, Letters, and Opinions* (1880), exhaustively researched with the help of Whitman and other people who knew Poe. Both books shed light on Poe's reputation in the decades immediately following his death, but Whitman's memoir reveals little about Poe's character, and Ingram's fawning attitude toward his subject (for instance, he believes that "unveiling" Poe's drinking problem "almost resembles sacrilege") is more a reversal of emotionally charged poles than a corrective to Griswold's memoir.

George E. Woodberry's *The Life of Edgar Allan Poe, Personal and Literary* (1885) set the standard for responsible, thorough Poe biographies. Woodberry's objectivity and judicious use of evidence give him a credibility earlier commentators on Poe lacked; moreover, his clear, straightforward writing style still makes for an enjoyable read over a century later. James Harrison's less elegantly written but thorough and generally factual biography accompanied his edition of Poe in 1903. These early biographers quote primary sources at length, anticipating to a limited extent the documentary approach of Dwight Thomas and David K. Jackson's *The Poe Log* (1987) but sacrificing much of the novelistic appeal of later biographies.

Hervey Allen's *Israfel: The Life and Times of Edgar Allan Poe* (1926) has considerably more narrative pull, perhaps to a fault. Allen indulges in conjecture and melodrama, committing a number of factual errors in the process, yet he tells a compelling and, for the most part, credible story. Allen is also true to his subtitle, placing Poe in the context of his "times" more thoroughly than any biographer prior to the 1990s. In the year of its first publication, *Israfel* was joined by Joseph Wood Krutch's psychoanalytic biography *Edgar Allan Poe: A Study in Genius.* Krutch rather scandalously argued that, among other things, Poe was impotent. He would soon be outdone by Marie Bonaparte, a student of Sigmund Freud, who in *The Life and Works of Edgar Allan Poe* (1933) treated Poe's works as dreams, painstakingly analyzing the details of his fictions to produce a complex psychoanalytic interpretation of Poe himself. Not only was Poe impotent, but through his stories he expressed necrophilic impulses resulting from his passionate attachment to his mother (who died before he was three years old). It sounds simplistic, but Bonaparte's readings of individual stories are nuanced and often persuasive. Only the first two hundred pages offer straight chronological biography (based, as she tells us, on Hervey Allen), but her approach to Poe's fiction renders the entire seven-hundred-page analysis a kind of psychobiography, using the works to explain the man.

Arthur Hobson Quinn's painstakingly researched biography of

1941 raised the standard set by Woodberry. Quinn, like his predecessors, relies on long quotations from letters, memoirs of acquaintances, and Poe's published works for its heft (over eight hundred pages), but he is more careful and more objective in his
handling of evidence than any of his predecessors, and his formalist interpretations of Poe's works are more sophisticated and more
useful to scholars than those of any previous biographer, with the
possible exception of Bonaparte. Quinn's Poe remained definitive
until Kenneth Silverman published *Edgar A. Poe: Mournful and
Never-ending Remembrance* in 1991. Silverman's book is more stream-
lined and more novelistic than Quinn's; drawing not only on Bonaparte but also on more recent theories of grief and mourning in
young children, Silverman sees Poe's sense of loss and the need for
"never-ending remembrance" as the central issue in Poe's life.
Some Poe specialists still prefer Quinn, partly because he took
fewer interpretive liberties, but most reviewers saw Silverman's as
the best overall biography of Poe to date. Preceding Silverman by
four years, Thomas and Jackson's *The Poe Log* may be more valuable than any narrative biography, although it would be a tough
cover-to-cover read. By carefully editing the documentary evidence of Poe's life (adding brief biographies of relatives and acquaintances and overviews at the heads of chapters), Thomas and
Jackson allow their readers to weigh the evidence—nine hundred
pages of it—for themselves. While it hardly makes conventional biographies obsolete, *The Poe Log* helps to put them all in perspective.

CRITICISM

Two book-length bibliographies cover Poe scholarship through
the early 1970s: J. Lasley Dameron and Irby B. Cauthen Jr.'s *Edgar
Allan Poe: A Bibliography of Criticism, 1827–1967* (1974) and Esther F.
Hyneman's *Edgar Allan Poe: An Annotated Bibliography of Books and
Articles in English, 1827–1973* (1974). Students might also survey the
most influential essays (and parts of books) on Poe through
the 1960s in two excellent collections: Robert Regan's *Poe: A Collection of Critical Essays* and Eric W. Carlson's *The Recognition
of Edgar Allan Poe: Selected Criticism since 1829* (both 1967). Two
decades later Carlson updated *The Recognition of Edgar Allan Poe*

with another solid collection, *Critical Essays on Edgar Allan Poe* (1987).

Most researchers will pursue more recent titles on Poe through the MLA International Bibliography in print, or, more likely, on-line or on CD-ROM, but readers will also benefit from the annotations and bibliographic thoroughness of the "International Poe Bibliography" published periodically in the journal *Poe Studies/Dark Romanticism* (last updated through 1993). The evaluative bibliographic essays in the annual *American Literary Scholarship* (current through 1997) are an extremely valuable guide; Poe is currently included under the heading "Early Nineteenth-Century Literature." For less thorough searches, annotated and selected bibliographies appear in David Ketterer's useful guidebook *Edgar Allan Poe: Life, Work and Criticism* (1989) and my *Edgar Allan Poe Revisited* (1998). Two fine complementary bibliographic essays devoted to scholarship on *Pym* are also worth noting: Douglas Robinson's "Reading Poe's Novel: A Speculative Review of *Pym* Criticism, 1950–1980" and David Ketterer's "Tracing Shadows: *Pym* Criticism, 1980–1990."

As with early Poe biography, the bulk of Poe criticism through the 1950s concerned itself primarily with Poe's reputation (both personal and literary). Even so, while Poe was dismissed by Henry James and (with some qualification) T.S. Eliot as juvenile, denigrated by Yvor Winters in *Maule's Curse* (1938), and virtually ignored by F. O. Mathiesson in his canon-forming *American Renaissance* (1941), some of the best commentary on his work from the first half of the twentieth century came from modernist literary icons: D. H. Lawrence (1923), William Carlos Williams (1925), and Allen Tate (1949 and 1951). Cutting against the conventional view of Poe as only accidentally American, Williams persuasively places Poe in his own version of the American tradition: "Poe gives the sense for the first time in America, that literature is serious, not a matter of courtesy but of truth" (216). Emphasizing Poe's theory and criticism more than his poetry and fiction, Williams pioneered the study of Poe as postmodernist (before that term had been coined) as well. Lawrence, anticipating Bonaparte, openly discussed the incest theme in "Usher" in terms of his larger concern with the decadent, narcissistic artist-figures in Poe, and Tate saw the significance of *Eureka* long before Poe's prose-poem cosmology began to attract serious commentary.

In the 1950s, Poe began to receive more detailed critical analyses and more respect. Charles Feidelson compares Poe's aesthetics to those of other "American Renaissance" writers in *Symbolism and American Literature* (1953), and Harry Levin devotes two substantial chapters to Poe in *The Power of Blackness* (1958). But two book-length critical works published in 1957 raised Poe scholarship to a new level: Edward H. Davidson's *Poe: A Critical Study* and Patrick F. Quinn's *The French Face of Edgar Poe*. Davidson offers straightforward, insightful close readings of representative texts, informed by numerous references to intellecutal history and to other writers (before, during, and after Poe's time). His extensive commentary on the poetry is particularly valuable; the book is also notable in devoting entire chapters to both *Pym* and *Eureka*, making Davidson one of the first critics (along with Quinn and Levin on *Pym*) to recognize those longer works' centrality to the Poe canon. He sees *Pym* as a coherent symbolic journey, albeit one that "left the human mind as mysterious as before. . . . What Poe did succeed in doing, to a rather remarkable degree, was to present a drama of natural forms: the world, as it had a complex physical history, became the main protagonist, and *Pym* himself was so far lost in the physical dimension that he nearly ceased to have any existence at all" (179). *Eureka* epitomizes Poe's validation of art as "man's one instrument for making some order out of the infinitude of empirical formlessness" (252), virtually a rejection of scientific knowledge rather than an attempt to unify it with intuition or artistic vision. Quinn surveys French criticism on Poe, making plain the fact that it was considerably more sensitive and sophisticated than Anglo-American commentary up to that point. But Quinn's own new-critical interpretations also broke new ground, emphasizing particularly Poe's use of the double as a model for human consciousness and, like Davidson, recognizing the importance of *Pym*. The third breakthrough reading of the late 1950s came from poet Richard Wilbur, who in his lecture "The House of Poe" (1959) and his introduction to a paperback collection of Poe's poetry (1959) presented a coherent symbolic reading of Poe, uniting the poetry and the fiction in an overarching mythology that (according to Wilbur) governs his artistic vision. The personae of Poe's poems, like the protagonists of many of his stories, are living in a kind of fallen state, detached from the realm of pure ideality, and their stories center on their attempts to regain that higher consciousness. Wilbur finds this mythology, this aesthetic, "insane," as he explains in "The House of Poe": "To say that art should repudiate everything human and earthly, and find its subject-matter at the flickering end of dreams, is hopelessly to narrow the scope and function or art." And yet, he contends, "Poe is a great artist, and I would rest my case for him on his prose allegories of psychic conflict" (277).

Poe's place in the canon would never be seriously questioned after the 1950s; although critics continued to mention Poe's unstable position among major writers, usually they did so to preface yet another reading that would show how sophisticated his fiction actually is. In a 1963 essay, James W. Gargano usefully dispelled the notion that Poe expressed himself directly through the narrators of his stories, arguing a point that teachers still struggle to convey to students, that Poe nearly always undermines the narrative point of view. Commentators began offering more aggressive analyses of the narrators of the "dying woman" tales in particular; for example, Joel Porte, in *The Romance in America* (1969), broke new ground by examining the misogyny in stories such as "Berenice" and "Ligeia." Meanwhile, the issue of which elements of narration to take at face value became the subject of numerous articles and chapters on individual works, reaching a high-water mark years later with a debate between G. R. Thompson and Patrick Quinn on the reliability of the narrator of "The Fall of the House of Usher" (1981).

The most important books on Poe published in the 1960s placed a higher value on scholarly footwork than on ingenious new readings of Poe's "timeless" tales. As T. O. Mabbott prepared the seemingly exhaustive introductions and notes to the Harvard edition, other Poe specialists were investigating Poe's journalism, influences, and struggles with other writers. In *Poe: Journalist and Critic* (1969), Robert Jacobs provides lucid, workmanlike discussions of Poe's nonfiction: the book is indispensable for a full understanding of Poe's career, although it does not make his critical work seem particularly compelling. Sidney Moss's *Poe's Literary Battles* (1963) chronicles Poe's feuds with Longfellow and Lewis Gaylord Clark particularly, shaping a bewildering tangle of evidence into a coherent and readable story. Similarly, Michael Allen analyzes the influence of *Blackwood's Edinburgh Magazine* and other British periodicals on Poe's style, producing an important and readable monograph, *Poe and the British Magazine Tradition* (1969). A broad overview of the Poe canon, Stuart Levine's *Edgar Poe: Seer and Craftsman* (1972) reflects the painstaking contextual scholarship of Jacobs, Moss, and Allen. Levine used various contexts—mostly historical—to explicate Poe's fiction and poetry, often with original insights. His erudite but informal style creates the effect of listening to a series of engaging lectures on Poe as craftsman; like Davidson, he demonstrates the strengths of traditional approaches.

Throughout the 1970s critics sought more innovative ways to look at the fiction and poetry, often arguing for the centrality of a particular theme, technique, or critical orientation. The most celebrated book on Poe from this period is Daniel Hoffman's *Poe Poe Poe Poe Poe Poe Poe* (1972). Although grounded in psychoanalysis, Hoffman's work is a far cry from Bonaparte's. His approach is anything but clinical—like Wilbur, Hoffman's response to Poe is unabashedly personal, but it rings true for scores of other readers—and his own irreverent style reveals his appreciation for Poe's verbal playfulness. Meanwhile, his detective-like grappling with the odd details of Poe's stories and poems evokes Poe himself at his analytical best. While it has not shared *Poe [x 7]*'s good fortune to remain in print, G. R. Thompson's *Poe's Fiction: Romantic Irony in the Gothic Tales* (1973) has also changed the way many people read Poe. Thompson went well beyond pointing out Poe's ironic treatment of his narrators to argue that "Poe is the preeminent American follower of the European 'Romantic Ironists'" (xi). He devotes much of the book to explicating concepts vital to Poe's art, such as romantic irony, "explained gothic" fiction, or grotesque and arabesque modes. His application of these concepts to individual tales is often stunning, as he uncovers layer upon layer of irony, doubling, and deception until "a total pattern of ironic mockery of absurd self-delusion is all that remains" (104). Though less original than Hoffman and Thompson, David Ketterer's *The Rationale of Deception in Poe* (1979) is another landmark reading from this era, centered on the concept of "arabesque reality," achieved by "looking at the world through half-closed eyes . . . destroy[ing[the external universe as usually perceived and eradicat[ing] the barriers erected by time, space, and self" so that "the world of imagination can take over" (28). *Eureka* is, of course, a key text for Ketterer's thesis, but, impressively, he reads virtually the entire Poe canon in light of the pervasive theme of deception and reenvisioning the physical world.

The emphasis on such tendencies in Poe's work—exploiting the slipperiness of language to undermine the authority of language, questioning the very notion of stable, knowable truths— presaged more overtly deconstructionist readings of Poe in the 1980s. By that time Poe already held a prominent place in the history of poststructuralist theory: Jacques Lacan's 1957 "Seminar on the Purloined Letter," which was not translated into English until 1972, used the character relationships that determine the movement of the letter as a model to demonstrate elements of his language theory, and responses by Jacques Derrida (1975), Barbara Johnson (1978), and others made Poe's story an unstable signifier of the always-already deconstructed text. John P. Muller and William J. Richardson's collection of essays on "The Purloined Letter" and deconstruction, *The Purloined Poe* (1988), chronicles this ongoing discussion. Throughout the 1980s and into the 1990s, more wide-ranging readings of Poe influenced by deconstruction aroused new debate and yielded new insights. Along with "The Purloined Letter," *Pym* became a focal point, receiving extended treatment from John Carlos Rowe in an article revised for his book *Through the Custom House* (1982), and John T. Irwin in *American Hieroglyphics* (1980). Irwin grounds his elaborate reading on nineteenth-century fascination with deciphering Egyptian hieroglyphics, regarding *Pym's* journey as a futile quest for origins of writing and selfhood. Like Irwin, J. Gerald Kennedy, in *Poe, Death, and the Life of Writing* (1987), combines historical scholarship (much of it on nineteenth-century attitudes toward death) with a deconstructionist approach to the nature of writing and to individual texts. Proceeding from the claim that "[w]riting carries within itself 'the principle of death' in its transformation of the verbal sign from a living utterance to a fixed mark on a lifeless page," Kennedy provides intricate, provocative readings of a wide range of texts, devoting chapters to Poe's letters and to *Pym*, as well as the motifs of premature burial, the death of a beautiful woman, and revenge. Probably the most thoroughly deconstructive book-length analysis of Poe is Michael J. S. Williams's *A World of Words* (1988), which convincingly demonstrates the degree to which "language itself is a topic of [Poe's] texts" (xv) through a wide reading of the Poe canon.

Along with deconstruction, sociological criticism addressing issues of race, class, and gender, usually by "historicizing" Poe's texts, became much more prominent in the 1980s and has continued to draw new attention and controversy to Poe. In her essay "Romance and Race" in the *Columbia History of the American Novel* (1991), Joan Dayan claims that critics have overlooked and in some instances covered up "the way the romance of the South and the realities of race were fundamental to his literary production" (93), and she proceeds to a discussion of race and racism in a number of Poe texts, concluding with *Pym*, which for most critics has been the key text on Poe and race. Dayan's argument is flawed by her claim that Poe wrote the overtly pro-slavery "Paulding-Drayton Review," which J. V. Ridgely (1992) and Terence Whalen (1999) have virtually proven to have been the work of Beverley Tucker (albeit written for the *Southern Literary Messenger* when Poe served as editor). But even so, Dayan shows race to be more of an issue in Poe's work than most critics have allowed, and her linking of race and gender through Poe's endorsement of an ideology of sentimentalized master-slave relationships, or "amorous bondage" (as she titles her 1994 essay), deserves serious consideration. Similarly, John Carlos Rowe has argued that Poe's writing and his place in American literary history should be reassessed in light of his having been a pro-slavery Southerner (1997). Few other recent discussions have gone substantially beyond Sidney Kaplan's 1960 essay on race in *Pym*, but some have cast Poe as a deconstructor of racialist ideology, his own racism notwithstanding. Dana Nelson, in *The Word in Black and White* (1992), argues that the Tsalal episode undermines the racist assumptions of the white colonizers of the *Jane Guy*. In *Gothic America* (1993), Teresa Goddu challenges the tendency to see the concern with race in *Pym* as part of Poe's "Southernness," while arguing that "even as *Pym's* color symbolism seems constantly to create difference, it elides that difference while articulating a discourse of racial identity that is constructed, and hence vulnerable to change" (85).

Analyses of gender in Poe's poetry and fiction have proceeded somewhat similarly: since the 1970s, critics have moved beyond merely acknowledging the misogyny in Poe's exaltation of the "death of a beautiful woman" to offer subtle analyses of the bizarre relationships between men and women in Poe's stories. In *Aesthetic Headaches* (1988), Leland S. Person explores the male characters' tendency to regard women as art objects, but he reads "Ligeia" as a cautionary tale against that objectification; the story depicts "a battle of wills finally won by a woman" (30). Also focusing on "Ligeia," J. Gerald Kennedy in a 1993 essay describes a "neurotic paradigm" that characterized Poe's male narrators: "The pattern of violence against women throughout Poe's fiction repeatedly betrays the male protagonist's outrage at his own helplessness and insufficiency" (126). And in her book *Second Stories* (1989), Cynthia S. Jordan sees a progression in Poe from "one-sided male-authored fictions" towards the "androgynous mind" of Dupin (135, 149).

Although many essays on Poe and gender, and nearly all on Poe and race, position Poe within his own cultural environment, more overtly "new historicist" readings have tended to focus more on issues of class and politics (which are never entirely divorced from race and gender, of course). Terence Whalen has broken considerable new ground in this area; his *Edgar Allan Poe and the Masses* (1999) is the most important recent monograph on Poe. Whalen combines old-fashioned sleuthing with shrewd analyses of the interplay between literary and broader economic realms. For instance, he decodes a Poe cryptogram ("essentially a new Poe text") from *Graham's Magazine* as part of a larger argument focusing on "The Gold-Bug," secret writing, and their relationship to the debate over monetary policy after the Panic of 1837. Whalen also corrects Poe's audacious claim to have increased the circulation of the *Southern Literary Messenger* from under one thousand to over five thousand; but, more importantly, he dissects the motives and methods behind the circulation of this particular myth—on the part of biographers as well as Poe himself. Other critics have been working in this vein as well, notably David Long, who analyzes Poe's rather obscure political leanings in "Poe's Political Identity: A Mummy Unswathed" (1990); Jonathan Elmer, whose *Reading at the Social Limit: Affect, Mass Culture, and Edgar Allan Poe* (1995) offers some new, historically attuned insight into traditional Poe topics such as hoaxing, horror, and plagiarism; David Leverenz, who in "Poe and Gentry Virginia" (1995) explores Poe's tendency to both honor and undermine "gentry constructions of social identity" (233); and Dana Nelson, who in a 1997 essay argues that "Some Words with a Mummy" dismantles (or "unwraps") a conception of white manhood constructed through fraternal ritual and "the scientific production of otherness" (515).

Other historically minded critics have focused on the antebellum literary world and issues of authorship. Dozens of essays over the years have been devoted to source and influence studies, but recent critics have gone well beyond traditional source hunting. In "Poe's Secret Autobiography" (1985), Louis Renza argues that the "verbal static," the word-games and self-referential gestures in Poe's fiction, create an uncanny autobiographical effect, "a prematurely buried . . . subtext whose self-referential significance becomes discernible only through a purely speculative, self-alienated act of reading" (65); David S. Reynolds discusses Poe in light of contemporary sensational literature in *Beneath the American Renaissance* (1988), arguing that Poe enforces morality and control over a genre usually characterized by "irrational excesses" (242); in a 1993 essay, Timothy Scherman analyzes Poe's jockeying for position in the literary world, particularly in his packaging of "Tales of the Folio Club"; and, focusing partly on Poe's appropriation of a passage from Dickens's *Sketches by Boz*, Stephen Rachman claims in "'Es lässt sich nicht schreiben': Plagiarism and 'The Man of the Crowd'" (1995) that "Poe uses plagiarism to question the very nature of authorship itself, not to 'tie together' but to untie 'originating contradictions'" (83).

Meanwhile, critics in the 1980s and 1990s have continued to examine Poe's work in terms of intellectual history, sometimes emphasizing philosophy, at other times specific cultural phenomena. Important books such as Joan Dayan's *Fables of Mind* (1987), John T. Irwin's *The Mystery to a Solution* (1994), and Shawn Rosenheim's *The Cryptographic Imagination* (1997) draw upon historical knowledge but could not be described as "new Historicist." Similarly, these writers display a poststructuralist awareness of issues of textuality and language but do not come across as deconstructionists; rather, they explore what might best be described with an old-fashioned phrase, "history of ideas." In *Fables of Mind*, Dayan, like Davidson, Wilbur, and Ketterer, sees the bulk of Poe's work as engaged in a philosophical enterprise; responding to the ideas of Locke and Jonathan Edwards particularly, Poe is "a skeptical writer who uses dogmatic supposition and visionary rhetoric to debunk the cant of idealism and what he called the 'doggerel aesthetics' of his contemporaries" (9). Irwin's *The Mystery to a Solution* primarily concerns Jorge Luis Borges's "doubling" of Poe's detective stories, but Irwin's fascinating labyrinthine analyses place Poe within a wide range of cultural and intellectual contexts, going far beyond the Dupin stories in exploring the nature of detection in Poe. Rosenheim proceeds in a similarly ambitious fashion to explore Poe's interest in secret writing, drawing connections backward (from Poe) to Bacon and Defoe and forward to cold-war decoding, cyberpunks, and the Internet. The recent trends I have outlined here are well represented in three important collections, which together contain many more worthwhile essays that I have not mentioned specifically: *Poe's Pym: Critical Explorations* (1992), *New Essays on Poe's Major Tales* (1993), and *The American Face of Edgar Allan Poe* (1995).

BOOKS BY POE PUBLISHED DURING HIS LIFETIME

Tamerlane and Other Poems. Boston: Calvin F. S. Thomas, 1827.
Al Aaraaf, Tamerlane, and Minor Poems. Baltimore: Hatch and Dunning, 1829.

Poems by Edgar A. Poe . . . Second Edition. New York: Elam Bliss, 1831.

The Narrative of Arthur Gordon Pym. New York: Harper and Brothers, 1838.

The Conchologist's First Book. [By Thomas Wyatt.] Philadelphia: Haswell, Barrington, and Haswell, 1839.

Tales of the Grotesque and Arabesque. Philadelphia: Lea and Blanchard, 1840.

The Prose Romances of Edgar A. Poe. Philadelphia: William H. Graham, 1843.

Tales. New York: Wiley and Putnam, 1845.

The Raven and Other Poems. New York: Wiley and Putnam, 1845.

Eureka: A Prose Poem. New York: Geo. P. Putnam, 1848.

POSTHUMOUS EDITIONS

Baudelaire, Charles, trans. *Histoires Extraordinaires.* Paris: Michel Lévy, 1856–.

———, trans. *Nouvelles Histoires Extraordinaires.* Paris: Michel Lévy, 1857.

———, trans. *Aventures d'Arthur Gordon Pym.* Paris: Michel Lévy, 1858.

———, trans. *Eureka.* Paris: Michel Lévy, 1864.

———, trans. *Histoires Grotesques et Sérieuses.* Paris: Michel Lévy, 1865.

Benton, Richard P., ed. *Eureka: A Prose Poem.* Hartford, Conn.: Transcendental Books, 1974

Griswold, Rufus Wilmot, ed. *The Works of the Late Edgar Allan Poe.* 4 vols. New York: J. S. Redfield, 1850–56.

Harrison, James A., ed. *The Complete Works of Edgar Allan Poe.* 1902–1903. Reprint, New York: AMS Press, 1965.

Levine, Stuart, and Susan Levine, eds. *The Short Fiction of Edgar Allan Poe: An Annotated Edition.* 1976. Reprint, Champaign: University of Illinois Press, 1990.

Mabbott, Thomas Ollive, ed. *The Collected Works of Edgar Allan Poe.* 3 vols. Cambridge, Mass.: Harvard University Press, 1969–78.

Ostrom, John Ward, ed. *The Letters of Edgar Allan Poe.* 2 vols. 1948. Reprint, New York: Gordian, 1966.

Pollin, Burton R., ed. *The Collected Writings of Edgar Allan Poe*. 5 vols. New York: Gordian Press, 1981–97.

Quinn, Patrick F., and G. R. Thompson, eds. *Poetry, Tales, and Selected Essays*. New York: Library of America, 1996.

Quinn, Patrick F., ed. *Poetry and Tales*. New York: Library of America, 1984.

Thompson, G. R., ed. *Essays and Reviews*. New York: Library of America, 1984.

Varner, John Grier, ed. *Edgar Allan Poe and the Philadelphia* Saturday Courier. Charlottesville: University Press of Virginia, 1933.

Wilbur, Richard, ed. *Poe: Complete Poems*. New York: Dell, 1959.

BIBLIOGRAPHY, BIOGRAPHY, AND CRITICISM (INCLUDING ALL WORKS CITED IN BIBLIOGRAPHIC ESSAY)

Allen, Hervey. *Israfel: The Life and Times of Edgar Allan Poe*. New York: Farrar and Rinehart, 1926; revised 1934 and 1943.

Allen, Michael. *Poe and the British Magazine Tradition*. New York: Oxford University Press, 1969.

Auerbach, Jonathan. "Poe's Other Double: The Reader in the Fiction." *Criticism* 24 (fall 1982): 341–61.

———. *The Romance of Failure: First-Person Fictions of Poe, Hawthorne, and James*. New York: Oxford University Press, 1989.

Bonaparte, Marie. *The Life and Works of Edgar Allan Poe*. Paris, 1933. Trans. John Rodker. London: Imago, 1949.

Byer, Robert H. "Mysteries of the City: A Reading of Poe's 'The Man of the Crowd.'" In *Ideology and Classic American Literature*, ed. Sacvan Bercovitch and Myra Jehlen. 221–46. New York: Cambridge University Press, 1986.

Carlson, Eric W., ed. *Critical Essays on Edgar Allan Poe*. Boston: G. K. Hall, 1987.

Carlson, Eric W., ed. *The Recognition of Edgar Allan Poe: Selected Criticism since 1829*. Ann Arbor: University of Michigan Press, 1967.

Cavell, Stanley. "Being Odd, Getting Even (Descartes, Emerson, Poe)." In *The American Face of Edgar Allan Poe*, ed. Shawn Rosenheim and Stephen Rachman. 3–36. Baltimore: Johns Hopkins University Press, 1995.

Charvat, William. "Poe: Journalism and the Theory of Poetry." In *The Profession of Authorship in America, 1800–1870: The Papers of William Charvat*, ed. Matthew J. Bruccoli. Columbus, Ohio: Chicago Press, 1985.

Dameron, J. Lasley, and Irby B. Cauthen, Jr., eds. *Edgar Allan Poe: A Bibliography of Criticism, 1827–1967*. Charlottesville: University Press of Virginia, 1974.

Davidson, Edward H. *Poe: A Critical Study*. Cambridge, Mass.: Harvard University Press, 1957.

Dayan, Joan. *Fables of Mind*. New York: Oxford University Press, 1987.

———. "Romance and Race." *Columbia History of the American Novel*, ed. Emory Elliott, 89–109. New York: Columbia University Press, 1991.

DeJong, Mary. "Lines from a Partly Published Drama: The Romance of Frances Sargent Osgood and Edgar Allan Poe." In *Patrons and Protegees: Gender, Friendship, and Writing in Nineteenth-Century America*, ed. Shirley Marchalonis. New Brunswick, N.J.: Rutgers University Press, 1988.

Derrida, Jacques. "The Purveyor of Truth." Trans. Alan Bass. In *The Purloined Poe: Lacan, Derrida, and Psychoanalytic Reading*, ed. John P. Muller and William J. Richardson, 173–212. Baltimore: Johns Hopkins University Press, 1988.

Eliot, T. S. "From Poe to Valéry." *Hudson Review* 2 (1949): 327–42.

Elmer, Jonathan. *Reading at the Social Limit: Affect, Mass Culture, and Edgar Allan Poe*. Stanford, Calif.: Stanford University Press, 1995.

———. "Terminate or Liquidate? Poe, Sensationalism, and the Sentimental Tradition." In *The American Face of Edgar Allan Poe*, ed. Shawn Rosenheim and Stephen Rachman, 91–120. Baltimore: Johns Hopkins University Press, 1995.

Feidelson, Charles. *Symbolism and American Literature*. Chicago: University of Chicago Press, 1953.

Gargano, James W. "The Question of Poe's Narrators." *College English* 25 (1963): 177–81.

Gilmore, Michael T. *American Romanticism and the Marketplace*. Chicago: The University of Chicago Press, 1985.

Goddu, Teresa. *Gothic America*. New York: Columbia University Press, 1993.

Harrison, James A. *Life and Letters of Edgar Allan Poe*. New York: Thomas Y. Crowell, 1903.

Hirsch, David H. "Poe and Postmodernism." In *A Companion to Poe Studies*, ed. Eric W. Carlson, 403–424. Westport, Conn.: Greenwood Press, 1996.

Hoffman, Daniel. *Poe Poe Poe Poe Poe Poe Poe*. 1972. Reprint, Baton Rouge: Louisiana State University Press, 1998.

Hyneman, Ester F. *Edgar Allan Poe: An Annotated Bibliography of Books and Articles in English, 1827–1973*. Boston: G. K. Hall, 1974.

Ingram, John H. *Edgar Allan Poe: His Life, Letters, and Opinions*. 2 vols. London: John Hogg, 1880.

Irwin, John T. *American Hieroglyphics*. New Haven, Conn.: Yale University Press, 1980.

———. *The Mystery to a Solution*. Baltimore: Johns Hopkins University Press, 1994.

Jacobs, Robert. *Poe: Journalist and Critic*. Baton Rouge: Louisiana State University Press, 1969.

Johnson, Barbara. "The Frame of Reference: Poe, Lacan, Derrida." In *The Critical Difference: Essays in the Contemporary Rhetoric of Reading*, 110–46. Baltimore: Johns Hopkins University Press, 1980.

Jordan, Cynthia S. *Second Stories*. Chapel Hill: University of North Carolina Press, 1989.

Kaplan, Sidney. Introduction. *The Narrative of Arthur Gordon Pym*. New York: Hill and Wang, 1960.

Kennedy, J. Gerald. *Poe, Death, and the Life of Writing*. New Haven, Conn.: Yale University Press, 1987.

———. "Poe, 'Ligeia,' and the Problem of Dying Women." In *New Essays on Poe's Major Tales*, ed. Kenneth Silverman, 113–29. Cambridge: Cambridge University Press, 1992.

———. "The Violence of Melancholy: Poe against Himself." *American Literary History* 8 (fall 1996): 533–51.

Ketterer, David. *Edgar Allan Poe: Life, Work and Criticism*. Fredericton, Canada: York Press, 1989.

———. *The Rationale of Deception in Poe*. Baton Rouge: Louisiana State University Press, 1979.

———. "Tracing Shadows: *Pym* Criticism, 1980–1990." In *Poe's Pym: Critical Explorations*, ed. Richard Kopley. 233–72. Durham, N.C.: Duke University Press, 1992.

Kopley, Richard, ed. *Poe's* Pym: *Critical Explorations.* Durham, N.C.: Duke University Press, 1992.

Krutch, Joseph Wood. *Edgar Allan Poe: A Study in Genius.* New York: Knopf, 1926.

Lacan, Jacques. "Seminar on 'The Purloined Letter.'" Trans. Jeffrey Mehlman. In *The Purloined Poe: Lacan, Derrida, and Psychoanalytic Reading,* ed. John P. Muller and William J. Richardson. 28–54. Baltimore: Johns Hopkins University Press, 1988.

Lawrence, D. H. *Studies in Classic American Literature.* 1923. Reprint, New York: Penguin, 1977.

Leverenz, David. "Poe and Gentry Virginia." In *The American Face of Edgar Allan Poe,* ed. Shawn Rosenheim and Stephen Rachman, 210–36. Baltimore: Johns Hopkins University Press, 1995.

Levin, Harry. *The Power of Blackness.* New York: Knopf, 1958.

Levine, Stuart. *Edgar Poe: Seer and Craftsman.* Deland, Fla.: Everett/ Edwards, 1972.

Long, David. "Poe's Political Identity: A Mummy Unswathed." *Poe Studies* 23 (1990): 1–22.

Mathiesson, F. O. *American Renaissance.* New York: Oxford University Press, 1941.

Miller, John Carl, ed. *Poe's Helen Remembers.* Charlottesville: University Press of Virginia, 1979.

Moss, Sidney P. *Poe's Literary Battles.* 1963. Reprint, Carbondale: Southern Illinois University Press, 1969.

Muller, John P., and William J. Richardson. *The Purloined Poe: Lacan, Derrida, and Psychoanalytic Reading.* Baltimore: Johns Hopkins University Press, 1988.

Nelson, Dana D. "The Haunting of White Manhood: Poe, Fraternal Ritual, and Polygenesis." *American Literature* 69 (1997): 515–46.

———. *National Manhood: Capitalist Citizenship and the Imagined Fraternity of White Men.* Durham, N.C.: Duke University Press, 1998.

———. *The Word in Black and White: Reading "Race" in American Literature, 1638–1867.* New York: Oxford University Press, 1992.

Peeples, Scott. *Edgar Allan Poe Revisited.* New York: Twayne, 1998.

Person, Leland S., Jr. *Aesthetic Headaches.* Athens: University of Georgia Press, 1988.

Porte, Joel. *The Romance in America*. Middletown, Conn.: Wesleyan University Press, 1969.

Quinn, Arthur Hobson. *Edgar Allan Poe: A Critical Biography*. New York: D. Appleton-Century, 1941.

Quinn, Patrick F. *The French Face of Edgar Poe*. Carbondale: Southern Illinois University Press, 1957.

———. "A Misreading of 'The Fall of the House of Usher.'" In *Ruined Eden of the Present: Hawthorne, Melville, and Poe*, ed. G. R. Thompson and Virgil Lokke, 303–312. West Lafayette, Ind.: Purdue University Press, 1981.

———. "'Usher' Again: Trust the Teller!" In *Ruined Eden of the Present: Hawthorne, Melville, and Poe*, ed. G. R. Thompson and Virgil Lokke, 341–53. West Lafayette, Ind.: Purdue University Press, 1981.

Rachman, Stephen. "'Es lässt sich nicht schreiben': Plagiarism and 'The Man of the Crowd.'" In *The American Face of Edgar Allan Poe*, ed. Shawn Rosenheim and Stephen Rachman, 49–87. Baltimore: Johns Hopkins University Press, 1995.

Regan, Robert, ed. *Poe: A Collection of Critical Essays*. Englewood Cliffs, N.J.: Prentice-Hall, 1967.

Renza, Louis. "Poe's Secret Autobiography." In *The American Renaissance Reconsidered: Selected Papers from the English Institute, 1982–83*, ed. Walter Benn Michaels and Donald E. Pease, 58–89. Baltimore: Johns Hopkins University Press, 1985.

Reynolds, David S. *Beneath the American Renaissance*. New York: Knopf, 1988.

Ridgely, J. V. "The Authorship of the 'Paulding-Drayton Review.'" *PSA Newsletter* 20, no. 2 (fall 1992): 1–3, 6.

Robinson, Douglas. "Reading Poe's Novel: A Speculative Review of *Pym* Criticism, 1950–1980." *Poe Studies* 15 (1982): 47–54.

Rosenheim, Shawn James. *The Cryptographic Imagination: Secret Writing from Edgar Poe to the Internet*. Baltimore: Johns Hopkins University Press, 1997.

Rosenheim, Shawn, and Stephen Rachman, eds. *The American Face of Edgar Allan Poe*. Baltimore: Johns Hopkins University Press, 1995.

Rowe, John Carlos. *At Emerson's Tomb: The Politics of Classic American Literature*. New York: Columbia University Press, 1997.

————. *Through the Custom House.* Baltimore: Johns Hopkins University Press, 1982.

Saltz, Laura. "'(Horrible to Relate!)': Recovering the Body of Marie Rogêt." In *The American Face of Edgar Allan Poe,* ed. Shawn Rosenheim and Stephen Rachman, 237–70. Baltimore: Johns Hopkins University Press, 1995.

Scherman, Timothy. "The Authority Effect: Poe and the Politics of Reputation in the Pre-industry of Antebellum American Publishing." *Arizona Quarterly* 49 (1993): 1–19.

Silverman, Kenneth. *Edgar A. Poe: Mournful and Never-Ending Remembrance.* New York: HarperCollins, 1991.

————, ed. *New Essays on Poe's Major Tales.* Cambridge: Cambridge University Press, 1993.

Tate, Allen. "The Angelic Imagination." In *Essays of Four Decades,* 401–23. Chicago: Swallow Press, 1968.

————. "Our Cousin Mr. Poe." In *Essays of Four Decades,* 385–400. Chicago: Swallow Press, 1968.

Thomas, Dwight, and David K. Jackson, eds. *The Poe Log: A Documentary Life of Edgar Allan Poe, 1809–1849.* Boston: G. K. Hall, 1987.

Thompson, G. R. "Poe and the Paradox of Terror: Structures of Heightened Consciousness in 'The Fall of the House of Usher.'" In *Ruined Eden of the Present: Hawthorne, Melville, and Poe,* ed. G. R. Thompson and Virgil Lokke, 313–40. West Lafayette, Ind.: Purdue University Press, 1981.

————. *Poe's Fiction: Romantic Irony in the Gothic Tales.* Madison: University of Wisconsin Press, 1973.

Walker, I. M., ed. *Edgar Allan Poe: The Critical Heritage.* London: Routledge, 1986.

Walsh, John. *Poe the Detective.* New Brunswick, N.J.: Rutgers University Press, 1968.

Weidman, Bette S. "The Broadway Journal (2): A Casualty of Abolition Politics." *Bulletin of the New York Public Library* 73 (February 1969): 94–113.

Weiss, Susan Archer. *The Home Life of Poe.* New York: Broadway Publishing, 1907.

Whalen, Terence. "The Code for Gold: Edgar Allan Poe and Cryptography." *Representations* 46 (1994): 35–58.

————. "Edgar Allan Poe and the Horrid Laws of Political Economy." *American Quarterly* 44 (September 1992): 381–417.

————. *Edgar Allan Poe and the Masses.* Princeton, N.J.: Princeton University Press, 1999.

Whitman, Sarah Helen. *Edgar Poe and His Critics.* 1860. Reprint, New York: Gordian, 1981.

Wilbur, Richard. "The House of Poe." In *The Recognition of Edgar Allan Poe: Selected Criticism since 1829,* ed. Eric W. Carlson, 255–77. Ann Arbor: University of Michigan Press, 1967.

Williams, Michael J. S. *A World of Words.* Durham, N.C.: Duke University Press, 1988.

Williams, William Carlos. *In the American Grain.* 1925. Reprint, New York: New Directions, 1956.

Winters, Yvor. *Maule's Curse.* New York: New Directions, 1938.

Woodberry, George E. *The Life of Edgar Allan Poe, Personal and Literary.* 1885; revised 1909. Reprint, New York: Chelsea House, 1980.

Contributors

J. GERALD KENNEDY is William A. Read Professor of English at Louisiana State University and former Chair of the English department. He is the author of *Poe, Death, and the Life of Writing* and *"The Narrative of Arthur Gordon Pym" and the Abyss of Interpretation* as well as co-editor of the forthcoming *Romancing the Shadow: Poe and Race* (Oxford University Press).

DAVID LEVERENZ is Professor of English at the University of Florida. His publications include *The Language of Puritan Feeling* (1980) and *Manhood and the American Renaissance* (1989), as well as many essays on American literature.

LOUIS A. RENZA is Professor of English at Dartmouth College. In addition to numerous articles on Poe and other American writers, he has published *"A White Heron" and the Question of Minor Literature* and co-edited *The Irish Stories of Sarah Orne Jewett*; his current project, *A Poetics of American Privacy*, focuses on Poe and Wallace Stevens.

SCOTT PEEPLES is Assistant Professor of English and Coordinator of American Studies at the College of Charleston. He is the author of *Edgar Allan Poe Revisited* (1998), and his essays have appeared in *Southern Quarterly*, *Biography*, and *ATQ*.

LELAND S. PERSON is Professor of English and the head of the English Department at the University of Cincinnati. He is the author of *Aesthetic Headaches: Women and a Masculine Poetics in Poe, Melville, and Hawthorne* and of many articles on nineteenth-century American literature.

TERENCE WHALEN is Associate Professor of English at the University of Illinois at Chicago. He is the author of *Edgar Allan Poe and the Masses: The Political Economy of Literature in Antebellum America.*

Index

1844 (English), 54

A New Home, Who'll Follow?
(Kirkland), 133

abolition movement, 36, 48

"Al Aaraaf," 27, 28, 154
and use of name "Ligeia," 143
read at Boston Lyceum, 53

Al Aaraaf, Tamerlane, and Minor Poems, 28, 153

Alexander's Weekly Messenger, 43, 173

Allan, Frances Valentine (foster mother), 20, 129
death of, 26

Allan, John (foster father), 20, 27, 28, 32, 35, 37, 38, 66, 72, 129, 130, 151, 154–56
condemnation of Poe, 22, 24
death of, 32
financial reverses of, 21
illegitimate children of, 33
inheritance of, 22
last will of, 33

refusal to pay Poe's debts by, 24
remarriage of, 28

Allan, Louisa Patterson, 28

American Anti-Slavery Society, 36, 193

American Copyright Club, 50

American Museum (Baltimore), 41

American Whig Review, 63

"Anastatic Printing," 82, 89
and democratic culture, 84

"Annabelle Lee," 58

Anthon, Charles, 75

Arthur, T. S., 48

"Assignation, The," 32
Aphrodite as idealized type in, 138

Astoria (Irving), 43

Auld, Hugh and Sophia, 31

Auster, Paul, 15

"Autography," 36

Babbage, Charles, 10

Bacon, Delia S., 30

"Balloon Hoax, The," 13, 50
Barth, John, 15
"Bartleby the Scrivener"
    (Melville), 9
Baudelaire, Charles, 56
    translation of Poe, 15
"Beloved Physician, The," 54
Bennett, James Gordon, 107
"Berenice," 7, 68, 69, 72, 79, 97,
    99, 107, 138, 141, 158
    and teeth of Berenice, 139
    dubious taste of, 34
    problem of identity in, 108
    woman as abstraction in, 139
Biddle, Nicholas, 33, 40, 44, 190
"Birthmark, The" (Hawthorne),
    139
    and sexual politics of idealiza-
        tion, 138
Bisco, John, 52
"Black Cat, The," 4–5, 7, 49, 97,
    121, 134
    black–white crossings in, 119
Black Hawk War, 27
Blackwood's Magazine, 21, 101, 104
Bliss, Elam, 29
Bogart, Elizabeth, 132
"Bon-Bon," 103
book prices (U.S.), 74
Bransby, Rev. John, 21
Briggs, Charles F., 52–54, 80
Broadway Journal, 52, 53, 80
    suspension of, 53
Brooks, Nathan C., 41
Brother Jonathan, 75
Brown, Charles Brockden, 4
Bryant, William Cullen, 39
Burling, Ebenezer, 22, 25
    death of, 30

Burton, William, 42
    dismisses Poe, 43
    sells *Gentleman's Magazine*, 44
Burton's *Gentleman's Magazine*,
    41–44
"Business Man, The," 8, 152, 158,
    159, 161
Byron, George Gordon, Lord,
    25

Carey, Henry C., 33, 40
"Cask of Amontillado, The," 152
Casket, The, 44
Cass, Lewis, 57
Child, Lydia Maria, 132
Chivers, Thomas Holley, 44, 81
    offers Poe financial support,
        54
"City in the Sea, The," 12
City of Angels, 14
Clark, Lewis Gaylord, 52, 54
    attacks on Poe, 53
Clarke, Joseph H., 21
Clarke, Thomas C., 47, 48, 49
Clay, Henry, 26, 50, 51
    American System of, 23
Clemm, Maria Poe (mother-in-
        law), 29, 31, 50, 57, 58, 136
    pleading letter to Poe, 35
"Coliseum, The," 32
"Colloquy of Monos and Una,
    The," 14
Colton, George, 53
Columbia Spy, 50
"Conqueror Worm, The," 12
Conrad, Robert T., 44, 155
"Conversation of Eiros and
    Charmion, The," 14
Cooke, Philip Pendleton, 42

Cooper, James Fenimore, 4, 45, 190, 196
Corman, Roger, 3
Crèvecoeur, Hector St. Jean de, 8

daguerreotype, 174
  of Poe, 175
"Decided Loss, A," 30
Declaration of Independence, The, 24
Democracy in America (Tocqueville), 104
Democratic Party, 51
Democratic Review, 34, 46, 51, 52
depression of 1837–43, 44, 48, 73, 74
"Descent into the Maelstrom, A," 45
"Devil in the Belfry, The," 42
"Diddling Considered as One of the Exact Sciences," 8
"Doings of Gotham," 50
Dollar Newspaper, 49
Don Quixote (Cervantes), 24
Doom of the Drinker, The (English), 47, 49
"Doomed City, The," 29
Douglass, Frederick, 3, 31
Dow, Jesse E., 47
Drake-Halleck review, 168
"Duc de l'Omelette, The," 30, 103
DuSolle, John S., 49
Duyckinck, Evert, 50
  and Young America group, 52
  as publisher of Poe, 53

Eaton, John Henry, 27
Edgar Poe and His Critics (S. H. Whitman), 143
Edinburgh Review, 66
elections of U.S. presidents, 26, 33, 39, 44, 50, 51, 57
"Eleonora," 45, 148, 149
Eliot, T. S., 15
Ellet, Elizabeth F. (Mrs.), 53
Ellis, Charles, 20
Embury, Emma C., 132
Emerson, Ralph Waldo, 11, 49, 82, 107, 184
English, Thomas Dunn, 53, 54
  attacks on Poe, 56
  satirizes Poe as drunk, 47
Eureka, 13, 14, 55, 56, 89, 177, 178
  and mass audience, 90
Evelith, George, 54, 55, 146
Evening Mirror (New York), 51, 53, 54

"Facts in the Case of M. Valdemar, The," 12, 53, 97, 98
  racial and sexual implications of, 118
  social meanings in, 118
"Fall of the House of Usher, The," 16, 21, 42, 111–15, 180
  psychological disintegration in, 7
Fargo, 6
Fay, Theodore, 36
Fitzhugh, George, 82
"For Annie," 57
Free-Soil Party, 57
Fuller, Hiram, 54
Fuller, Margaret, 53, 54, 131, 132, 135, 142

"Gaffy," 24
Galt, John, 22
Garrison, William Lloyd, 36, 48,
    193
Gil Blas (Lesage), 24
Gilman, Charlotte Perkins, 146
Godey's Lady's Book, 32, 34, 132,
    209
    and Poe's "Literati" sketches,
    54
gold, California discovery of, 55
"Gold-Bug, The," 26, 49, 67, 97
    master-slave relations in, 116,
    117
Gove, Mary, 132, 133
Graham, George, 15, 48, 63
    and *Graham's Magazine*, 44
    proposed partnership with
    Poe, 45
Graham's Magazine, 44, 49, 51, 75,
    76
Graves, Samuel "Bully," 27, 28
Griswold, Rufus W., 46
    obituary of Poe, 15

Halleck, Fitz-Greene, 162n
Harper and Brothers, 40, 41, 72
    rejection of "Folio Club"
    tales, 38
Harrison, William Henry, 44,
    196
"Haunted Palace, The," 7, 41,
    97, 112, 113
    social meanings of, 113, 114
Hawks, Rev. Francis Lister, 39
Hawthorne, Nathaniel, 46, 138,
    139, 207
Herring, Elizabeth (cousin), 32
Herron, James, 46

Hewitt, Mary E., 132
"Hop-Frog," 5, 57, 97, 98, 118,
    119, 152
    exploitation and revenge in,
    82
"How to Write a Blackwood
    Article," 4, 21, 41, 97, 116
    as satire of sensational tale,
    137
Hurst, Henry B., 15
Huxley, Aldous, 15

immigration (U.S.), 33, 65
"Imp of the Perverse, The," 95
    patricide in, 115
    sensation as escape from feel-
    ing in, 121
Indian removal project, 5, 26, 27,
    157
Indian wars, 157
information, economic value of,
    66
international copyright law, 46,
    50, 51, 74, 86
Irving, Washington, 39, 42, 43, 45

Jackson, Andrew, 26, 33, 51,
    192–94
    and rights of common man,
    65
    and Robards affair, 107
    denounced as bigamist, 107
    presidency of, 65
    reelection of, 33
    Specie Circular of, 39, 73
    war on the Bank of the
    United States, 39, 65
Jacksonian era, 33, 65, 97
    and mass press, 172

Jefferson, Thomas, 23
  death of, 24, 191
Jewett, Helen, 107
"Journal of Julius Rodman,
  The," 5, 10, 13, 43

Kennedy, John Pendleton, 32, 33,
  44, 45, 130, 151
  aid to Poe, 34
  as literary patron of Poe, 32
Kirkland, Caroline M., 54, 132,
  133
Knickerbocker Magazine, 34, 52
  attacks on Poe, 53

Lafayette, Marquis de, 22, 29
Lea, Isaac, 27
Legaré, Hugh Swinton, 25
Leslie, Eliza, 48
Lever, Charles James, 78
Lewis, S. Anna, 132
Liberator, The, 36
"Liberian Literature" (Minor),
  70
  Poe's revisions of, 71
Library of American Books, 53
"Ligeia," 7, 12, 21, 41, 109, 115,
  142, 143, 158
  and revenge of domestic
    Angel, 145
  and "Real Womanhood,"
    135
  as parody of "separate
    spheres" ideology, 135
  as reversal of spousal rela-
    tions, 135
  inventory of Ligeia's features
    in, 144–45
  Ligeia's force of will, 136

"Lionizing," 16, 114
  satire of nose-pulling in, 103
Lippard, George, 48, 49
  tribute to Poe, 63
"Literary Life of Thingum Bob,
  The," 8, 51
  as parody of literary entre-
    preneur, 155
"Literati of New York City,
  The," 54, 132, 144, 167, 173,
  202
Locke, Jane Ermina, 56, 131
London Ladies' Magazine, 66
Longfellow, Henry Wadsworth,
  42, 43, 45, 49, 51, 173
"Loss of Breath," 97, 115
  burlesque of sensationalism
    in, 101
  misogyny in, 137
  sexual innuendo in, 101, 102
Lowell, James Russell, 49, 50
  as editor of *Pioneer*, 47
Lynch, Anne C., 53, 55, 130, 132, 147

Madison, James, 19
madness
  in modern culture, 6, 7
  satire of treatment, 7
"Maelzel's Chess Player," 36
"Man of the Crowd, The," 9, 16,
  44, 104, 158, 175, 180
  as unreadable text, 183
  fantasy of privacy in, 184
  narrator as voyeur in, 175, 176
  narrator as voyeuristic object,
    177
"Man That Was Used Up, The,"
  6, 49, 97, 99, 152, 157–59,
  161, 180

"Man That Was Used Up, The"
  (*continued*)
  as critique of military man-
    hood, 156
  master-slave relations in, 116
  racial ideology in, 157
manhood
  and economic success, 154
  and employment, 158
  and male neurasthenia, 162n
  and self-made man, 150
  nineteenth-century concepts
    of, 130, 150
Manifest Destiny, 52, 65, 199
"Marginalia," 51
market revolution (U.S.), 8, 9, 33,
  66, 171
"Masque of the Red Death,
  The," 4, 13, 180
Mathews, Cornelius, 50
"Mellonta Tauta," 10
"Mesmeric Revelation," 14, 50,
  56
metempsychosis, 99
"Metzengerstein," 30, 97, 99, 101
  and gentry rituals of
    vengeance, 100
  sensational crossings in, 100
Mexican War, 54, 55, 57, 65
Minor, Lucian, 37, 70, 71
  lauds African colonization, 70
Missouri Compromise, 21, 190
"Morella," 12, 97, 107, 139, 141,
  158
  gender and power in, 140
  problem of identity in, 140
"Morning on the Wissahiccon,"
  172
Mowatt, Anna Cora, 132, 133, 144

"MS Found in a Bottle," 25, 32,
  178, 179
  secrecy and privacy in, 179
"Murders in the Rue Morgue,
  The," 9, 45, 49, 85, 111, 152,
  161, 168
  Dupin's desire for truth in, 86
"Mystery of Marie Rogêt, The,"
  9, 47, 86, 110
  as critique of tabloid journal-
    ism, 109
"Mystification," 24, 39, 152, 153
  Von Jung as trickster in, 152

*Narrative of Arthur Gordon Pym,
  The*, 5, 11, 13, 25, 39, 75, 89
  delay in publication of, 40
  Messenger installments of, 38
  publication of, 41
Natural Born Killers, 6
Neal, John, 28, 153
"Never Bet the Devil Your
  Head," 96
New England Magazine, 34
New World, 75
New York City
  mob violence in, 39
  Poe's observations about, 50
New York Herald, 107
New York Sun, 50, 74
newspaper industry (U.S.), 74
Nietzsche, Friedrich, 12

Osceola, Chief, 27
Osgood, Frances S., 52, 53, 132,
  143
"Outis" papers (Poe), 173
"Oval Portrait, The," 46, 134
  and male gaze, 141

O'Sullivan, John L, 51, 199
  defines American "Manifest
  Destiny," 52

Panic of 1837, 40, 41, 73, 76, 77
  and mass culture, 73
  and penny press, 74
Patterson, Edward H. N., 57
Paulding, James Kirke, 39, 41, 72,
  73, 91n
Paulding-Drayton review
  (Tucker), 37, 71, 81
  misattributed to Poe, 71
Pease, Peter Pindar, 25
Penn magazine, 43–45, 75, 78
Peterson, Charles, 48
*Peterson's Lady's National
  Magazine*, 48
"Pfaall, The Unparalleled Ad-
  venture of One Hans," 34
Phantasy-Pieces, 46
Philadelphia
  anti-Irish sentiment in, 48
  cultural growth of, 48
  economic vitality of, 40
  Nativist demonstrations in,
  48
  racial conflict in, 40, 48
  Whig control of, 48
"Philosophy of Composition,
  The," 63, 79, 87
  and death-of-a-beautiful-
  woman theory, 138
  and sources of Poe's sensa-
  tionalism, 122
Pioneer, The, 47
"Pit and the Pendulum, The,"
  46
Poe, David Jr. (father), 19

Poe, David Sr. (grandfather), 19,
  130
Poe, Edgar Allan
  achievements of, 64
  anatomizing of women by,
  142, 144, 145, 148
  and allegory, 182, 183
  and American privacy, 16,
  162–88, 167
  and American publishing industry, 63–93
  and *Broadway Journal*, 52, 53
  and Burton's *Gentleman's
  Magazine*, 42, 43
  and cryptography, 10, 43, 143,
  169, 173
  and Democratic Party, 53
  and economics of literature,
  69, 72, 77, 79, 84
  and gender constructions, 16,
  129–65
  and gentlemanly ideal, 151
  and *Graham's Magazine*, 45,
  46, 75
  and "heresy of The Didactic," 80
  and hoaxing, 43, 50
  and illness of Virginia, 115,
  146
  and international copyright
  law, 46, 50, 51, 74, 86
  and magazine age, 67
  and "magazine prison-
  house," 82, 185
  and masculine identity, 130,
  149, 150
  and mass audience, 79, 88,
  168, 177
  and misogyny, 137

Poe, Edgar Allan (*continued*)
and money, 67, 154
and mother's death, 129
and mystification, 153
and patriarchal ideology, 138
and "political economy," 77,
80
and politics of editing, 70
and religious doubt, 11, 12, 14
and sensationalism, 16, 95–127
and slavery, 20, 21, 23, 31, 37,
157
and *Southern Literary Messenger,* 34–36, 38, 70, 71
and *The Stylus,* 76
and tale of ratiocination, 45,
67, 85, 86, 110, 173
antidemocratic politics of, 78,
182
appearance at Boston
Lyceum, 53
appointment to West Point
of, 26, 27, 28
apprentice tales of, 30, 31
apprenticeship as magazinist,
70
as agent in slave transfer, 31
as "gentleman publisher,"
132–33
as lecturer, 49, 52, 56, 58
as littérateur, 159
as magazinist, 69, 71, 75, 77
as poet, 28, 153
as ostensible editor of con-
chology text, 41
at University of Virginia, 23,
24
attacks on Longfellow, 42, 43,
49, 51

childhood of, 19–21
collapse in Baltimore, 58
commercial origins of, 66
commercial versus artistic
aims of, 80, 82
conflict with John Allan, 21,
24, 26, 28, 33, 130, 151
contemporary influence of, 3,
15
court-martial of, 29
criticism of women writers,
133
cultural politics of, 81, 82, 84
death and resurrection of
women in, 146, 147
death of, 15, 58, 63
defense of, 15
defense of "Berenice," 69, 107
desire for artistic autonomy,
87
desire for remarriage, 56, 148
desire to found magazine, 42,
43, 44, 50, 54, 57, 75, 76, 132,
154, 155
devotion to Virginia, 35
dismissal at *Southern Literary
Messenger,* 38, 73
drinking sprees of, 46, 47, 57
early poetry of, 21
education of, 21, 23–24, 28–29
enlistment in U.S. Army, 25
expulsion from West Point,
29
female characters of, 132–49
gambling of, 24
gentry aspirations of, 22, 151
Gothic imagination of, 14
grotesque transformations in,
98

in Boston, 25, 53
in Baltimore, 29–31, 58
in Charleston, 25–26
in New York, 39, 46, 51, 54
in Philadelphia, 40, 47–48, 57
in Richmond, 35
journalistic attacks on, 56
lecture in Providence, 57
letter to Mrs. Clemm, 136
letters to John Allan, 24, 151,
    157
letters to Mrs. Whitman,
    147–49
literary career of, 64, 85, 90, 154
male characters of, 103, 149–61
male verbal power in, 143, 160
male-female relationships in,
    131, 134, 137
marriage proposal to Mrs.
    Whitman, 56
marriage to Virginia, 37
metaphysical speculations of,
    14
military experience of, 25–27,
    68, 156, 157
mind-body crossings in, 101
mockery of self-made man,
    159
on genius and productivity, 88
opinion on daguerreotypes,
    174
opinions about Margaret
    Fuller, 131, 132, 142
parody of business manhood,
    158
parody of Irving, 42
parody of military manhood,
    156
possible suicide attempt of, 56

poverty of, 76
proposal to Mrs. Shelton, 58
quarrel with Thomas W.
    White, 38
quest for fame, 168
quest for government job,
    45–47
relationship to brother
    Henry, 29
rhetorical war on manly
    ideal, 152
romance with Sarah Elmira
    Royster (Shelton), 22, 23, 25
satirized as drunk, 54
sensationalism and boundary
    crossings in, 96, 97, 99, 100,
    108, 111, 115
sensationalism and literary
    development of, 114
sensationalism and manly
    control in, 98
sensationalism and racial
    crossings in, 115, 116, 119
sensationalism as escape
    from feeling in, 98, 99
survival of shipwreck by, 25
theory of divided text, 79, 80,
    89
theory of poetry (death of
    beautiful woman), 138, 161
theory of single effect, 46, 89,
    182
theory of single sitting, 182
transcendental idealism of, 14
violence in, 4, 5, 96
ward of Allan family, 20
wins lawsuit, 54
wins literary competitions,
    32, 49

Poe, Elizabeth Arnold Hopkins (mother), 19
  impact of her death on Poe, 129
Poe, Elizabeth Cairnes (grandmother), 27, 29, 31, 35
Poe, Josephine Clemm (wife of Neilson), 35
Poe, Neilson (cousin), 35, 136
Poe, Rosalie (sister), 19, 20, 32
Poe, Virginia Clemm (wife), 29–31, 35, 50, 136
  consumption of, 45, 46, 54, 146
  death of, 54
  marriage to Poe, 37
  Poe's mourning for, 56
Poe, William Henry Leonard (brother), 19, 22
  decline and death of, 29
  dissipation of, 27
Poems by Edgar A. Poe, 29
"Poetic Principle, The," 58
"Politian," 36
Polk, James K., 50, 51, 52, 57, 199
"Power of Words, The," 52, 82, 87, 89
"Predicament, A," 6, 41, 98
  race and sexual innuendo in, 116
"Premature Burial, The," 10, 50, 97
  social destabilizations in, 111
Price, Vincent, 3
privacy
  and literary value, 178
  and reprinting of literary texts, 86
  and surveillance, 170

and U.S. geography, 170
  effect of transportation changes on, 171
  legal definition of, 180, 186n
  threats to, 171
pro-slavery ideology, 36, 71
Prose Romances of Edgar A. Poe, The, 49
publishing industry (U.S.), 16, 64, 66, 73, 75, 77, 185
  and mass reader, 78
  and overproduction of texts, 90
  and pirating of British works, 74
  as determinant of Poe's career, 85, 87, 89, 97
  capitalist basis of, 73
  growth of, 74
  Poe as advocate of, 82
  Poe as critic of, 82
Pulp Fiction, 6
"Purloined Letter, The," 51, 152, 160, 161
  Dupin as hired intellectual in, 86
  information value in, 87

Raven and Other Poems, The, 53
"Raven, The," 3, 11, 51, 52, 58, 80, 121, 122
Republican Party, 57
Reynolds, Jeremiah, 38
Richmond, Nancy "Annie," 56, 57, 141, 143, 148
  Poe's idealization of, 149
"Right to Privacy, The" (Samuel Warren and Louis Brandeis), 180

rock music, and cult of death, 12
Rogers, Mary, 110
Royster, Sarah Elmira (Shelton),
   25, 58, 148
  agrees to wed Poe, 58
  early romance with Poe, 22
  engagement and marriage of,
   24

Sartain, John, 58
Saturday Courier (Philadelphia),
  30
Saturday Visiter (Baltimore),
  30–32
Scott, Winfield, 22, 55
Scott, Walter, Sir, 21
"Secret Writing," 45
Sedgwick, Catharine Maria, 4,
  132
"Self-Reliance" (Emerson), 184
Seneca Falls Convention, 57
sensationalism, 95–127
  and convertibility of identity,
   110
  and fragmentation in, 109
  and tabloid journalism, 105,
   110
  as defense against sentiment,
   120
  body detachment and control
   in, 103
  first uses of, 104
  grotesque transformations of,
   98
  Poe's burlesque of, 101
  power and powerlessness of,
   122
  social effects of, 107
Shakespeare, William, 21, 25

Shew, Marie Louise, 54, 56, 147
Sigourney, Lydia Huntley, 132
"Silence—A Fable," 39
Simms, William Gilmore, 25
slavery, 5, 21, 36, 38, 48, 57, 70, 72
  and abolitionism, 36, 48
  and colonization, 37, 70
  and fugitive slaves, 55
  discussed in *Southern Literary
   Messenger*, 71
  extension of, 51, 52, 55
  in Baltimore, 31
  pro-slavery ideology, 36
Smith, Elizabeth Oakes, 132
Snodgrass, Joseph Evans, 42, 44
"Some Secrets of the Magazine
  Prison-House," as critique
  of publishing industry, 82
"Song of Myself" (Whitman),
  158
"Sonnet—To Science," 11
South (U.S.), gentry rituals of
  honor in, 102, 123n
South Sea exploration, 38, 41
Southern Literary Messenger, 44,
  47, 68–72, 76, 107
  handling of slavery contro-
  versy, 37
Specie Circular, 39, 73
"Spectacles, The," 148
  as parody of male gaze, 141,
  142
Spirit of the Times, 48, 49
Stanard, Jane Stith, 22, 129, 143
"Star Spangled Banner, The"
  (Francis Scott Key), 20
Starr, Mary, 32
Stephens, Ann S., 132, 133
Stowe, Harriet Beecher, 82

Stylus, The, 47, 55–57, 75, 76
  Poe's epigraph for, 89
"System of Doctor Tarr and
    Professor Fether, The," 7

tale of ratiocination, 67
"Tale of the Ragged Mountains,
    A," 24
"Tales of Mystery and Imagina-
    tion" (Alan Parsons Pro-
    ject), 3
"Tales of the Folio Club," 31–34,
    72
  rejection by Harper and
    Brothers, 38
*Tales of the Grotesque and
    Arabesque,* 42, 43
Tamerlane and Other Poems,
    25
Taylor, Zachary, 57
"Tell-Tale Heart, The," 4, 47
Texas, annexation of, 51, 52, 55,
    65
Thayer, Sylvanus, 29
Thomas, Frederick, 45, 155,
    159
"'Thou Art the Man,'" 160
  as critique of amiable gentle-
    man, 161
"To Helen," 22, 55, 143
Tocqueville, Alexis de, 104, 105,
    167, 169, 172
Tucker, Nathaniel Beverley, 37,
    71
Turner, Nat, 31
Twain, Mark
  The Mysterious Stranger, 12
Twice-Told Tales reviews, 46, 182,
    184

Tyler, John, 44–47
  resignation of cabinet, 46
Tyler, Robert, 46

"Ulalume," 55, 58
Uncle Tom's Cabin (Stowe), 121
Underground Railroad, 48
Union Magazine, 58
United States
  anti-Catholic hostility in, 48
  capitalist culture of, 67, 73
  communication revolution,
    66, 67
  community and privacy, 176
  higher education in, 23
  individualism and mass soci-
    ety in, 168
  internal improvements in, 23
  low newspaper postal rates
    in, 74, 105, 172
  lyceum movement in, 49
  mass culture of, 67, 68, 77
  monetary crises in, 38, 39, 45,
    73
  population growth of, 33, 64
  privacy in, 16, 167–88
  public and private spheres,
    169, 184
  public sphere and voyeurism,
    175
  railroad growth, 65
  religious life in, 34
  transportation revolution in,
    66
  urbanization and privacy in,
    170
  westward expansion of, 23
United States, Second Bank of,
    33, 40, 45, 65

University of Virginia, 23, 51, 68
"Unparalleled Adventures of
     One Hans Pfaall, The," 13
Upshur, Abel Parker, 155

"Valley of Nis, The," 29
Van Buren, Martin, 44, 51, 57, 73,
     116
  election of, 39, 194
Verne, Jules, 14
Virginia slave insurrection, 31
"Von Kempelen and His Experi-
     ment," 57
voyeurism and public sphere, 175

Wallace, William, 46
Walsh, Robert, 27
War of 1812, 20
Washington, George, 10
Webster, Daniel, 46, 104
West Point (U.S. military
     academy), 26, 28, 29, 68,
     157
What Dreams May Come, 14
Whig Party, 39, 44, 51
White, Eliza, 35
White, Thomas W., 34, 37, 47,
     69, 70, 72
  doubts about Poe, 35
  intention to fire Poe, 38
  refusal to name Poe editor, 36

Whitman, Sarah Helen, 11, 53,
     55, 56, 141, 143, 147
  and dark side of Poe, 151
  calls off marriage to Poe,
     57
  Edgar Poe and His Critics, 15,
     143
  on Poe's personality, 150
  Poe's fantasy of dying with,
     149
Whitman, Walt, 15, 158
Wilkes Expedition, 41
"William Wilson," 7, 16, 21, 42,
     174
Willis, Nathaniel Parker, 15, 55,
     162n, 163n
Wilmer, Lambert, 25, 30
Wilmot Proviso, 54, 55
Wirt, William, 27, 193
Woman in the Nineteenth Century
     (Fuller), 131, 142
"Womanhood, Real,"
     nineteenth-century
     ideal of, 135, 162n
Wyatt, Thomas, 41

Yeats, William Butler, 104
"Yellow Wallpaper, The"
     (Gilman), and female con-
     finement, 146
Young America group, 52

Printed in the United States
69807LV00002B/153